IMMORTAL BOY

Immortal Boy

A PORTRAIT OF LEIGH HUNT

ANN BLAINEY

ST MARTIN'S PRESS
New York

ISBN 0-312-40945-1

CONTENTS

For my daughter, Anna

ACKNOWLEDGEMENTS

Few biographies of Leigh Hunt have been written, and none in recent decades. The most notable is Edmund Blunden's *Leigh Hunt, A Biography* (1930), a charming and beautifully written account. Blunden, however, did not have access to the wealth of letters collected by the inveterate Leigh Hunt collector, Luther Brewer and presented by him to the University of Iowa, nor was Blunden interested in the troubled and depressive side of Hunt's nature. Another distinguished life of Hunt was written in 1935 by Louis Landré as a doctoral thesis, *Leigh Hunt, Contribution à l'histoire de Romantisme anglais*. It was published in a small edition and has never been translated into English. Professor Landré's work is voluminous and meticulous, a book to which all students of Hunt will turn again and again. He was not however greatly concerned with Hunt the man.

Hunt has left behind a wealth of biographical material, enough for many volumes. To write only one I have had to be ruthlessly selective. My aim has been to show Hunt the man, sometimes engaging, sometimes infuriating, but always surviving: as a reviewer in the *Palladium* put it in 1850, an 'immortal boy'.

I wish to record my thanks to the Henry E Huntington Library and Art Gallery, the Pierpont Morgan Library, Harvard University Library, the Brotherton Library, University of Leeds, the National Library of Scotland, the Bodleian Library, Oxford, and the British Library. In particular I thank Mr Frank Paluka, Head of Special Collections, University of Iowa Libraries, and his staff, and I gratefully acknowledge the friendship and assistance of three Leigh Hunt scholars: David Cheney, Richard Russell and Desmond Leigh Hunt. The last two are direct descendants of Leigh Hunt. Finally I give thanks to my husband and to my daughter, and to my publisher, Christopher Helm.

1 BLUECOAT

Leigh Hunt considered himself in all respects English, though neither of his parents had been born in the British Isles. The Hunts were a colonial family. A relative once noted that their very appearance — mother and children — was distinctly un-English, and that their blue-black hair and olive skins betrayed them even before they spoke: Mrs Hunt never entirely lost her American accent and traces of it were discernible in her children. Many years later, when Nathaniel Hawthorne, the celebrated American novelist, visited Leigh Hunt, he at once noticed this colonial quality and declared him 'thoroughly American'.

Leigh Hunt had much to say of his colonial ancestors in his *Autobiography*, tracing their origins and associations with English families, frequently regretting that his evidence was vague. The Hunts had emigrated to the West Indies in the sixteenth century, and many of them had been clergymen, including Hunt's paternal grandfather, Rev. Isaac Hunt of St Michael's, Bridgetown, Barbados. His mother's family had settled in Philadelphia, becoming wealthy, well-known Quakers: the ships of his maternal grandfather, Stephen Shewell, traded with England, Holland and the West Indies. Hunt's parents, Isaac and Mary, met when Isaac was sent to study at the College of Philadelphia. Isaac was then about 18 years old, not tall, with delicate features, blue eyes, a small acquiline nose, a fresh fair complexion, and an amiable and 'graceful address'. Most notable was his voice: it either captivated or repelled, depending on whether its hearers were won over by its extraordinary charm or suspicious of its possible insincerity.

Leigh Hunt described his father as 'the scapegrace who smuggled in the wine, and bore the brunt of the tutors' at college. But Isaac seems to have been a good student, gaining his Bachelor of Arts in 1763, his licence to practise law in 1765, and two degrees of Master of Arts — one from Philadelphia in 1771 and the other from King's College, New York, in 1773. While studying he was also a pamphleteer, and under the pseudonyms of Isaac Bickerstaff and Jack Retort had published satires against the Pennsylvanian authorities. Isaac had many other talents. 'When he spoke at the farewell oration on leaving College', wrote Hunt, relating a family legend,

1

'two young ladies fell in love with him, one of whom he afterwards married'. The two ladies were Mary Shewell and her young aunt Elizabeth Shewell, both of whom were under the care of Stephen Shewell. Mary was a dark beauty, Elizabeth a fair one. It is possible that Isaac passed over Elizabeth in favour of her dark-haired niece, for there seems to have been a long-term animosity between him and Elizabeth, and she was to ignore entreaties to come to his death-bed. Elizabeth married the rising American painter, Benjamin West, in London in 1765, after reputedly escaping from Stephen Shewell's house by stealth.

Mary, still in her early teens, was courted by Isaac. If family tradition can be believed she had been brought up in 'so retiring a manner after the American fashion, that she became too bashful to avail herself of an offer of Dr Franklin who would have taught her the guitar'. Tall, gentle, shy, warm-hearted, with a 'love of nature and of books', Mary was also intensely religious; although not a Quaker herself, she 'used to talk with delight of the heavenly calm she felt going to their meetings, and sitting still during the silence'. Her character was a complete antithesis to Isaac's, she timid and reserved, he 'shrewd, spirited, and shewey'. She was overwhelmingly attracted to him, and with the support of her mother gradually overrode her father's objections. On 17 June 1767 they were married in Philadelphia. Mary then being about 15 years old. The couple seem to have lived together happily for almost ten years. In that time six children were born: Isaac, Stephen, Robert and John who survived, and Elizabeth and Benjamin who died in infancy.

Though Stephen Shewell entertained Thomas Paine and was intimate with Benjamin Franklin, neither the Shewells nor the Hunts were willing to abandon Britain in a struggle over the American colonies. In fact pamphleteer Isaac went further. In 1766 he had written *The Political Family* in which he had pointed out the reciprocal advantages of union to both Britain and the colonies, thus uncompromisingly proclaiming his Tory politics. The work lay on his desk for nine years until early in 1775 he decided to publish it. The timing was dangerous. This pamphlet and his attempts as a lawyer to defend loyalists precipitated an uproar in September 1775. According to his own account, Isaac was seized by a mob and paraded 'for the greatest part of the day in the most ignominious manner through all the streets of Philadelphia', expecting 'every moment to be torn to pieces by a multitude spirited up to a phrenzy'. A stone hit his head and is said to have weakened his sight for the rest of his life. After a spell of imprisonment, he was quietly shipped aboard a Shewell vessel bound for Jamaica, where he endured severe sickness. Arriving in England, weak and penniless, in the summer of 1776, he lamented that his American property, worth some £3,000, had been confiscated, but it is not completely certain that he was the owner.

While Isaac was enduring his ordeal, Mary and her children remained at her father's house in Philadelphia. Her later life was to be a history of illness and her first attack of jaundice is said to have occurred when she saw Isaac thrown into the cart. Those rough scenes left her with a 'frightened aversion' to even the most trivial violence: the sight of two men scuffling in the street was enough to drive her in tears down another road. Her family would henceforth regard this fear as one of her idiosyncrasies.

Mary's time at her parent's home in Philadelphia was a brief interval of security. But a wife's duty was to follow her husband and the rest of Mary's life was to be a long and weary testimony to this belief. Despite his own financial losses during the revolution, Stephen Shewell did his best to help his daughter, reputedly arranging not only her passage to England but providing a gift of £500. Years later Leigh Hunt would accuse his grandfather of niggardly conduct towards his mother. In the crisis Shewell could not have been more generous, though later when impoverished himself he may have resolved to cease pouring into the bottomless pit of Isaac's easy spending.

It was nearly two years after the cart incident that Mary and her four sons — the oldest no more than ten years — boarded the *Earl of Effingham*, bound for England. Her son would later record that the captain, seeing the forlorn little party come aboard, was moved to pity, the more so because the ship was old and the voyage dangerous. Off the Scilly Isles in a heavy storm the ship almost foundered. Here, according to family legend, Mary thrust aside her own nervousness and did all she could to calm her fellow passengers, even reprimanding a cowering woman for lack of faith. The ship was driven into Swansea Bay and Mary and her sons hastened on to London.

Isaac had not prospered. His legal training was not recognised in England, and he had been obliged to find another profession. He had toyed with the theatre, where his superb voice would have been an asset, but discarded this in favour of the family calling of the church. On 24 February 1777 he was ordained a deacon at the

Chapel Royal, St James's Palace, and when Mary arrived later that year she found him at Bentinck Chapel, Lisson Grove, preaching once on Mondays and twice on Sundays.

Isaac had many natural talents for the church: his voice, his dramatic sense, his love of the Bible and sermons. He was neither witty nor profound, but what he lacked in quickness and depth he made up in eloquence and theatricality. He was soon popular. But his over-optimism, his easy conviviality and his love of pleasure led him into laxness and debt. His constant pamphleteering made enemies. His superiors began to distrust him, and his parishioners, who had once presented him with money and a portrait, eventually spurned him. Hunt wrote that his father would have been more suited to a pulpit in Barbados, where he might have preached 'and quoted Horace, and been gentlemanly and generous, and drunk his claret, and no harm done'. As it was, Isaac 'sank from distress to distress, always scheming, never performing and too well able to seize a passing moment of enjoyment, till he grew acquainted deeply with prisons, and became irritable with conscious error, and took hope out of the heart that loved him, and was glad to escape out of its society'.

Alarmed by his debts, Isaac appealed to friends and relatives. Friends generously sent three of the boys to school and supported the fourth. Mary turned to her uncle by marriage, Benjamin West. His phenomenal career as a Court painter and his kind and controlled disposition had won him many highly placed admirers. First instructed in art by a Cherokee Indian — so it was said — West became a member in his mid-twenties of the academies of Parma, Florence and Bologna, and a favourite of George III. He welcomed his American relations into his large house in Newman Street, and set about interesting his patrons in Isaac Hunt's unhappy situation.

With a gradual easing of their poverty, the Hunts were able to set up house in Hampstead Square, Isaac preaching where he could, making occasional visits to the church in the village of Southgate, north of London. One of these Southgate sermons was heard by the Duke of Chandos whose house was nearby, and so impressed was he by Isaac's learning that he engaged him as a tutor for his nephew, James Henry Leigh. Relieved at this change in fortune, the family moved to a delightful house at Southgate, and Mary reclaimed the children to their parental home.

In Southgate Mary became pregnant again, a trying discovery for a woman in her mid-thirties, in chronically bad health, and already worn out by a recent pregnancy which had resulted in the birth of an ailing girl. At their new home, Eagle Hall, on 19 October 1784, she gave birth to a boy and 'subsequently to great care and sickness'. To Isaac the birth was a source of pleasure and a possible means of advancement in ducal favour: it was doubtless with this in mind that he named his son after his pupil, James Henry Leigh.

Isaac, alas, did not long remain in ducal favour. The reasons for his fall are not completely clear, but by 1787 he was back at Bentinck Chapel, again in debt and — as a dispossessed loyalist — petitioning the government for help. From Southgate the family moved to Finchley and then to Hampstead, where there was increasing concern for Mary's health. Though still in her thirties, dark-haired and trim in figure, Mary seemed to be a worn out woman. Her complexion was jaundiced, her cheeks sunken, her mouth drooped. 'I do not remember', wrote Hunt, 'to have ever seen my mother smile, except in sorrowful tenderness. Mary worried continually over little Leigh who had 'almost every disorder to which infancy is exposed', no sooner recovering from one illness then falling into another. A costly convalescence in France after a severe attack of measles turned into a nightmare when he caught smallpox. At Finchley he was diagnosed as suffering from incurable dropsy of the head, for which 'a profusion of leeches' effected a remarkable cure. A few months later it was said that he would die prematurely, an idiot, or live to a ripe age with the additional blessing of considerable intellect. If he reached 15, all would be well! With a devoted mother, and a 'scarcely less affectionate,' older brother, Robert, to nurse his sickness, little Leigh survived.

Isaac meanwhile drank his claret and owed more and more money — until the family left Hampstead and moved to that most dreaded of habitations, the King's Bench Prisons for Criminals and Debtors. Significantly Hunt's earliest recollection is of a room in prison: 'Here was a game of rackets, giving the place a strange and lively air in the midst of its distresses; here I first heard, to my astonishment and horror, the verse of a song sung out as he tottered along, by a drunken man, the words of which appeared to me unspeakably wicked'. The effect of such scenes on an obsessively timid woman and on her small child must have been calamitous. Mary's recourse was withdrawal, depression and anxiety and it is scarcely surprising that in childhood Hunt would suffer nightmares and fear of the dark, would stammer and sigh compulsively, and be unable to stand up for himself. Anxiety and depression would burden him through life.

Released from prison, the family 'struggled on', wrote Hunt feelingly, 'between quiet and disturbances, between placid readings and frightful knocks at the door, and sickness and calamity; and hopes which hardly ever forsook us'. Yet some good times were etched upon his memory. On quiet evenings Mary would brew coffee and Isaac would read aloud in his enchanting voice; they would sit by the fireside and talk agreeably of literature, politics and religion. Mary's taste — unlike her more orthodox husband — inclined to the emotional and radical, to sentimental novels, republicanism and the Universalist sect. On quiet afternoons they would visit Mary's friends. Hunt would later remember in particular Miss C., in whose 'poor sitting room in the year '89 or '90' he would stand beside the harpsichord and sing at his mother's bidding, his little sister Mary, 'with her round cheeks and blue eyes, wishing me to begin': 'Dans votre lit' was small Mary's favourite, for she believed that 'lit' was Leigh. At home, the two small children would sit with picture books, reading with indescribable pleasure *Little Jack and Jemima Placid* and *Pilgrim's Progress*. On occasions the little boy would pinch up his hat with pins, put on his father's clerical bands and mount a chair with a wooden sword in his hand to deliver a sermon. To be a soldier was one ambition inspired by the soldiers he saw drilling in the park. To be a clergyman was his main intention: 'My chief delight', he told his American Aunt Lydia when he was six, 'is studying Holy Scripture', and he promised to send her his sermons 'if I am not a very poor parson'. His mother applauded his religious ambitions: his military ones only filled her with horror.

The home of Benjamin West continued to be a haven to Mary and her children, especially the gallery at the back where, dressed in a white gown, the painter received his friends. Much of Hunt's later enthusiasm for art undoubtedly came from these early visits. He and Mary would go down the gallery as if they were 'treading on wool', pausing reverently to examine their favourite pictures with 'a countenance quite awe-stricken'. Later they would join their aunt in the parlour to talk about family, friends and books. Young Leigh, left to amuse himself, would wander about the room to examine the treasures, gazing intently on the firescreen painted with the 'Loves of Angelica and Medora' which he could have 'looked at from morning to night'.

In that parlour, Hunt wrote later, he 'learned to unite the love of freedom with that of the graces of life', for West, though 'not so warm in his feelings as those about him', still united them both in his character. He would always have mixed feelings about his grand-uncle, failing to understand that West's coldness concealed a highly emotional nature which its owner — once the victim of a nervous breakdown — feared to indulge. West was perfectly happy, Hunt drily remarked, 'because he thought himself immortal'. With Mrs West there was no such reserve: she was all auntly affection and she tried to encourage her nephew to overcome his nervous childhood habits. As they sat in her parlour she would offer him a reward if he could refrain from holding his breath and sighing for more than a certain time. Many years after she was still fussing over his health and sending him cold cures. When the Newman Street house was auctioned a generation later, Hunt felt all his boyhood come over him in a rush of tenderness for its now dead occupants and vanished treasures, as though part of himself was up for sale. 'May a blessing be upon that house', he wrote then, 'and upon all who know how to value the genius of it'.

A little security was now at hand for the family. Probably through the efforts of Benjamin West at Court, Isaac began to receive a loyalist pension of £100 a year, supplemented by his smaller earnings from preaching and the sales of his pamphlets and sermons. Intermittently, they were also helped by gifts from Mary's family, for her American brothers visited London at least twice during the 1790s. 'I cannot', wrote six-year-old Hunt to his Aunt Lydia, 'part with my uncles without begging the favour of them to put this letter in their bag and deliver it to you when they arrive at Philadelphia a city I should be very happy to visit as it is the place where my dear good mama was born, and my grandpapa, grandmama and all my relatives and friends whose Health and Happiness I pray for night and morning'. Later, when Isaac's sisters, the wealthy, widowed Elizabeth Dayrell and Ann Courthope Hunt, arrived from Barbados, Isaac's finances were considerably assisted, and the Dayrell town house in Great Ormond Street and country house in Surrey became holiday havens for the Hunt family. Isaac, only too happy to sink back into a leisurely colonial life, spent increasingly long spells in his sister's household.

Such memories were on the credit side. Mary's poor health continued, and she was plagued by jaundice and by rheumatism first contracted, it was said, on a freezing day in Blackfriars Road when she took off her thick petticoat and gave it to a beggar woman. Her emotional health was also precarious. Life was made bearable only by her children and by her ever-deepening religious faith, as a letter to her eldest son Isaac bears witness: 'if we act uprightly there is peace of Conscience, and joy that I would not exchange for all the Kingdoms of this world or the glory of them'.

Mary's faith was soon to be tested. When Hunt was about five years old his sister Mary died. The effect on his mother was overwhelming. Her anxiety became focused on her other sickly child. She cossetted him and he responded with an intense love and dependence. As she fearfully watched over his childhood, he in turn watched over her. He dreaded her disfavour, he dreaded her illness, he dreaded any form of separation from her. Her pain, her fears, her helplessness, her concern were his also.

Under such a regime, the child began to adopt many of his mother's fears. Once 'an irritable little fellow', capable of kicking his bullying brother Stephen in the shins, he was rendered timid, he wrote later, by 'illness, imagination, and an ultra tender and anxious rearing'. She set me, he recalled, 'an example of such excessive care and anxiety for those about us, that I could not see her bite off the ends of her threads while at work without being in pain till I was sure she would not swallow them'. His mother's protectiveness extended even to words: with what horror, following her example, little Leigh regarded swearing. He well remembered the 'fearful joy' with which he uttered one such daring word, only to be overcome with remorse so that 'for some time afterwards I could not receive a bit of praise, or pat of encouragement on the head, without thinking to myself, "Ah! they little suspect that I am the boy who said d—n it" '.

Relating these incidents in later life, Hunt observed, 'Some of the bad consequences to myself were indeed obvious'. His adult capacity for overanxiety was one effect. However, Mary also gave him an unusual capacity for loving and caring, which he acknowledged by adding, 'Dear Mother! No one could surpass her in generosity'.

Isaac and Mary Hunt had already set up the older boys as best they could. John was apprenticed to a printer, Robert to an engraver — 'and I heard the old folks say he will soon make a better

picture than his Master', wrote Leigh Hunt confidently. Stephen
was to be a lawyer. Only the eldest, Isaac, so 'cordial, open,
careless' like his father, had dared to go his own way and taken ship
to America, to enter the army and never to return. 'I am very sorry',
wrote Hunt, no doubt echoing his parents' opinion, 'that my
brother Isaac did not come back from New York — for a rolling
stone gathers no moss'.

Hunt's future remained in doubt and here the parents' greatest
skill was required, for he had already begun to show unusual signs of
intelligence. He had taught himself to write by copying his father's
sermons — his handwriting always resembled Isaac's — and his
mother carried his writings in her pocket to show to admiring
friends. Proud Isaac mapped out a demanding course of study for
his child. 'My mother', wrote Hunt looking back, 'taught me
reading, and he the Latin grammar. At one time, he would never let
me taste anything at table, till I repeated the Latin for it.' Hunt's
later dietary fads may perhaps be traced to the tension of those
mealtimes. Writing to his aunt in March 1791, he described his
lessons with evident pride: 'I have recovered my health, and can
devote myself to my studies which consist at present in learning the
Latin Nomenclature of which I can perfectly repeat 2063 words.
Writing also fills up some of my time. Books of amusement I read at
my leisure.' Since he worked so diligently, he can have had little
leisure. And here one must touch on a side of Hunt's nature that
would become more noticeable with age. Ingrained in his thinking
was the idea that love must be earned by obedience and industry, or
it would be forfeited; a belief to which he would add the heartfelt
rider: '*Experience* has taught *me* to beware'. The child, who feared
that his parents might withdraw their love if he proved unworthy,
carried this fear into adulthood.

It was obvious to both parents that, poor though they were, they
must give this son a superior education. To his credit, Isaac devised
a sensible solution. On 1 April 1791 he petitioned the governors of
Christ's Hospital in their 'usual Pity and Charity to distressed Men,
and poor Widows and Fatherless Children, to grant the Admission
of his said Child into Christ's Hospital . . . there to be Educated
and brought up among other poor Children'. Isaac appended a
certificate attesting to his poverty and honest origins, with the
required signature of the minister, churchwarden and three householders of the parish of St Pancras, and promised to leave the 'said
Child' with the governors until the age of 15, to be apprenticed to

whatever trade or calling they decided. At the end of October, in accordance with the school rules, Leigh Hunt was baptized; this belated baptism — so at variance with his father's vocation — has justifiably puzzled biographers. On 24 November he put on the distinctive Tudor-style blue and yellow uniform, which earned the pupils the name of 'Bluecoat Boys', and began his schooldays.

Standing in Newgate Street, its entrance next to Christ Church, Christ's Hospital had been founded by the Charter of Edward VI to combat the destitution of sixteenth-century London. Its aim was not merely to feed, clothe and form the moral character of its poor pupils, but to educate them in commerce and the arts. In the seventeenth century Charles II had founded a navigation section which supplied the Navy and Merchant Service with able officers. Thus for two and a half centuries it had produced generations of successful merchants, divines, sailors and scholars, with for good measure, a poet dramatist, a mystic and a martyr. Both Samuel Taylor Coleridge and Charles Lamb had attended there in the years immediately preceding Hunt's entry.

What could it have been like for a 'young delicate pet child' to leave an over-sheltered home and enter the hurly burly of 600 boys from all classes and backgrounds? Not surprisingly, he 'suffered a great deal'. The beatings in the schoolroom and violence in the playground terrified a child brought up with an aversion to all violence. The punishment of a fellow pupil could make him weep, but he also inherited from Mary a stoicism — perhaps even a masochism — which enabled him to bear his own punishment with little outward fuss. Even at that early age he was proud of his 'spirit of martyrdom'. He was proud also of his ability to fight for a friend or for a cause; the impersonal righteousness of a quarrel seemed to drive away his fear. There was another side of his nature which gave him support. Emotionally he was the child of both parents, deriving from his father a capacity for pleasure as strong as his mother's for melancholy. He would call his father an 'unhappiness-producing person', but he owed to him the blessing of ebullience. 'In the midst of my quiet looks and melancholy feelings', he wrote, 'I had animal spirits, ready to take advantage of any gaiety that should arrive.' To take into himself a positive enjoyment of pleasure, and throw off the underlying melancholy of his nature with bursts of exuberance, would henceforth be prominent in his behaviour. Only this capacity, he recalled, made his early years at school tolerable.

Under the strain of school life his nervous stammerings and

sighings increased in a vicious circle: 'the worse my stammering, the worse the illtreatment', and the worse the illtreatment, the worse the stammering. His master in the upper school was Rev. James Boyer, 'a proper tyrant, passionate and capricious'. Immortalized in kinder recollections by Coleridge and Lamb, Boyer had little good to say of Hunt, or Hunt of him. Boyer hated the boy's mind for its unruliness and liberalism — opinions gleaned, wrote Hunt, 'from what I heard at home, to the contradictions I had already begun to feel elsewhere, and perhaps in some degree to the tempest of the French Revolution'. Violence of feelings between master and pupil flares across the pages of Hunt's remembrances. Hunt's stammering drove Boyer to a fury with which the child, afraid of violence, was helpless to cope. In despair Hunt had his fellow pupils hear his lessons in advance, but to no avail; he continued to stammer. One day Boyer, in a fever of anger, seized a copy of Homer and hit the boy in the mouth, knocking out a tooth. As the blood gushed out, Hunt watched with wonder as Boyer's tone became alarmed, remorseful and finally paternal. After this revelation, he began to see his master's behaviour in 'all its unhandsomeness; and at length as my respect for him lessened, my fear lessened with it, and I did not stammer so much'. From endurance, he had learned, came strength and eventual victory. It was a valuable lesson.

Physically and mentally, the spartan school regime tried Hunt's health and spirits. In his memoirs the tedious rigidity of routine is a prominent theme, and at school the time-table was inflexible: rising at six, washing, breakfasting, lessons, play, dinner, lessons, supper, bed, with endless intermissions of prayers and Bible reading. Even pious young Leigh was temporarily turned from religion by this example. He was similarly turned from his enthusiasm for learning. Because he could read on entering school he was placed in the classics class and ignored all other forms of education. (To the end of his life he would blame Christ's Hospital for his inability to do the simplest sum.) 'Few of us cared', he recalled, 'for any of the books that were taught: and no pains were taken to make us do so'. Slowly his precocity and enthusiasm faded to lethargy, and it is perhaps no wonder that he failed to gain a place at university. It was his free reading which aroused him: Spenser, Collins, Gray, with whom he fell 'passionately in love', and illustrated books on classical mythology and art which provided mental, emotional and visual stimulation. He haunted the bookstalls: 'When the master tormented me', he remembered, 'when I used to hate and loathe the sight of Homer, and Demosthenes, and Cicero — I would comfort myself with thinking of the sixpence in my pocket, with which I would go out to Paternoster Row, when school was over, and buy another number of an English poet'. He tried his own hand at numerous writings. Though in class Boyer would throw away his essays with sarcastic comments, in his free time Hunt was dashing off serious verses which Mary would enclose with pride for his grandfather in America.

The pain and boredom of school life were offset by school friend-ships. 'Friendship was a romantic passion with me', Hunt wrote, and Christ's Hospital would 'ever be dear' because of those early relationships. In the fullest of his school accounts, written in 1827 when he was 43, he recalled in detail the network of friendships of those years, emphasising the uniqueness and closeness of his loyalties and affection, which even after that laspe of time retained much of their original excitement.

The 'romantic passion' of friendship was no passing adolescent fancy but one which would last his entire life, at times elevated into almost a religious observance. And those schoolboy friendships in many ways foretold the pattern of his adult relationships. At school it was his custom to have a group of close friends, perhaps half a dozen, with whom he shared outings, conversation and intellectual interests: so it would be later in his life. Among these groups was always one special friend, the recipient of the most intense emotion. The first such friendship was the most compelling: a shattering hero-worship which threw him into a 'kind of Sabbath state of bliss'. The chosen boy was a 'kind of angel', in whom he saw again the candour, truth, gentleness and courage of Mary Hunt. Within Christ's Hospital this timid lonely little boy had found a soul-mate, cast in his mother's image, with whom he might partially recreate the close daily relationship of childhood. He responded whole-heartedly. 'I would have been torn to pieces', he recollected, 'rather than not stand by my friend'. In another place he wrote, 'I am sure I could have died for him'. Many years later when he again found such an angelic soul-mate the effect was similarly shattering.

During his schooldays Hunt had three such favourites. Of the second he recounts nothing, and the third was very different. Now it was Hunt who was looked up to, while he in turn gave out a possessive, somewhat domineering affection. This boy was called William Papendiek, of a cultured, musical and hospitable family in service at court; it was at their musical soirees that Hunt first heard the music of Mozart. William was fragile, blue-eyed, helpless and docile. He admired Hunt's opinion, looked to his protection and obeyed his wishes. Hunt was affectionate but superior and aloof. When William passed around his food hampers of apples and cakes, he commended his generosity but loftily refused to partake. Hunt met William's two sisters, the elder handsome and accomplished but independent, the younger a frailer version of her brother and dying of consumption. It was the younger who attracted him and they briefly fell in love. His friendship with the family lasted well into his twenties, and he visited them often before a final falling out and William's early death.

It was undoubtedly such absorbing experiences which made up Hunt's happiest early memories. With what delight he would recall chats and verse over the teacups in the senior studies, or bathing in the New River, or shouting Italian poetry through the fields of Hornsey — this time with a friend named Thomas Barnes — or chanting Collins's Odes as they boated on the Thames at Richmond. Mary Hunt would always welcome his companions at home. She would come to collect him for excursions, and he would long remember with a pang the sadness of her face as she came along the cloisters, the weary hang of her head and her melancholy smile. One outing he especially anticipated. It was to the home of a wealthy merchant at Austin Friars, whose family was close to Mary. In the charming garden of Godfrey Thornton's solid, rambling house, in the dining room which boasted the best cranberry tart ever tasted, thawed by the warmth of this gentle loving family, the timid bluecoat boy discovered a freedom and security unknown in his own household. It became a domestic model for him. For a time he even fell slightly in love with young Almeria Thornton.

In all his school years Hunt was permitted only one real holiday, a period of three weeks when he was not obliged to sleep in his dormitory bed. These rare August days he spent at Merton, near London, at his rich Aunt Dayrell's country house. Here he roamed the fields in ecstasies of freedom, dressed to the villagers' astonishment in his blue school skirts. He slept in a soft bed, ate exotic tropical food, and entered into the populous household of aunts, cousins, tutors, visitors and black servants. Used to the crowded dormitories, his nervousness again manifested itself: for a time he could not sleep alone, and required the presence of one of the servants.

His younger cousin flavoured his memories of the Merton

holiday: 15-year-old Fanny with dark laughing eyes and a plum-like mouth. Though only 13 himself, he hung about her in a fit of love, while she flirted with a 23-year-old suitor and, well aware of his infatuation, treated him like a naughty little brother. In the orchard she would mount the ladder like a fairy and throw down the fruit with contemptuous exclamations to her clumsy 'petit garcon'. He long treasured a heart-shaped locket she casually gave him.

Isaac Hunt, always hopeful, courted all influential contacts, taking his son to call on the politician Horne Tooke at Wimbledon and to visit Parliament to hear William Pitt. The lack of pretension surprised Leigh Hunt — the members 'lounging on the benches and retaining their hats' — for he did not yet realise how 'very simplicity' could in effect exalt 'the most potent assembly in Europe'. His adolescent imagination was fed by other excursions. On free days he would go alone to the Jewish synagogue in Duke Place, fascinated by the ritual, and at school he was noted for organising impromptu religious processions, his friends chanting the psalms in Hebrew at his instruction. Ignoring the tedium of school devotions he went his own religious way with stimulating effect. 'I mooted', he would later confess, 'points of faith with myself very early'. His school career, however, was less auspicious. At 15 he became first Deputy Grecian, next in line to the three most senior and respected boys in the school. He never became a full Grecian, attributing his failure to his stammering. Grecians were required to speak in public and this he could not do.

Looking back, Hunt was anxious to come to terms with his school. He was grateful for its 'old cloisters, for its making me acquainted with the languages of Homer and Ovid, and for its having secured to me, on the whole, a well-trained and cheerful boyhood'. Yet when one looks at his several accounts, even those written with the detachment of 50 years, the negativeness of the recollection and the faintness of the praise are striking. What sort of an experience was it when one of its happiest memories was of a slow recuperation from a severe scalding of the legs? He lay for several weeks in the school infirmary and the 'getting well was delicious. I had no tasks — no master; plenty of books to read'. The nurse's daughter brought tea and buttered toast and taught him how to play the flute: 'we used to play and tell stories, and go to sleep, thinking of the blessed sick holiday we should have tomorrow, and of the bowl of milk and bread for breakfast, which was alone worth being sick for'. Hunt's overall comment on his school was also negative: 'It did not hinder', he wrote, 'my growing mind from making what excursions it pleased into the wide and healthy regions of general literature'.

FIT FOR NOTHING BUT AN AUTHOR

'For some time after I left school', wrote Leigh Hunt, 'I did nothing but visit my schoolfellows, haunt the book-stalls, and write verses'. Accustomed for eight years to the continuous discipline of Christ's Hospital, Hunt found the transition to the wider world was bewildering. He went often to see friends still at school. 'It seemed', he wrote in retrospect, 'as if I lived during the rest of the day, purely to carry them accounts of what I saw and heard'. Such evenings were now his happiest. Hands were clasped as if their owners 'had not met for a week', Souchong tea was produced, boys with kettles were summoned, and over the teacups Hunt took up again the comforting threads of his school days. 'I missed even the regularity and restriction of my hours', he confessed, 'and I felt the pressure of my hat, like a head-ache'.

Leisure for such visiting could not last. Aunt Dayrell's death had plunged the Hunts once more into financial difficulty and it was essential that Leigh find work. None of his brothers could help, for they were doing, as Mary confided, 'only tolerably well'. John had been ill during the winter of 1798, swelling up 'so much that he could not sit down', his physician blaming his occupation as compositor which forced him to stand for hours in the extreme cold. Robert, an engraver, was suffering from the wartime recession, which left 'no surplus for luxuries'. Wandering Isaac, soon to desert from the American Army to join the British Army in Canada, lived a life of improvidence and seldom wrote. Of all the brothers Stephen was closest to money, being now married to Aunt Dayrell's eldest daughter and executor of her will, but even he was poor, lacking the £15 licence fee to practice at the King's Bench until the arrival of his remittance from Barbados. It was imperative that Leigh work, and for this his father had plans.

At school Hunt had been busy in writing verses, and with more leisure his output multiplied. Old poems were reworked, new ones written. Entering a literary competition in the *Monthly Preceptor*, he won first place for a translation of Horace, his prize qualified by the advice that to become a good writer Master Leigh Hunt needed only 'a little arrangement, and to study the art of arts, the art to blot'. Urged on by such success, he threw off several imitations of his lifelong favourite, Spenser's *Faerie Queen*, along with a poem inspired by Thomson's 'Winter' and a piece 'founded on Gothic mythology'. While the mature Leigh Hunt would later blush for these juvenile trifles, Isaac was intensely proud and would not rest until they were placed before the world. In 1801, he enlisted subscribers, and the juvenile effusions were published in a book, aptly titled *Juvenilia*, the frontispiece designed by his cousin Raphael West, the subtitle reading 'A Collection of Poems. Written between the Ages of Twelve and Sixteen . . . Dedicated by permission, to James Henry Leigh', containing miscellanies, translations, sonnets, pastorals, elegies, hymns and anthems.

Juvenilia was an instant success. The leading literary reviews praised it and the *Monthly Mirror* declared that it contained 'proofs of poetic genius, and literary ability, which reflect great credit on the youthful author, and will justify the most sanguine expectations of his future reputation'. Isaac meanwhile was in a flurry of excitement, canvassing old acquaintances on both sides of the Atlantic for one guinea subscriptions to finance another three editions. It was an impressive array of subscribers that he mustered: dukes, marquises, and earls, archibishops, judges, artists led by Benjamin West, statesmen headed by Charles James Fox and even old teachers from Christ's Hospital. Leigh Hunt was firmly launched on the literary tide.

Later, Hunt would blame *Juvenilia* for giving him a spurious sense of his own importance, for having made him suppose that he had 'attained an end, instead of not having reached even a commencement'. He blamed it, too, for having caused him to waste many years in imitating Pope, Gray and Collins when he should have been studying 'poetical art and nature'. No one could doubt that *Juvenilia* was imitative and yet there were already signs in it of his future distinctive style. The explorative reading, the artistic idealism, the celebration of friendship, the gossipy preface, were all, as his distinguished critic, Edmund Blunden, has pointed out, foreshadowings of the later Hunt. For a boy of 17 it was an achievement, and if it went to his head this was understandable. The shy schoolboy whose poems were despised by his teacher had become a literary lion-cub. Without the confidence imparted by his first book, his career could have been very different.

Hunt grew an infant beard and went to literary parties. He was paraded by his jubilant father as 'the example of the young gentleman and the astonishment of the young ladies'. But beneath the fame, the shy schoolboy still existed. The face which looks out from two youthful portraits by Bowyer and by Jackson is vulnerable. Its contours are still a child's, with plump cheeks, a high forehead, firm dark brows, an overfull, petulant mouth, and brilliant brown eyes. Also evident is his tall, athletic build, large head, and the dark skin and hair, which Benjamin West declared always set the Hunts apart in an English crowd. Later many people thought that Hunt had Negro blood. Hunt himself said that his dark complexion was due to the effect of climate on his colonial English ancestors, and his unembarrassed discussion suggests that he had no suspicion of black ancestry. His *Autobiography* recalls the family tradition that in infancy his brother Stephen was almost kidnapped by Red Indians who mistook his dark looks for a child of their own. At this distance one cannot know the truth. What concerns a biographer more is that his looks gave him a feeling of difference which perhaps reinforced his lack of confidence.

Young and unsure of himself, he was given to temperamental outbursts, and many of them centred around his future employment. Not knowing his own ambitions, he was quick to deride the suggestions of others. He refused his grandfather Shewell's offer to 'make a man' of him in Philadelphia, and at the same time resisted his brothers' efforts to find him work in London. During the first four years of the century *Juvenilia* ran into four editions in England and one in America, and a dozen or so of his poems appeared in literary magazines, but he did no other work. In desperation John sent him to Gracechurch Street to see a printer, but Leigh would not co-operate. While no member of the Hunt household had felt it demeaning for John to accept apprenticeship and live in the house of his master, Leigh considered it unthinkable for himself. It was now artist Robert's turn to try, but a term in his studio taught this youngest brother nothing: 'I do not remember', Hunt later recalled, 'even taking the graver in my hand'. Finally lawyer Stephen took him as clerk into his chambers, and here young Leigh continued to idle and scribble, reading the *Biographica Britannica*, versifying on the blotting paper and 'drawing caricatures instead of deeds'. The plan was doomed from the start, for Stephen 'had not lost his spirit of domination' and Leigh was just finding his.

In this troubled relationship there also existed sympathy, for Stephen encouraged his brother's writing and enlarged his imagination. One evening in March 1800 they went together to an ephemeral comic opera called the *Egyptian Festival*, the first theatrical performance Hunt had ever seen. It was 'a haven of light and pictures' and it virtually changed his life. Thereafter he went incessantly to the theatre and began to write plays — tragedy, comedy and farce. Armed with an introduction from the musical Papendieks, he even asked the celebrated opera singer, Michael Kelly, at his music shop at Pall Mall to use his influence to have the farce put on. He was the first singer or actor Hunt ever beheld off a stage, and for that reason, as well as for his courtesy in refusing, that Kelly always had a place in his affections. By this time the disgruntled brothers had largely abandoned plans for Leigh Hunt's career. 'I proclaimed aloud to my family', wrote Hunt later, 'that I was fit for nothing but an author: and I believe that they were all of that opinion'. His determination had triumphed.

Half out of affectation, half out of laziness, he wrote most of the night and slept most of the day. Isaac, aware of his own infirmities, turned a blind eye as long as his son was contriving to keep up his reading and writing. Mary, consoled that he was spending his nights safely at home and that his poems were often on 'moral subjects', accepted his routine, although her austere spirit did not easily tolerate his rising at three in the afternoon. He would then have dinner, visit the bookstalls, call on friends for tea, and return home to his studies. Mary would welcome him with the 'never-failing coffee pot', and so he would read through the night on a course of authors of his own devising. He was a 'glutton of novels', and devoured Smollet, Mrs Radcliffe, and the work of Henry Fielding. He read 'every history' that came to hand from Herodotus to Gibbon. But the writer who made the most impression was Voltaire: *The Philosophical Dictionary* 'was for a long time my text book'. 'Bred up (in my home circle) to look for reforms in religion', and to question 'every doctrine, and every statement of facts, that went counter to the plainest precepts of love', he took to Voltaire's religious scepticism, marvelled at his 'gay courage and unquestionable humanity' but managed to retain his mother's deep but unorthodox religious faith. Thus he would read and write through the night, his lamp burning until Old Sally the maid, whom Mary Hunt had taken in as a young pregnant outcast, would open the shutters at daybreak and exclaim that he was as thin as a weazel and pale as a ghost.

Thus Hunt remembered in 1827, but if one turns to his fuller account in the *Autobiography* a different picture emerges. Admittedly the *Autobiography* was written over 20 years later and draws

heavily on his 1827 reminiscences, but its wealth of detail, cor-
roborated by those few letters which survive from the time, lends it
authenticity. From the *Autobiography* one learns that he spent
many evenings at the theatre, and even more with friends from a
widening social circle. And so he first met Barron Field, the son of
the school apothecary, a literary lad studying law at the Inner
Temple, and he also met the brothers John and Henry Robertson,
who were 'all for books, music and plays'. With these brothers he
attended an informal group called the Elders, whose members
drank elderberry wine, and with Barron Field he went briefly to a
young lawyers' society for public speaking. Nor was Mary Hunt
always sitting serenely with her welcoming coffee pot, as he fondly
remembered. Her life was disjointed, and her letters to her son
Isaac — who had suddenly surfaced in Newfoundland — betray
many anxieties and illnesses. John was ill and troubled by an
increasing family, two boys shortly to be joined by a third;
Stephen's only child was delicate and would have been 'nursed out
of his life' but for the care of an aunt. Mary herself, 'poor mortal',
was continually ill with a bilious complaint and 'not able to walk any
distance without support'. When 'I tell you', she concluded, 'I have
for near four months been resident with your Brother Stephen's
Family, and your other Parent in Surrey, you will know I have
enough to make me bilious'. Was she, one wonders, referring to
Surrey Gaol where her husband, that chronic debtor, may well have
been a reluctant inmate?

A portion of Hunt's time was also compulsorily given to military
duties. 'What am I to do', Mary bewailed to her far-off son, 'when
Bonaparte thinks proper to bend his steps on the City of London'. It
was not only her own safety for which she feared: it was also for that
of her boys and, with her hyperaversion for fighting, the threat was
vivid. To her sons it was more nuisance than threat, for they had to
join a volunteer regiment or be fined. Busy and independent John
chose to pay the fine; the others joined. Mary saw her beloved
Stephen and Robert made officers, while young Leigh became 'a
common man in Lord Amherst's regiment'. There they marched
and countermarched, invaded bakers' baskets and beermen's casks,
made fun of their superiors, and, unlike poor Mary, never had 'the
slightest belief in this coming of Bonaparte'. Hunt well remembered
a grand parade in the courtyard of Burlington House when their
gallant colonel was tossed over his horse's head into the dirt; no
more hilarious farce had he seen in the theatre.

As Hunt joked with his fellow soldiers or sat down late at night to write his versions of Collins, Gray and Pope, his imagination raced. He thought about love, and his thoughts were torn this way and that. He had inherited Mary's severe conscience and need to idealise, and her readiness to question 'the mass of inconsistency and injustice' which an egotistical society had 'confounded with an universal necessity'. He had inherited also, as he was fond of remarking, his father's warm West Indian blood, and consequently a generous adolescent sexuality. The blend did not make him comfortable. His feelings were inflamed by the sights he daily saw, and the books he daily read, for these were times of sexual licence in life and in literature. Looking back he did not doubt that disciplined occupation and robust exercise would have cured many of his problems. Furthermore, knowing few women, his attitudes came out of books, especially *Tom Jones*, and were related more to fantasy than reality. Desirable females he classed as remote and chaste heroines like Sophia Western, or warmhearted and available servants like Molly Seagrim. He dreamed both of heroines and servants, and combined the two into a torturing vision of a goddess who was at once inviting and heroic. But goddesses, as he knew, were not the stuff of daily life, and in his inner struggles the realities of fear and conscience always won. To 'think of those feelings, which nature prompted, imagination fired, and which love of books and an affectionate disposition conspired to render graceful, and then of the awful faces of Shame, Deception, Disease and Violated Conscience, which threatened them if they obeyed the impulse' — all this was too much for his faint heart.

In this tortured state he fell in love for the third time, with a hoyden named Harriet. Daughter of an honest East End tradesman, a practised flirt 'more knowing than artless' she may well have been expected to fit into the second of his fantastical categories. He had met her through a schoolfellow who then went to sea. Hunt, expecting her to be heartbroken, had tried to console her; and she replied with 'romps and laughter'. He was soon a regular visitor to her house, where they would sit chastely in the back parlour, he serious and adoring, she flirting, teasing, even plunging 'her little shock head in a great tub of water' to shake it provocatively in his face like a mop. But her provocation was in vain. In the end the affair broke up largely because she found him cold. For some time he continued to love her sentimentally from afar, and news of her unhappy marriage and early death distressed him.

Hunt consoled himself with books. He haunted bookshops in Oxford Street, Covent Garden and Holborn, collecting poetry and biography and little editions of the classics. One November he stayed out all night, wandering about aimless and penniless, too late to go home and alarm his nervous mother. Many years later he vividly recalled this experience. 'I shall never forget that night because so many objects were new to me . . . Good Gods! how I walked': from Knightsbridge to Barbican, to Oxford Street and through the squares, and down to the Thames to watch the barges coming up with their blacked bodies and with lights like 'monsters with fiery eyes'. He rested on church steps and in doorways, afraid of being arrested. In Oxford Street at dawn he was heartened to see a blacksmith open up his forge, where he warmed himself — in imagination. An hour later he warmed himself in the reality of his brother's house, reprieved from his vagrancy but with the experience firmly etched on his imagination: he had laid the foundation for observations of London life.

Through his love of books he met Thomas Maurice, librarian and poet, once the prim-eyed, enamel-faced, poetical protegé of Dr Johnson, but now a chubby, dishevelled old scholar who lamented his weak eyes, widowed state, constant colds, and impossible task of completing his manuscript catalogue. Maurice's rooms were in the first-floor turret nearest Museum Street, and Hunt came to love his dinners of roast fowl and claret. At the librarian's encouragement he would read for hours in the British Museum and then, stale with reading, he would crave physical exercise. At Oxford, visiting Papendiek, he was almost drowned while boating; at other times his nervous energy erupted in walking tours. In the autumn of 1801 he and John Robertson planned a walking tour from Margate to Brighton. They set out from London on a river boat filled with Methodists, whose ungenerous behaviour towards a cold and wet female passenger, not of their persuasion, stayed long in Hunt's memory. A few years later he would call it to mind as he wrote scathing articles on Methodism. After reaching Margate the two tourists put vexations behind them, and 'chattering, laughing and eating prodigious breakfasts' they set out to walk 112 miles in four days.

John Robertson tended to idealise his friends, especially female ones, and Hunt did not always accept these valuations. Nevertheless one such friend lived up to the glowing preamble: a Miss Kent whose house Hunt first visited with Robertson probably in

1801. Her father had been a linen draper of Brighton, of 'fast' disposition with 'more taste for pleasure than business'. He had died leaving a mass of debts to his widow Anne, a dressmaker and former Court milliner. Luckily Mrs Kent was a woman of 'clear-sighted energy, clear management and unflinching will', and she resumed work to support her three children, Mary Anne, Elizabeth and Thomas. Elizabeth, an avid writer and observer of nature, was Robertson's particular friend, and he was eager for Hunt to meet her. Though she wrote poetry she was far too shy to attempt to publish, and Robertson hoped that a meeting with Hunt — whose work she had admired in the *Monthly Preceptor* — might give her confidence.

Robertson was not disappointed. Leigh Hunt and timid but tempestuous young Bessy took to one another at once, but it was the sister two years older, who captured even more of his attention. Mary Ann or Marian* was aged about 13 (her birth at Pershore in Worcestershire is given as 28 September 1787 or 1788, the latter date being almost certainly correct) and she had the type of sexual attraction which is probably at best in adolescence. 'Her shape', Hunt wrote lyrically, 'was allowed to be beautiful, being no less delicate in the waist than plump where it ought to be; with shoulders fit for one of Titian's portraits, and an ankle which bore it all, like roses on the stalk'. Her face was not pretty but her dark eyes were attractive and her long luxuriant black hair, when unwound, fell to her knees. She was also 'piquant and genial'. Though not in the least bookish, she had a pleasant voice and a small talent for reading aloud, for modelling in clay and cutting silhouettes. She had about her something of Harriet: her manner, confident and bright, encouraged the shy suitor, and her prattling required no effort in return. But he was Mary's son as well as Isaac's and so it was her moments of seriousness which most captivated him. Marian was a seamstress, helping to support her family, sewing from 'morning to night, till she sometimes fainted on her chair'. The sight of her dark head bent over her work had an overwhelming effect on him. 'I had

---

*Mary Anne was her baptismal name, but about 1803 she seems to have turned it, like many other girls of her time, into the more fashionable form of Marian. Throughout his courtship and during the first months of their marriage, Leigh Hunt addressed her as Marian. In October 1810 Hunt began to call her Marianne, and she retained this spelling for the rest of her life. One wonders if this change to a more ornate, poetic-style spelling is not connected in some way with Hunt's other attempts to transform her into a more ornate poetic-style woman.

acquired a reverence for needle and thread in connection with domestic necessities', he wrote, 'from seeing it in the hands of my mother'. Though Marian lacked Mary Hunt's temperament and intellect, this common vision of the two needlewomen was profoundly moving. 'I found myself needle and threaded', he confessed, 'out of my heart by a girl of fourteen'.

Leigh Hunt was already in love, and an accident of fate made doubly sure of it. On a visit to the Kent household he was taken ill, and at once put to bed by an anxious Mrs Kent, who summoned a physician. St Anthony's Fire was diagnosed and Hunt began a ten-week convalescence carefully nursed by Marian. Such bliss was it to be cared for by his beloved that when the time came to leave he could not bear it. He accepted two rooms and became a boarder. How, one wonders, did Mary Hunt accept this arrangement, and how did she take the news that he was nightly remembering two mothers in his prayers? With Isaac's debts again mounting she may have been too harrassed to take it entirely to heart, but she cannot have favoured it.

Marian was undoubtedly flattered to have attracted such a suitor, the more so if she suspected that her sister also wanted him. His attentions, too, may well have been reassuring at what was an unsettling time for her, for her widowed mother married Rowland Hunter, a prosperous bookseller of St Paul's Churchyard, on 3 December 1802. Each Sunday from then on Hunt would hurry to the Hunter household in Little Tichfield Street, Marylebone, and sit by his beloved's side, the two of them so silent that 'the crackling of the fire was audible', and he would introduce her to the books he loved: 'my favourite became accustomed to sit on a little stool near me, with her glossy head in my reach; while I held my book in one hand, I was diverting my attention from it with the other . . . I have made love over the gravest of the pages . . . I was now as happy as I well could be, though not so much so as I could have wished'.

Hunt was not always as happy as he could have wished. Already there were tensions in the relationship which he understood barely if at all, and some at least would seem to have been sexual. When both were in London they met or wrote almost daily. The strain on what he called his 'warm West Indian blood' can only be guessed at. How warm it was can be seen from his frank surviving love letters. After their marriage neither would hesitate to voice openly a longing to go to bed with the other, and during their courtship he often wrote of his wanting to touch and kiss her. It would seem that strong sexual feelings ran between them, but that the spectres of shame and violated conscience made consummation unthinkable. So for the eight years of their courtship they exercised self-control, and some of that frustration must surely have been vented in the anger Hunt sometimes expressed to Marian.

At first Hunt was bathed in bliss. 'I rose every morning with the consciousness of loving somebody, which is much; and of being beloved, which is more.' He was filled with the joy, energy and purpose that only love can bring. He wrote Marian his first surviving love letter from Oxford where he visited Papendiek and it was chatty, tender and natural. Her 'idea', he told her, 'soothes my slumbers at night and wakes with me in the morning'. When they conversed he felt a 'stillness and seriousness, a kind of gravity which I cannot account for . . . a divine calmness of the spirit'. In trouble his first impulse was to turn to her. When he capsized in the Isis and took cold — 'a hand full of blisters, a body full of pain, and a head full of confusion' — he grew ten times better when he read her letters.

In a short time Marian became a necessity. She resembled a drug to which his system was addicted; any lessening of the dosage and he was in agonies. Then that miraculous stillness of spirit gave way to the doubts and feelings of insecurity. Marian, he was to discover, could be loved neither from afar nor domineered. His letters express his 'anxieties'. She was not sufficiently attentive, she was not writing at sufficient length or with sufficient promptness, she was not telling him what he longed to hear. 'Do me the favour', he wrote crossly, 'of sitting down to your pen and ink immediately you receive this epistle, and writing me a letter somewhat if possible longer than your last'. It was with good reason that Marian began to call him 'captious'.

When the first rapture began to fade he realized that Marian was scarcely literate and as the months passed this disturbed him. Her youth and his poverty were additional obstacles to an early marriage but meanwhile he must secure her. They must become engaged, but an engaged relationship soon aroused pressing worries. He already had in mind a firm, if not obsessive, picture of his ideal wife, a compound of what he had read in books and seen in his mother. An intelligent woman, engrossed in politics, religion and literature, capable of independent thought, Mary Hunt's more radical ideas were the genesis of his own, and her rather sentimental taste in literature would colour his taste throughout his life. Hunt believed that his ideal woman — and he would not allow Marian to be anything short of ideal — should possess taste and education, should have a gentle and polished manner, should converse intelligently but not aggressively — he loathed aggression in a woman — and be able to write a graceful letter and pursue artistic interests.

These qualities were presented as requirements, but really they were demands arising from his emotional depths. He required not only a wife but a soul mate, who would share his most intimate fears and longings, and whose constantly reassuring love would banish the isolation and despair which always seemed imminent. In other words, he wished to recreate the intense daily relationship with the mother of his childhood, whose lips he had tremblingly watched as she bit off her thread. In return he would give the care and devotion of that far-off child. This is the picture that emerges from the letters sent to Marian over the next six years.

Marian did not match these requirements. Many years later her son Thornton would describe her intellect as 'childlike', incapable of following the depth of Hunt's conversation. She did, however, offer the two great virtues of youth and love, and she might be educated into the type of woman he demanded. Not for a moment did it enter his head that Marian might not want or might not be capable of absorbing his instruction. He argued that he was offering a precious service and that if she truly loved him she would wish to please him. In the early spring of 1803 he began his campaign. 'My dearest Marian', he wrote persuasively, 'will do so and so for me because our wishes and hearts are one'. But immediately he encountered difficulties. Marian had merely attended a dame school, her spelling was weak, her writing poor, her expression limited, and her capacity for putting blots on the page large. Presumably to set an example, he began to take pains with his own letters, polishing his style and turning his neat spiky writing into a careful bold copperplate. Marian, for her part, was bewildered. Only Hunt's correspondence survives, but between the lines of his letters a picture of her reactions begins to emerge. She seemed to feel that Henry, as she called him, was making a fuss about nothing, which is scarcely surprising, for few females of her time were formally educated. Nevertheless to humour her dear Henry, to whom it seemed to mean so much, she tried. If she neglected to write prompt answers, or dropped blots or misspelled words or failed to make entries in her commonplace book, he became so angry. If only he were not so cross!

In August 1803 an incident, trivial in itself, illustrated this touchiness. Marian was about to make a short visit to Brighton with her mother and Hunt called at Little Tichfield Street to say good-bye, having by this time relinquished his rooms in the house. Busy, presumably with preparations, she kept him waiting for some time, and his sulks were out of all proportion even after she had apologized. 'Tis true', he wrote her, 'I stayed but a minute with you when you sent for me, and persisted in leaving the room when you entreated me to stay; I did not so much as look at you; but it was because I knew, that if I trusted myself a single glance at the face I doted on, I should have folded you to my bosom, and begged that pardon which I thought I ought not to beg; for you must confess, that if you *did* leave me, when you came down, for the reason you assigned, yet you might have come down before a *quarter to nine*, considering I was not to see you for a week.'

Hunt's insecurity caused him to fear close relationships, and as closeness was achieved his fears erupted in gestures that both pulled towards him and pushed away the unfortunate object of his affections. On the one hand he demanded complete control; on the other he aggressively found fault, partly to achieve a safe distance, partly to turn that person into a facsimile of the safe 'ideal' of his imagination. It seemed that he could only achieve his security by making the other person insecure. It was this process Thornton had in mind when he wrote that his father set up a 'standard of ideal elevation' for those he deeply loved, and exhibited anger and doubt as the relationship progressed. Where his feelings were less deeply engaged, however, he could be charitable and tolerant.

About a year after their engagement the first explosion came. Marian, with her 'reserve of independence' as Thornton later termed it, at last rebelled. Unexpectedly she broke off the engagement — not as Thornton claimed in September 1803, for in mid October Hunt was still writing her tender letters — but more likely in November or December. Over Christmas they were estranged and finally, at the start of February, Hunt wrote in fearful agony from his brother's house, imploring her forgiveness. 'I sit down to write to you, Marian, with a beating heart', he told her wretchedly, 'perhaps it is the last time I may thus address you'. Without her he was nothing, like a desert without water; he could keep silent no longer but must confess his need. He was convinced that to renew their love was in their both interests or he would not thus presume to beg: 'Dearest girl, refuse not what I ask'. His 'errors' were conquered; would she not at once dispel this black cloud and take again to her bosom her 'dear Henry, now no longer fretful and melancholy, but prepared to be happy himself and to do everything he can to make you happy too'. He enclosed this ardent appeal inside a somewhat ambiguous letter to her mother, Mrs Hunter, suggesting that if Marian would not have him back he would transfer his court to the sister Bess. His letter did not entirely convince Mrs Hunter, though it did move the more susceptible Bessy who, on his behalf, unselfishly used her influence on Marian.

Marian forgave him almost at once. Thirteen days later he was dashing off a tender love letter which left no doubt that all was mended. But Marian continued to 'resent dictations', so that for several years he had the disquieting conviction that 'the love was chiefly on my side'. Marian was no pliant schoolboy, and the storms of their courtship were far from over.

3 THE STORMY COURTSHIP OF MISS KENT

Quietly absorbed in his personal affairs, Hunt did not yet see that he was an actor on a larger stage. Living now in the intellectually alert household of his brother John, he must have been aware that socially and politically England was changing. The industrial revolution had begun to transform society, spawning industrial towns in the North and Midlands and phenomenally increasing wealth and hardship. An anxious government, attempting to quench the resulting instability, was itself unstable. The two great statesmen, Fox and Pitt, died within a year of one another while the King slipped into permanent insanity. In Europe war broke out again, and Prussia and Austria collapsed before Napoleon's armies, and England was threatened and felt threatened.

Control of the press in England seemed necessary if morale was to be maintained. The turn of the century had seen a revival in radical journalism and the emergence of papers independent of political parties: Cobbett's *Political and Weekly Register* had shown what could be done. Despite government control, the press was becoming an independent voice which half a century later would trumpet across the nation as the great organ of the public mind.

It had long been John Hunt's ambition to start a paper of his own. Like his father, John was a dedicated political propagandist, although their politics differed. Raised in a home where political pamphleteering was admired and reform of church and state were advocated, it was natural that he incline to radicalism but he far surpassed his mother, being a self-proclaimed deist and republican. Moreover, as a skilled printer, it was natural that he should dream of publishing his views. Nevertheless it was a courageous move when early in 1804 he set up a paper, taking advance orders from addresses of influence including Buckingham Palace. His hopes died quickly, for in the very week that Leigh Hunt and Marian were reconciled, his backers withdrew. In May 1805 he tried again — more successfully — with a weekly paper called the *News*, and proposed that Leigh should write the drama notices.

As a journalist young Leigh Hunt was not entirely untried. In the last year he had shown an enthusiasm for prose, being inspired by a set of the British classics given to him by his father. He had progressed to periodicals, and while he spurned the more celebrated *Spectator*, required reading during his schooldays, his imagination was caught by the lively pages of the *Connoisseur*, a magazine of vitality and wit which he discovered with 'all the transports of first love'. He could not wait to dash off imitations of it. From his pen came a series of papers which he even signed with his hero-authors' *nom de plume*, Mr Town, Critic and Censor-General: Hunt added a 'junior' as his own humble differentiation. These he took 'with fear and trembling' to the editor of a new evening paper where to his astonished joy they were at once accepted, with six free copies of the newspaper, the *Traveller*, in lieu of payment. 'Fortunately', he would write many years later, no one noticed these precocious contributions, or his prose head may well have been turned as disastrously as his poetic one. Yet here, as in his comment on *Juvenilia*, Leigh Hunt does himself less than justice. His *Traveller* essays are significant in English literature and history. With them he revived the largely forgotten model of the light, discursive essay of the mid-eighteenth century, and these first imitative attempts laid the foundation of his own distinctive essay style.

John Hunt was therefore taking on no novice when he offered his youngest brother employment on his new paper. He had a shrewd and realistic view of the boy's capacities, and Leigh, with his capacity for hero worship, had come to venerate his brother John. Every night he prayed for three people: his mother, Marian and John. They were the ones he longed to meet again in heaven, or so he told Marian. His worship of John was not misplaced: tall, dignified, unselfconscious, conscientious, a man of 'calm, deliberate integrity', John was the rock to which the entire family clung. He, of all Mary's children, had inherited the largest share of her enthusiasm, integrity and spiritual purpose. While he lacked her sweetness and tenderness — he was said to be 'somewhat hard and severe' — he also lacked her crippling anxiety and melancholy, and his Shewell virtues were combined with a salutary stiffening of stability, equanimity, capability and commonsense. Married to a thrifty, serious wife, and living a regular and comfortable life, it was little wonder that John drew to his ordered household both Robert and Leigh, and that in 1805 Leigh moved permanently with the family to their new house in Brydges Street, Covent Garden.

John Hunt was an exacting master. His watchword was independence, and all his life he would insist on it, both for himself and for those he employed. That critics should fraternise with actors, accept free meals and tickets, and respond with complimentary notices, was anathema to him, and he infected his brother with his disdain. There was then no such thing, Leigh Hunt would later write, as impartial newspaper criticism. What passed as criticism was 'a draft upon the box-office, or reminiscence of last Thursday's salmon and lobster-sauce'. To know an actor personally 'appeared to me a vice not to be thought of; and I would as lief have taken poison as accepted a ticket'. Leigh Hunt was fired with John's principles beyond the call of duty. Established actors, actresses and dramatists were criticised in the pages of the *News* with a moralising zeal which, he admitted much later, was downright bumptious. One dramatist called him, on stage, a 'pertling' and John Kemble called him that 'damned boy'. However, his work also had merit: he wrote perceptively and carefully, and he was invariably lively. If he condemned pretension, he applauded excellence, and if he tended to write with self-conscious ostentation and pedantry, there was always substance enough in his reviews to command attention. At a time when most reviews were short and adulatory, Hunt's notices were revolutionary. The drama critic of the *News* had something to say. Indeed so well known did his criticisms become that they deserved a life outside the ephemeral pages of a newspaper. Late in 1807 he worked them into a perceptive book called *Critical Essays on the Performer of the London Theatres, including General Observation on the Practice and Genius of the Stage*. This was gratefully dedicated to and printed by his brother John, who rejoiced as he read the unstinted praise which flooded in from readers and reviewers — his gamble had proved worthwhile.

Thanks to John, Leigh Hunt found himself a success. Often he called on his brother's newspaper friends such as John Bell, the gentlemanly, high-living proprietor of the *Weekly Messenger* at whose house in the Strand he first heard talk of politics and literary criticism and of the persons who wrote them. At brother John's house he also made new contacts, heard much new discussion and involved himself in new ventures. In 1806, John again enlisted his brothers' skills and began to bring out — under his imprint and that of his former master and relation by marriage, the printer Reynell — a five-volume anthology of eighteenth-century writers, with critical essays by Leigh Hunt and illustrations by Robert Hunt. Called *Classic Tales, Serious and Lively*, it was well received. In 1806 John Hunt launched another newspaper, the Whig-supported evening *Statesman* whose theatrical column was once more written by

Leigh. There seemed no end to the brothers' literary ventures.

It was a demanding life that Leigh Hunt led. In the evening he was frequently at the theatre, now a duty rather than a pleasure; never again, while he had his 'critical pen' in hand, would play-going be an 'unembarrassed delight', and he would often long for those carefree evenings when he 'went only to laugh or be moved'. From his play-house seat he would hurry home to compose his review, and it would be the early hours before he reached his bed. In the day he had other work. Isaac, disturbed that Leigh lacked a steady job, early in 1805 had petitioned the influential statesman, Henry Addington, for a post for his son as a clerk in the War Office. Hunt would long remember Addington's kindness when he called at the politician's home in Richmond Park to thank him for the job, and how he afterwards sat dazed upon the grass, wondering how he would reconcile literary life with humdrum clerkship. The two lives were not easily reconciled and he often slept in, and fooled and day-dreamed over his tasks and did his sums incorrectly.

Now more than ever Marian was a necessity, for in 1805 Mary Hunt fell seriously ill. She would gaze at the setting sun, ponder on Heaven and fancy her dead children beyond the sunset, where all would soon be reunited. Supported by an intense piety, she waited for the end. Her children visited her to varying degrees. Sweet-natured, homely Robert visited her constantly; indolent, generous Stephen less often; busy, dutiful John when he could; and Leigh much less often than he ought. The accusation is his own. 'I was young . . . I was giddy' he wrote by way of explanation, but nobody reading his earnest reviews in these months or his heartfelt letters to Marian could believe so shallow an excuse.

Why then did he not visit his mother? Her suffering was no doubt harrowing, but he had never shirked pain where duty to another was involved. No doubt, too, his attachment to Marian and his journalistic life had caused him to grow away from her; and here a possible explanation presents itself. Did he fear that attendance at her deathbed might renew those slackening emotional ties and renew demands with which his emancipated self could not cope? What is certain is that at her death he collapsed into an intense grief, and that for years to come he kept by him two of her last letters to him written with 'failing eyes, a trembling hand, and an aching heart'. At first they had devastated him: 'the recollection of her sufferings and virtues tended to embitter the loss'. Later their reading produced 'a sacred and strengthening grief'. Later he would write:

'knowing what she was, and believing where she is, I now feel her memory as a serene and inspiring influence, that comes over my social moments only to temper cheerfulness, and over my reflecting ones to animate me in the love of truth'. If 'any circumstances of my life could give me cause for boasting, it would be of having such a mother'. For the rest of his life her grave in Hampstead churchyard would be a place of pilgrimage to which he would go for spiritual sustenance. In her last months his failure to visit her, whatever his reasons, must have occasioned considerable guilt. In 1827 he would write 'my mother' and add, 'I never can write those words without emotion'.

Mary Hunt died in November 1805, a few weeks after Hunt's twenty-first birthday. By January he himself was acutely ill, emotionally and physically, with extreme manifestations of anxiety, in what can only be interpreted as a nervous breakdown. Curiously, he did not seem to associate his illness with her death, though to modern eyes there would seem to be a connection. He began to suffer from palpitations, which he diagnosed as evidence of a diseased heart; he feared he might die in his sleep and slept sitting up to minimise the danger. He felt he was about to choke, and his head pounded with intolerable pressure. He was giddy, rheumatic, had flickerings before the eyes and suffered from nausea. Everything worried him: he could not pick up a book, pursue a random thought or recollect a memory without beginning a line of fears. That he could find 'no cause whatsoever' for these feelings terrified him. Though his rational mind did not believe in Hell — as Mary's son he had been brought up emphatically to disbelieve in it — emotionally he now felt himself a candidate, hopeless and worthless. 'I plagued myself', he wrote later, 'with things which are the pastimes of better states of health, and the pursuits of philosophers. I mooted with myself every point of metaphysics that could get into a head into which they had never been put. I made a cause of causes for anxiety, by enquiring into causation . . . Oh! what pain was it to me then!'

Today Hunt's physical symptoms would probably be seen as manifestations of his nervous condition. He saw the reverse, thinking his nervous condition the product of ill health and believing a suitable physical regime would cure both. He refused to see a physician, partly from fear of what he might be told, partly because he was determined to suffer to the end and wear 'out the calamity by patience'. He began to cure his palpitations by horse-riding. When he rode at break-neck speed to the brink of a chalk pit he found considerable improvement and felt sure his action had been the reason. All his life he would favour diets as a means to health and now starvation became the key to his self-treatment, or perhaps more accurately, self-punishment: he described it later as a 'ridiculous super-abstinence'. So he took 'wholly to a vegetable diet' which made him so weak and giddy that he could not walk along the street without holding on to the railings. He then decided to exist on milk, another mistake for he had inherited Mary's sickly liver and fell prey to a yellow jaundice and nausea. At last, since he was so weak, he allowed himself 'a modicum of meat, one glass of wine, no milk except in tea, and no vegetables'. He improved a little but his 'mental distress' continued. Applying the same self-punitive measures to his body, he discovered that physical and 'moral' excitement gave relief and he formulated the theory that violent exercise opened the pores and so relieved his maladies. He took icy plunges in winter and blistering baths in summer, supplementing this bizarre regime with energetic activity.

Though he looked ill, few of his friends realised the agony he was suffering. He kept to his work, often at frantic pace because this somewhat relieved his anxiety, writing his reviews and editorials, and doing his private study. Those closest to him bore the brunt of his irritability and outbursts, his recurring depression, and his constant need for reassurance and sympathy. Chief among these was Marian. Just before his mother's death he had felt moved to petition Mrs Hunter to help him in his inability to communicate with Marian, for he felt further from her than ever. After his mother's death the emotional barriers between them seem to have been swept away in the surge of his need. 'There is nothing', he told her, 'which my mother has left behind her, to which you are not the proper heiress in the truest sense of the word'. In some ways it would be a bitter inheritance, for the girl he sought was not the flesh and blood Marian but the soul-mate of his imagination, endowed with too perfect qualities. No real woman could occupy such a high and precarious pedestal.

At the same time, Hunt's letters suggest that the lesson in caution he had learned from their separation had not outlived the strain of his illness. Insecurity, and consequently a desire to reprimand, had returned. He was obsessed by two things. The first was Marian's illiteracy. 'Now, cannot you', he wrote in Frebruary 1806, 'sit down on Sunday, my sweet girl, and write me a fair, even-minded honest hand, unvexed with desperate blots and skulking interlineations'. This cry he would repeat in numerous letters over the next three and a half years. The second complaint was her unfaithfulness. She had left him once and she might do so again. In his helplessness he knew that such a loss would destroy him, and so Marian must at all costs be transformed into that ideal, faithful soul-mate on whom his sanity depended. To this end he employed every self-defeating weapon that he knew: lectures, rebukes, cajolery, threats, supplications and declarations. Marian must learn, as he had learned, that love was the reward of good behaviour. He assailed her with smothering possessiveness, he demanded proofs of her affection and her willingness to conform, and he hinted that if she did not behave *he* would be obliged to leave *her*. Such was the emotional pattern of his courtship letters between 1806 and 1809.

In February 1806 Hunt's family packed him off to Lincolnshire to stay with John Robertson's artist brother in the hope that fresh air and diversion might cure his illness and depression. He ate, slept, read and his spirits, at first low, rose past normality to an unnatural state of elation. He and Charles Robertson rode from Gainsborough to Doncaster, laughing, shouting and playing on words to the point where Hunt devised 150 rhymes on the word 'philospher'. Alas, the vapours returned, his spirits fell, and his palpitations recurred. The long daily letters to Marian changed from hopeful, excited travelogues — for he was seldom so ill that he could not take pleasure in sharp observation — into catalogues of her errors.

The next absence came a few months later, when Hunt had throat stiflings, rheumatism, melancholy, and giddiness. This time he went to William Papendiek at Barnes Terrace. Having heard rumours of William's growing snobbishness, he told Marian, he would examine his old school friend to see 'whether he was really worthy of my friendship or not'. With what dismay the gentle, generous Papendieks must have regarded this irritable young man who arrived on their doorstep. The parents, after many years at Court, retained a profound reverence for rank: a mention of the Prince of Wales brought forth ecstasies of praise. No brother of John Hunt could sit silent through such conversation. In his nervous extremity he broke out, and they were appalled. William was obliged to take his guest aside and beg him not to contradict, whereon Hunt burst out laughing and contemptuously said he would never be a hypocrite. Not surprisingly the visit was cut short. Hunt had yet to learn that aggression, so effective and even admirable in journalism, was less effective and admirable in human relations.

The visit to the Papendieks was a fiasco and, as his disenchantment grew, Marian received many rebukes, in his frequent letters.
At first, when he was happier, he interspersed his lessons with
praise, but as his anxiety increased so did his lack of humour and
proportion. What did she mean by calling him *Dr* Henry? If this
meant 'dear' she should have written out the words in full: he had
never written a prescription in his life. Poor Marian! Her clumsy
attempt to joke had failed completely. Two months later she set
jokes aside, and dared to retort to her beloved's complaints. To
Hunt's fevered and vulnerable mind this was gross disobedience,
and must at once be squashed. Stating by way of preface that he was
not 'angry', he let out several pages of tirade. Men desired in
women, he told her, 'a general *spirit of mildness*' which her abrasive
manner sadly lacked, shaming him in 'a most painful and indescribable way', and indeed alienating his affection. He might not even
continue to love her at all if she 'should *continue* that kind of
behaviour'.

It was clear in Leigh Hunt's mind that Marian must be at fault. If
he conceded for even one moment that *her* 'kind of behaviour' was
in any way provoked by his, the whole structure of their relationship
was threatened. If such an idea did dimly arise, he at once dismissed
it as unjustified. After all, how could he be in any way to blame,
when he only intended her improvement? But what of Marian's
side? Without her part of the correspondence one cannot be sure,
but she must have been disillusioned. She had tried humouring,
joking, even remonstrance and all had met a blanket of anger. Why
then did she not leave him? Again one can only speculate. It was a
socially advantageous match. Above all, it seems that she loved
him, and since he needed her so, she was prepared to stay.

By March 1807 Marian was so ill that her anxious mother sent her
to her uncle in Brighton where she stayed until late in the year. For
once Hunt seemed shocked into sympathy. He wrote his sweetest
letters — tender, amusing, cheering, full of anecdote, retailing with
zest a daring joke he played at a party of the Hunters where he
passed off Marian's baby step-sister Nancy as his own and Marian's
child. He sent her presents, including a box of oranges, but as the
weeks drew out he fancied himself again neglected. When in July he
decided to take a holiday, he did not go to Brighton but went instead
to Margate in the company of the head of his department in the War
Office, a Mr Stuart, and his pretty and accomplished unmarried

sister. Miss Stuart's name came increasingly into the letters, and Hunt was deliberate in his use of it. It is clear that he felt Marian was defying him by protracted absence and clear also that he had found, as he thought, a weapon to subdue her. Unhappy Marian eventually admitted to jealousy and he was jubilant. 'You need not be jealous of Miss S.', he wrote, 'or of any girl upon earth, while you try to improve yourself . . . produce a mild demeanour . . . *Always prefer scratching to hasty blots* . . . if neatness is not immediately to be obtained, carefulness always may'. They were transparent emotional games but that did not make them the less effective, or less pathetic.

The year 1808 followed the same pattern in letters and absences. Hunt continued giddy, sleepless, irritable and melancholy; Marian was weak and depressed, with backaches and headaches and other symptoms of 'nervous origin'. In June Hunt went to Nottingham for his paper. For a time he was more relaxed, and his letters even praised Marian's first attempts at modelling in plaster — he had longed for a wife with artistic accomplishments. He returned to a sweltering summer and soon both were ill, Marian so bad that she was treated with leeches and sent to relatives at Brompton. At this, Hunt's composure collapsed and he imagined her mother plotting to break their engagement. He may have been right, for Mrs Hunter's relationship with him had deteriorated and she had neither time nor understanding for his artistic nature or free-thinking mind. She had struggled with poverty, clung to principles, practised thrift, and achieved the victory of comfortable marriage with respectable Rowland Hunter, and she expected others to overcome their troubles. Furthermore, Hunt's unorthodox ideas on religion, which he was eagerly imparting to Marian, disturbed her narrow Christianity. But she had a loving and loyal heart, and she may only have been attempting to test the strength of the attachment by sending Marian away.

Hunt exploded, besieging her with letters. When a month later Mrs Hunter sent Marian on from Brompton to Ramsgate, Hunt severed all contact with her. At the same time he was concerned about his beloved, and his letters reveal tenderness and anxiety: one cannot doubt that he loved her and that he missed her. On the eve of his twenty-fourth birthday he wrote to her: 'I hope to God I shall never see another birthday without you, without my wife. Every-thing I do, and almost everything of which I think, looks towards that time.' At the same time he upbraided her for not answering his letters and for not — naughty child — doing her lessons.

The day of the marriage came closer. With his literary earnings and his salary from the War Office of £100 a year, he could expect a 'tolerable' married income. At the back of his mind was the wretched picture of his parents' poverty and he was determined to avoid it. He had seen his mother, 'the best woman of her time', worn out. How terrible to contemplate another beloved woman trembling to hear a knock at the door, or to meet a quarter day.

Marian returned from Ramsgate and Hunt was overjoyed. He could not keep his hands from her, even in public, and Barron Field was forced to speak to him about so ungentlemanly a display. Hunt, however, saw his own behaviour as sincere and natural, and indignantly 'cut him very short'. During Marian's absence he had carefully planned their future together, charting a time-table of their coming days: 'In the daytime you will sit by me while I write, and employ yourself as your own dear industry directs you, though you must always take advantage of the fine weather to go out with me: in the afternoon we shall be *en famille* for perhaps one half of the week, and during the rest you will see a few friends, Mr Haydon, Mr Gorton etc, who are all sensible men and *worthy to be in the society of a reasonable woman.*' On Sundays they would visit the Hunters. They should have no house of their own, which was '*just now*' impossible. Instead they would live with brother John and his family. Marian's character was entirely to John's taste, he reassured her, and they would all 'be comfortable' together.

In January 1809 Marian, so weak that she could scarcely walk, could not offer the reactions he craved. One evening they quarrelled, and she watched him storm once again from the room. He expected her to placate him but she did not. Next day, in a torrent of frustrated feelings, he chided her for her aloofness: '*you stopped in the room when I went upstairs and made not a single effort to prevent me.*' At the back of his mind was the old fear that Marian might still have a will of her own.

Marian's retirement to High Wycombe in May 1809 suggests she did have such a will. At the house of a family friend she sought to recover her health and peace of mind, and perhaps to come to some decision about the future. What went through her mind is not known, but what went through Hunt's is well documented. He bombarded her with letters seeking a date for the wedding. On Monday 12 June he confidently expected them to wed the following Sunday at his parish church of St Clement Dane in the Strand. Mr

Hunter was to help him obtain the marriage licence and interview the rector — those frivolous but necessary arrangements which so demeaned, in his opinion, the happiness of the event. After the wedding they would dine quietly with Marian's mother, and walk to their new home at John's house in the Strand.

Another two weeks would pass before their wedding day. Was Marian nursing sensible doubts? Thornton, writing long after, declared that the delay was due to Marian's age: being not quite 21, it was necessary for her to complete the formalities and obtain parental consent. Whatever the reasons, on 3 July 1809 the long and stormy courtship was terminated by marriage. It remained to be seen whether they would live happily ever after.

4　GLOOM AND CHEER

In 1807 John Hunt began to plan his most ambitious journalistic venture. His initiative and his sense of duty alike suggested a new style of paper: a serious political weekly, allied to no party and as impartial as he could make it. At a time of few newspapers, virtually none attempting reflective political articles, and an avid and increasing reading public, he felt he could not fail.

Family feeling and sense of economy suggested the use of his brothers as contributors. Robert — said by his nephew Thornton to be a 'thriftless, thoughtless, bookless, homely non-artist', devoid of all talent but 'digestion' — would cover the fine arts, while Leigh with proven skills would do the theatrical reviewing. For Leigh, John had additional plans. With remarkable speed, this youngest brother had made his name as a revolutionary theatrical reviewer of impartial, outspoken, witty and scholarly style. If those skills could be turned to the writing of politics, what fame or profit might be achieved for them all! It was a thought that John persistently aired and Leigh just as persistently resisted. Theatrical criticism, he said, was allied to literature, whereas politics were a world apart.

John Hunt was a persuasive arguer, and he had powerful arguments. He had seen the gratification that Leigh Hunt derived from educating the dramatic taste of his readers and in chastising the faults of actors and dramatists. He possibly realised that his timid brother found satisfaction and power in the critic's role, and relief from his sense of helplessness by making destructive attacks on those he believed deserved them. Although impotent in fighting personal battles, Leigh Hunt could endure the attacks of public enemies with a masochistic delight which, on his own observations, had been inculcated from his cradle. Under the banner of fearless impartiality he took pleasure in castigating shoddy actors and dull playwrights, and almost took pleasure when they retaliated. At one performance he sat in a box beside the stage while an actor only feet away delivered a vitriolic prologue attacking him, and it brought only elation. In later years he would be ashamed of such youthful pride, but now he delighted in it.

John Hunt had the wit to see that these personal characteristics, added to a sharp intelligence and fluent prose, could make his brother one of the finest political journalists of his day. Young Leigh's lack of political expertise did not dismay him, for John had enough for both: if they pursued general topics, Leigh might manage without ever requiring too close a knowledge of daily politics. By the end of 1808 John had persuaded Leigh Hunt to be co-proprietor, editor, political writer and theatrical critic of the new paper.

The *Examiner*, named after Swift's famous journal of the previous century, went on sale on the first Sunday in 1808. From the beginning a large proportion of its articles flowed from Leigh Hunt's pen, most signed with the mark he had already established for himself — a hand with a pointing index finger which he called the 'Indicator'. But his political journalism always went 'against the grain'. Each week he procrastinated over his articles, making the compositors wait, and when he did write, it was often hurriedly. He voiced his shortcomings in 1813:

> I have hitherto confined myself as a journalist, to very general politics, and principally to the ethical part of them, to the diffusion of a liberal spirit of thinking, and to the very broadest view of character and events, always referring them to the standard of human nature and common sense . . . In short the common sense — the moral part of my business — I know well enough, and am as enabled to detect the most wretched errors . . . which the ordinary politicians of the day would pass upon us for good government; but I want acquired learning — the details, the out-of-door experience.

Though Leigh Hunt lacked this experience, he never felt sufficient motivation to acquire it, and he could achieve his effects without it. In another way, this very lack of professionalism was his salvation. It brought to his work a freshness, sincerity, commonsense and scholarship which were as unusual in journalism in those days as in these. Francis Wrangham, the noted scholar and theologian, echoed many when he wrote to congratulate the brothers on their 'spirit and elegance' and to predict a meteoric rise of their paper.

By October 1808 the *Examiner* was selling over 2,000 copies a week; four years later Jeremy Bentham thought it the most highly regarded weekly among 'political men', selling in excess of 7,000 a week, and reaching thousands more in reading rooms and reading circles. John Hunt, though privately a radical, kept his paper on a moderate line. 'We had absolutely no views', wrote Leigh Hunt later, but 'those of a decent competence and of the public good; that others may speak and act like Englishmen is our sole political object'. The brothers upheld the Monarchy, recognised the connection between church and state, and as loyal Englishmen opposed Napoleon; they aimed for 'Reform in Parliament, liberality of opinion in general (especially freedom from superstition), and a fusion of literary taste into all subjects whatsoever'. The Constitution, 'with its King, Lords, and Commons', was their 'incessant watchword'. These impeccable principles did not prevent their launching sharp attacks on king, lords, commons, church and state, the conduct of the war, and any other policy or institution with which they disagreed. The fearless impartiality of Hunt's theatrical journalism was transmitted to his politics.

There were times when the *Examiner* flew perilously close to its respectable limits, and when its conservative rivals were quick to label it subversive. Hunt saw himself many times cartooned and pilloried in the pages of competing journals. These jibes were, in a sense, gratifying: the *Examiner* was making its mark. The threats made by the security-conscious government were more disquieting. As England was at war, the activities of the press were of intense concern. Direct censorship was less of a journalistic problem than the threat of an action for seditious libel. In the *Examiner*'s first two years, half the papers in London were so threatened though only just over half of these threats came to prosecution and trial. Possibly the government realised that no jury would convict them. The threat of prosecution was the deterrent: even if they won their cases, proprietors faced crippling costs, and even the preparation of a defence, when the trial was later abandoned, could ruin a newspaper's finances. Moreover, if proceedings were abandoned, they could be initiated again. The threat hung in the air, like a bond for future good behaviour.

The Hunt brothers soon experienced this threat. In the first year they supported the cause of a Major Hogan who, with personal bitterness, spoke out in a pamphlet against the favouritism and corruption of military promotion. In supporting Hogan the *Examiner* uncovered a scandal in selling commissions, involving the Commander in Chief of the Army, the Duke of York, son of the King, and his mistress, Mary Anne Clarke. The government was not slow to prosecute the proprietors. Before the Hunts could come to trial, however, a parliamentary enquiry found justice in the allegations. Prosecution was dropped and the paper prospered considerably from the publicity, although the brothers lost money in the abortive legal proceedings. Leigh Hunt, in particular, was a loser. He had been working as a clerk in the War Office, despite increasing embarrassment, but in December 1808, heeding the hints of his superiors and his own exhaustion and conscience, he admitted his twin careers were untenable and resigned.

The idea of two devoted brothers fighting for the public good, at risk to themselves, had caught the public's imagination: 'it will be their pride', thundered Leigh Hunt in his editorials, 'to be brothers in suffering, if they can do one atom of service to the Constitution and help to awaken the eyes, the hands, and the hearts of Englishmen to the only effectual means of resistance against the common enemy'. At 24 Leigh Hunt was a 'poliical oracle'. Prospective employers approached him, prospective friends flocked to him and literary circles embraced him. He stayed aloof, determined to remain independent. When John Murray, on behalf of the *Quarterly Review*, twice approached him for articles — for a generous payment of ten guineas a page — John Hunt sent back his brother's refusal that the politics of Murray's magazine too directly opposed his own. Murray regretted the refusal and predicted that if Leigh Hunt could curb his radicalism he would make an eminent critic.

Between 1809 and 1811 the *Examiner* suffered threats of further government prosecutions. In October 1809, in an article calling for a Whig ministry, Leigh Hunt hinted at the possible blessings of a Regency — seditious words to government ears. The pro-Whig *Morning Chronicle* printed the passage verbatim, thus obliging the government to prosecute the proprietors of both papers for seditious libel. The *Morning Chronicle* came to trial first. James Perry, its proprietor and editor, a former law student and actor, was an old hand at seditious libel cases. He had already won two, but had lost the third and spent three triumphant months in Newgate where he held political court. Perry, whom Hunt would describe as a 'warm friend', conducted his own defence in March 1810 with vigour and drama and earned an acquittal, thus automatically protecting the Hunt brothers from trial.

No sooner were the brothers free from this prosecution than they attracted another. In September 1810 they copied from a Stamford paper an article entitled 'One thousand Lashes!!', criticising the brutality of army flogging. The article was by the paper's ambitious young editor, John Scott, whose future fortunes were to be linked with those of the Hunts. Both Scott and the Hunts were charged, the Crown alleging that the article had implied that Bonaparte's men were more humanely treated than the British soldier — sentiment which, at time of war, threatened national safety. The case did not come to trial until January 1811, a delay of four long and anxious months — a government tactic, it was said, to sap the nerves of the accused. Lord Ellenborough, president at the Court of the King's Bench and, ironically, one of the subscribers to Hunt's *Juvenilia*, described the article as 'inflammatory' libel, likely to encourage military disaffection. This time the Hunts might well have been convicted had it not been for the efforts of their counsel, a new friend named Henry Brougham. Scottish-born, six years older than Leigh, he was a writer, an opponent of slavery and a Whig parliamentarian. In the Hunts he found a cause well suited for his eloquence and sympathies. He argued forcefully for the rights of free discussion on public topics and he condemned the high military authorities for their brutal punishment. Though the judge was hostile and had 'no hesitation in pronouncing this an inflammatory libel', the London jury was sympathetic and found the brothers innocent. Later, a Lincoln jury, in spite of Brougham's defence, found the Stamford paper guilty.

Trials, real or imminent, unstrung Hunt's already fraying nerves, and the prestige he was gaining as editor of the *Examiner* did not fully compensate. Yet despite his poor physical and mental health and a myriad of worries, these years saw a flowering in his career and character. His rapport with his readers was a source of confidence: he spoke to them as friends and drew strength from their ready and sympathetic responses. Announcements in the *Examiner* of his illnesses elicited medical advice, homely cures and invitations to recuperate at a country house. His readers had become his companions. New friendships also brought satisfaction. His closest friends wers still the old Christ's Hospital coterie. There was Thomas Barnes, in whose study Hunt was 'as much at home' as in his own: a good-looking, caustically witty friend as radical in view as Hunt, enamoured alike of boating and of Latin verses. There was James Scholefield, whom Hunt had first seen as a stout boy 'very neat and self possessed' on the school steps, who would win many prizes at Cambridge before taking holy orders. There were John Rogers Pitman, later a preacher, and Thomas Mitchell who, after a brilliant career at Cambridge, became celebrated for his trans-

lation of Aristophanes. Barron Field was also a close companion of
these years.

All these friends loved literature and humour, all were young and
all felt pleasure in their tight-knit group. They found Hunt was a
delightful companion. Dining, drinking, joking, arguing, speaking
on a wide range of topics with vitality and charm, he was the centre
of the circle. 'Your letter', wrote Field, 'gave me such delight this
morning, that I could eat no breakfast, and could think of nothing
but sitting down to answer it'. Most of Hunt's friends by no means
revered him; their clear-eyed friendship was a healthy counter-
balance to his heady fame and overdemanding nature. If Hunt
sometimes became dictatorial and spoke out, as Mitchell said, 'ex
cathedra examinantis', he was put in his place. When Hunt accused
Field of overfamiliarity with Marian and 'unthinkingness' and levity
towards himself, Field retorted with the firmness of a tried friend:
'You shall one day acknowledge Leigh, that *I am not a trifler*'.

Wider circles now opened to Hunt. On Sundays he went often to
Sydenham, sometimes taking Field or Barnes or Mitchell with him,
to the home of Thomas Hill, the proprietor of the *Monthly Mirror*
for whose pages he occasionally wrote. Here he met new acquaintances: the poet Thomas Campbell, the comic actor Charles
Mathews, the wit and versifier Theodore Hook, and two young
poetic brothers, James and Horace Smith. Though John Keats
would later call their company 'cold and inhumane', Hunt recalled
only the wit and fellowship: Du Bois, Hill's editor, full of jokes,
dimpled Campbell a 'merry companion, overflowing with humour
and anecdote', young Hook sitting at the piano hilariously imitating
opera with 'the most received cadences and flourishes', and James
and Horace Smith reciting their amusing verses 'with rhymes as pat
as butter'. The star performer was Charles Mathews — magic and
mimicry transformed his person to anyone he chose. No wonder
Hunt often stayed all Sunday and even overnight. When he could
not attend, he sent a witty token; once he sent a coconut inviting Du
Bois to 'cut it up with almost as much pleasure as he does his absent
friends'.

At the premises of his step father-in-law in St Paul's Churchyard
Hunt met a more serious type of friend. In 1809 Rowland Hunter
had succeeded to the business and clients of his adopted uncle, the
renowned bookseller and publisher Joseph Johnson, and he continued the tradition of Johnson's Friday dinners. At his table Hunt
would first meet William Godwin, the radical political philosopher,

and Henry Fuseli, the artist of nightmare fantasies whose head and beard of white hair caused small Nancy Hunter to christen him 'white lion'. There, too, came John Bonnycastle, professor of mathematics at Woolwich Military Academy and as much a rustic old horse as Fuseli was a lion, and John Kinnaird, a literary magistrate devoted to classics and the bottle. Of this group, Hunt remembered Fuseli best. The coarseness of his language, and the violence of his conversation, seemed an apt accompaniment to the violence of his pictures.

To the newly married Marian, excluded from such male activities, it was a lonely life. After uneasy months in John Hunt's house, where visitors noticed the tension, the couple moved into Gowland Cottage at Beckenham, near Sydenham, 'out of reach of coaches', on the outskirts of London. Her sense of isolation must have increased when in January 1810 Marian found herself pregnant and unwell. For Hunt it was also a time of problems and preoccupation, which even the joy of approaching fatherhood could not lighten. Isaac Hunt was mortally ill, and the painful conflicts of Hunt's childhood were once more revived. Leigh Hunt would always feel guilt that he had shirked his mother's last days: with his father he took a full share of responsibility and pain. It was left to him to try to invite to his father's deathbed old and paralytic Elizabeth West. 'She grasped my hand', Hunt remembered, 'looked at me as steadily in the face as her shaking head would allow, and said, while her eyes filled at once with tears and resentment, "Never" '.

Isaac Hunt in his last days was a pathetic figure. His thoughts turned continually to reunion with Mary: his eyes brimmed as he sighed. 'She is not dead, but sleeps'. By day he read his Bible and his beloved sermons. By night he puffed his pipe and reminisced about his gentlemanly past. These last gentle memories helped to soothe the parting and must have reassured Hunt as he followed the coffin to the churchyard in Bishopsgate's Street. Not surprisingly, his memory of his mother revived with intensity. In April and October 1810 he composed two eulogies to her; the first in a memoir in the *Monthly Mirror*, his earliest published autobiographical writing, the second in a poem called the 'Planet of the Poets' which was never published.

Mary Hunt had not lived long enough to see his marriage or his children, but she had taught him how much care and support an anxious woman craves, and these he gave to Marian through her tedious pregnancy. When he was away he wrote almost daily, detailing his numerous duties and pleasures and the symptoms of his illnesses. 'I am going with Mr Hunter directly after breakfast into the city,' he told her, 'where I plunge head and ears into books till dinner, which I take with him at St. Paul's Churchyard. Tomorrow ditto, and the theatre in the evening. My limbs are as well as they were but not better'. And he entreated her to 'Pray take care of yourself my love, for your own sake, for the sake of ours, and for the sake of your affectionate Henry'. Since their marriage, his relationship with Marian had become more secure, and he could speak with a new ease. More and more his letters would voice not disapproval but his increasing need for her, though occasionally he still tried to transform her. In autumn 1810 Marian assumed the more fanciful spelling of Marianne: one cannot be sure that Hunt was behind it, but in view of his past transforming efforts one can certainly suspect so.

On 10 September 1810 Hunt's first son was born. He was beside himself with joy, and companions and relations were eager with congratulations. Field called the babe a little 'Indicator', referring to Hunt's journalistic trademark, and religious Benjamin Haydon, an artist friend first met in 1807, prayed that he 'would be famous in the World, and immortal in the next'. Elizabeth West, more mundane, hoped that Marianne would prove a good nurse. The baby was named Thornton Leigh, after his father and his father's early friends, the family of the merchant Godfrey Thornton.

The years 1810 and 1811 were troubled for Hunt. The daily challenge of political writing tired him, the threat of seditious libel action harrassed him, and his father's death and the responsibilities of parenthood were a strain. The cumulative effect brought a breakdown. In September 1810 he was wracked by rheumatism, in October he caught a chill, and in November and December he felt a severe weakness. He worried continually about leaving Marianne alone in damp Gowland Cottage; he begged her to take care how she went about the house in wet weather. He was 'annoyed on a hundred accounts' that he could not be at home with his 'beloved wife and her darling little boy . . . Pray compose your spirits, my dearest love, and wait as cheerfully as you can the return of your patient and affectionate Henry'. By the start of 1811 he was so unwell that he was obliged to leave Marianne and baby Thornton alone even longer to visit James Scholefield at Cambridge, and gain the necessary strength for the coming libel trial.

It is testimony to Leigh Hunt's restless energy and to the relief that activity brought him that he should have launched another journal in 1810. The success of the *Examiner* had generated a desire for a serious quarterly magazine devoted to a more profound and reflective study of politics ('reflective' was a favourite word) and also of fine arts, theatre and, above all, literature. Discussion among Hunt's school friends yielded enthusiastic contributors: Field, Barnes, Scholefield and Mitchell all showed willingness to write. So much did Hunt identify it as a Bluecoat enterprise that he described it in the preface as the 'production of a set of Persons educated at one School' and valuable to each other for congenial taste and friendship. To these contributors he added other names: Thomas Moore, Octavius Gilchrist, Robert Hunt, George Dyer, John Aikin and Charles Lamb — Lamb and Dyer being Christ's Hospital men. Dyer and Hunt had known each other since 1808; Aikin, doctor of medicine and journalist, was probably a recent acquaintance; Lamb, nine years older and well ahead at school, had possibly just been introduced to Hunt, most likely by Field.

Charles Lamb became a close friend. Hunt found him fragile, melancholy, tolerant and kind, with sharp intelligence, abundant sociability, a keen observation and ebullient and pointed wit. Insanity clouded his life. He himself had been briefly insane and always feared its return; 15 years earlier his sister, Mary, had murdered their mother in a fit of dementia and he was now her devoted nurse and guardian. By day this small slight man worked as a clerk in East India House, by night he threw off depression through conviviality and humour, a philosophy that Hunt found particularly to his taste. Like Hunt Lamb hated injustice; unlike Hunt he was conservative and unspeculative, and despite charming verses no real poet. His literary strength lay in his essays, where his observations and wit were incomparable. When he joined the new magazine, for its second issue, he was an established writer of poems and stories, but his greatest work as an essayist was initiated, many believe, by this association with Hunt, and it began in this magazine.

Hunt called his magazine the *Reflector*, for it was designed to reflect on the mind of the times. For a biographer, it reflects another picture even more valuable: the changing mind and mood of Hunt himself. In past *Examiner* years an angry critical style of writing had suited his temper. In the *Reflector* another style became visible — softer, happier, less critical and more creative. He began to view pleasure differently, not as a respite from duty but as a goal in itself. Small pleasures began to assume a new importance: the frost, the fire, his books, Marianne's hands issuing from her sleeves, and the rural beauty of Hampstead where his mother lay buried. The fear that 'broods over and hatches fear' could be vanquished by the positive power of innocent enjoyment — 'conversation, cheerful society, amusements of all sorts'.

Hunt was beginning to see that fear was a major source of the world's ills and that sunny contentment was one of its most positive blessings. Therefore it was his — and everyone's — duty to cultivate enjoyment and cheerfulness in themselves and in others. He began to surround himself with cheerful objects, flowers, pictures, books, busts. He began to pursue cheerful pastimes. Above all he began to tell his readers that they, too, must be seekers after cheerfulness. Cheer is his key word: it appears repeatedly in his writings. Henceforth his dominant belief in artistic, religious and personal matters was a philosophy of *cheer*.

In the *Reflector* Hunt wrote one of the first pieces inspired by his new philosophy, an essay called 'A Day by the Fire'. He wooed his readers with a confidential, chatty charm hitherto unknown in the English essay, his aim to convert them to an appreciation of pursuits and objects 'promoting healthy, innocent enjoyment'. The reader sees Hunt's winter study, 'cosy' and 'snug': he almost cuddles the word 'snug'. Hunt is seated by the fire: 'firesider' is a word he himself coins. He and his reader are to spend the day together as trusted friends, an emotional and intellectual sauntering from pleasure to pleasure, with Hunt as knowledgeable guide. He then introduces the simple, life-enhancing delights of winter life: 'bright fires and joyous faces', the tea urn, twilight fireside talks, music and wine and good friends, favourite poets and reassuring historical anecdotes, and 'a neat delicate, good humoured female presiding at your breakfast table . . . retaining a certain tinge of the pillow'. By teaching readers to enjoy such pleasures, he believed he was creating a happier, healthier, more virtuous existence.

The *Reflector* was mainly intended as a political magazine, but Hunt did publish general essays and poetry. He contributed both, including one long poem in the last number, the rollicking, colloquial 'The Feast of the Poets'. In places it was a verse version of those dramatic reviews in which he castigated playwrights and critics. He also attacked the poet Pope, once his poetic idol, and many modern writers including the Lake School poets, Coleridge and Wordsworth. He did not yet understand their revolutionary poetic methods.

Nevertheless the 'Feast' showed an increasing poetic mastery. Hunt was re-adopting the role of poet, though it conflicted with his other career of political journalist. They were two different roles and moods: the 'elastic spirits' of the poetic philosopher of cheer, and the 'bursting wrath' of the reforming journalist. 'Politics and Poetics', another poem written for the same magazine, expresses this dilemma amusingly. Unfortunately the 'Feast' was such a bitter poem it alienated many fellow writers. Later Hunt would call it 'youthful presumption', and regret that he had written it.

Thus the *Reflector* mirrored Hunt's mind in 1811 and 1812. He wrote a large part of its four numbers — 230 of its 940 pages. The magazine had vitality, and its end in March 1812 was unexpected, its serials remaining unfinished. Hunt apologised to his readers that the magazine had lost money — the financial documents bear this out — but its circulation at the end was rising and its spark was unquenched. Though its brief career had been fraught with despair, its demise saddened both editor and contributors.

The Hunts were bitterly attacked by the Tory press, following their acquittal in the trial for seditious libel in February 1811. The *Courier* was so malicious that the poet Samuel Taylor Coleridge, who also wrote on politics for that paper, was forced to disown authorship. Hostility towards the Hunts was counterbalanced by a stream of encouraging letters. One came from an 18-year-old undergraduate at Oxford, who addressed the Hunts as 'fearless enlighteners of the public mind at the present time'. A high-flown letter full of passionate, youthful effusion, its real purpose was to propose a radical scheme for uniting disparate reform groups suppressed by the wartime government. The undergraduate even likened his idea to Illuminism, which must have surprised Hunt as this was a disreputable Jacobin society dedicated to revolution. Soon after, the letter-writer offered Rowland Hunter a manuscript. Hunter declined it, but suggested an introduction to Leigh Hunt. On a May morning in 1811 the youth presented himself at the Hunter's home at Carburton Street, Fitzroy Square, where Leigh Hunt was staying, and ate breakfast with the family. Thus it was that Leigh Hunt first met the man who would become his dearest friend, Percy Bysshe Shelley.

Of that first meeting, arresting descriptions remain. Hunt

remembered his young guest as a 'youth, not yet come to his full growth, very gentlemanly, earnestly gazing at every object that interested him, and quoting the Greek dramatists'. Shelley, at that moment preoccupied with questions of individual virtue in political reform and given to quoting *Antigone*, remembered Leigh and Marianne less visually and less accurately. Engrossed by atheism — he had just been expelled from Oxford for his pamphlet, *The Necessity of Atheism* — he saw his host and hostess almost totally as kindred spirits. Both had been, he mistakenly avowed, Wesleyan Methodists who had after marriage converted each other to unbelief: now they were deists and in all practical respects atheists. 'Hunt is a man of cultivated mind, and certainly exalted notions', he wrote admiringly, and 'Mrs Hunt is a most sensible woman, she is by no means a Xtian'.

Such sympathy would normally have generated further visits, but Shelley and Hunt did not meet again for several years. Nevertheless, this first muddled but rewarding meeting laid the foundation for what would be the most significant of all his friendships.

5 THE BIGOT OF VIRTUE

In January 1812, when Thornton was little more than a year old, Marianne became pregnant again. Nursing a baby and coping with her husband's illnesses, it was little wonder that she found herself faint and 'fearful of walking the length of the street'. Once she had 'scarcely gone a hundred yards from the door, when she was taken ill and obliged to go into a shop'.

The previous year the Hunts had abandoned Gowland Cottage and come to London, where they lived with the Hunters at Carburton Street before moving to their own lodgings at 37 Portland Street. These moves, along with other expenses, ran them into debt, and in February 1812 the butcher, baker, upholsterer and other tradesmen were pressing them. Hunt drew at once on an inheritance from his American grandfather Stephen Shewell, who had recently died, and turned also to generous relatives and friends. Bess Kent lent him £40, Henry Brougham a lesser sum, while William Knighton, his physician, agreed to treat him without fee. Hunt explained that his money troubles were temporary and came from the late arrival of the last instalment of his American inheritance, but he was not telling the entire truth. Moreover, his troubles would not be temporary.

By July 1812 Hunt's debts had grown to the 'very little' sum of £550, slightly more than the entire income he had received the previous year from the *Examiner*. To his anxious brother John he laid bare the 'little indulgences' and 'thoughtless habits' which in the past three years of married life had snowballed into this burdensome sum. It was a table of the money owed to tradesmen, the loss from the unexpired lease on Gowland Cottage (which he refused to re-let because of the damp), the overspending of an 'infamous servant', a holiday at Hastings, and loans to 'two or three friends who were distressed'. As well there was an unsettled bill of £38 to a bookseller, and a promissory note of £50 to an art dealer for an oil portrait by Cornelius Jansen of the poet Milton. Hunt was only partially contrite about this last purchase. 'It was madness, I allow', he confessed to John, but 'I ought, however, to tell you that now I have got the picture I would not take £500 for it.' Hunt's spendthrift ways had begun. When depressed he would often spend

52

recklessly to cheer himself up, and when elated, he would spend with equal recklessness to match his mood. All his life, in a meta-phorical sense, he would be purchasing portraits of Milton.

Hunt assured his brother that he could live within his weekly income were it not for the accumulation of debts from past years. To discharge those he was prepared to sell part of his share in the *Examiner*. Alternatively he would borrow against his share and pay off this loan, according to his optimistic calculations, by March next year. The arrangement reached between the brothers is not clear, though presumably Leigh Hunt did not sell his share.

Hunt had been brought up in the midst of debts. The debtor's prison was his earliest recollection, he had watched his father's improvident spending and his mother's decline amidst the tension of indebtedness, and had vowed that no wife of his would suffer thus. Marianne, too, had known a childhood of debt and the grind of sewing for a meagre payment. Yet perhaps the very familiarity with debt since early youth blunted both Hunt and Marianne to the anxieties of poverty. In their first years of marriage they spent at will, with only the barest regard for what they could afford; if credit could be obtained they obtained it, without thought for what they already owed. Marianne, moreover, lacked her mother's house-wifely competence and thrift, and to manage within a strict budget would always be beyond her. Hunt was not impervious to the danger. 'As long as I am in the right', he told John, 'and feel myself so, I may almost venture to say that I am immoveable to external adversity, but this money business in agitating me as it has done, has disclosed to me a secret, and I am quite aware that I can have no command of happiness till I reduce my expenses to obedience'.

Hunt had other anxieities to weaken his 'command of happiness': the *Examiner* was again under the gaze of the Attorney General. In 1811, in consequence of the King's insanity, the Prince of Wales had become Regent. Abandoning his liberal views he retained his father's Tory ministers. Once popular he became increasingly un-popular, his dissolute life and extravagance drew forth angry reac-tions, and his public appearances were marked by open dis-approval. In March 1812 he was castigated in the House of Lords for breaking his promise on the issue of Catholic emancipation. In the same month the *Examiner* began a concentrated attack upon him; for two numbers it made fun of the Prince in odds and ends and ridiculed him in anonymous verses called 'Triumph of the Whale' written by the enthusiastic punster Charles Lamb.

In March, at the formal St Patrick's Day Dinner, the Prince's health was proposed and his name drew hisses. Next day, in loyal overreaction, the *Morning Post* crammed its columns with flattery: the Prince Regent was said to be 'the *glory of the People* — the *Protector of the Arts* — You are the *Maecenas of the Age* — Wherever you appear, you *conquer all hearts*, wipe away tears, excite *desire and love*, and win *beauty* towards you — You breathe *eloquence* — *You inspire the Graces* — *You are an Adonis in loveliness!*'

At the *Examiner* offices, Hunt read this nonsense with fury and seized his chance. On 22 March his carefully constructed answer appeared. Though rumours later attributed the authorship to Lamb, there can be little doubt that it was primarily written by Hunt, with Lamb possibly assisting. It bore the title 'The Prince on St Patrick's Day' and so memorable is it in journalistic history that its highpoint should be set out in full:

What person, unacquainted with the true state of the case, would imagine, in reading these astounding eulogies, that this *Glory of the People* was the subject of millions of shrugs and reproaches! That this *Protector of the Arts* had named a wretched Foreigner his Historical Painter in disparagement or in ignorance of the merits of his own countrymen! That this *Maecenas of the Age* patronized not a single deserving writer! That this *Breather of Eloquence* could not say a few decent extempore words — if we are to judge at least from what he said to his regiment on its embarkation to Portugal! That this *Conquerer of Hearts* was the disappointer of hopes! That this *Exciter of Desire* (bravo, Messieurs of the *Post!*), this *Adonis in Loveliness* was a corpulent gentleman of fifty! In short, that this *delightful, blissful, wise, pleasurable, honourable, virtuous, true* and *immortal PRINCE*, was a violator of his word, a libertine over head and ears in debt and disgrace, a despiser of domestic ties, the companion of gamblers and demireps, a man who had just closed half a century without one single claim on the gratitude of his country or the respect of posterity!

This article made the government rejoice. So far the Hunts had faced two abortive prosecutions and an acquittal, but here was seditious libel, with little doubt. The Hunt brothers had published with 'intention to traduce and vilify His Royal Highness the Prince of Wales, Regent of the United Kingdom, and to bring His Royal

Highness into hatred, contempt and disgrace'. Thus ran the charge.

The charge against John and Leigh Hunt was taken seriously by their friends. The Christ's Hospital group, whether or not it sympathised politically, rallied with affection. Scholefield, at Cambridge, wrote with 'proud indignation' and 'communion of feeling', lamenting 'so villainous an occasion'. 'My dearest Leigh', wrote Field, 'you must be happy, with the consolation of a loving, healthy family and the admiration of distinguished supporters.' Thomas Moore, the young Irish poet whose opera, *Blue Stocking Revels*, Hunt had disparaged in the *Examiner* but whom he now called 'the most delightful person one could imagine', wrote commending his 'noble warfare'. Jeremy Bentham, the famous political philosopher, invited Hunt to a 'Hermit's dinner, at this my Hermitage . . . the gate that opens into Queen's Square from the Birdcage Walk and the Barracks'. The 'approbation of the good and the wise', replied Hunt, was a special reward: 'Pray do not take me for a mere enthusiast who deals in words'. When illness prevented Hunt from coming, Bentham visited him, giving the appearance of 'a father talking and laughing with one of his children'.

In reply to letters from the *Examiner*'s readers, Hunt was at pains to disclaim the role of eager martyr: 'Pray do not regard me as one who from mere want of better taste am in love with prisons and prosecutions; for candidly speaking, I really do prefer a freedom of range to a gaol-room.' Nevertheless there is no doubt that Hunt had entered the struggle both eagerly and with full knowledge of the consequences. At a party at Charles Lamb's on 16 March, a week before his contentious article appeared, he told the diarist Crabb Robinson that he was 'prepared for the worst . . . No one can accuse me of not writing a libel'. His lawyer friends, Barron Field and Henry Brougham in particular, had advised him to be cautious. 'I cannot but greatly applaud the boldness as well as the ability of your attacks', wrote Brougham, now a firm friend and literary confidant. 'But this makes me the more anxious that the press should be saved from the strong hand of power, which I fear will be raised against it . . . The country is in the most dangerous and unfortunate state, and all our prudence as well as courage is required to preserve what remains of liberty.' Brougham admitted to being 'frightened' by 'one passage in the last *Examiner*', but Hunt scorned his advice. Nor did he in any way mitigate his position during the rest of 1812. The struggle between the 'Licentious Example of the Court and the Voice of Public Virtue', as he proudly termed it, continued to be expressed in the *Examiner*'s pages.

If the side of the prosecuted was uneasy, so were the prosecutors. In July the libel trial was postponed, it was said, because the newly appointed Attorney General had not yet taken office. The truer reason, the Hunts learned, was the government's determination to select a jury certain to convict them. Special juries composed of civil servants, presumably more likely to convict, were not uncommon in such cases. Brougham, who had been retained for the defence, was heartened by the delay and believed the charges would probably be dropped. Fast on his predictions came offers from the government to 'buy off' the Hunts by withdrawing the charges in return for assurance of future good conduct. 'Really you are well rewarded for all your anxiety, for all your apprehension, for all your obloquy', wrote Field. The government offer, he added, was making a hero of Hunt and 'quashes and annihilates not only the pending, but all future prosecutions'. Brougham, too, was sure that a prosecution would harm the government, for the publicity of the trial would be a thousand times more damaging than the libel. Despite such hopes the trial went ahead, its opening set for early December.

To one always attracted to the notion of suffering for a cause, the heroic stand of the *Examiner* was undoubtedly a source of intense emotional satisfaction. However, while one part of Leigh Hunt welcomed suffering, another repelled it, and the strain of waiting for another five months was more than he could bear. Through the early months of the year his health had been somewhat better; indeed he had begun to put on weight and had been obliged to visit his tailor. He had also been aware of a withdrawal into himself, an aversion to all physical exercise, a feeling of lethargy and some difficulty with his eyesight. Visiting his mother's grave for strength and consolation, he had been aware of 'an additional placidity. . . a grateful sense of present existence, and an earnest of a still better one hereafter'. He would sit for hours in the churchyard, his legs dangling, a book in his lap, given up to 'nothing but leaves, and silence, and a pretty undulation of meadow ground'. In July this pleasant lethargy turned into active anxiety. His 'old nervous disorder' came back, and he was depressed, sleepless, feverish, without appetite, with spots before his eyes and palpitations of the heart. His family and friends were worried. He could not even write. His *Examiner* tasks were skimped, his responsibility abandoned. His family summoned Dr Knighton, who prescribed 'draughts' and advised a country holiday. A worried John Hunt wrote speedily to his relations, the Marriott family, with whom Hunt had once stayed happily at Taunton, to arrange a visit. In the meantime there was Marianne's confinement to be managed, and early in August she gave birth to John Horatio Leigh, a 'second edition of Thornton' according to Field. It was therefore late August before Hunt despondently boarded the coach for Bath, equipped with a packet of Marianne's biscuits for the long journey.

The country miracle was not forthcoming. Many of his letters from Taunton survive, and they are plainly those of a man 'in a kind of waking nightmare', harrassed by debts and work, lost without his family yet trying to appear cheerful. He had experienced, he would tell Marianne, a 'horrible nightmare' when he 'seemed to helloo out double the usual number of times', and a violent palpitation occasioned 'by rather too much exercise'; or he had had a 'considerable degree of fever yesterday, but am better this morning, though very weak and thin'.

He brooded on his family. 'I can fancy Thornton on his horse', he wrote plaintively, 'riding to see his papa, and only I lament that I cannot snatch the dear, affectionate, good-tempered little fellow to my heart'. He worried continually how Marianne would meet their expenses and was relieved when he was able to borrow from a local banker the sum of £50 which he remitted to Marianne at once. His tone to Marianne was noticeably relaxed, the insecure hectoring of his earlier illnesses no longer present. The roles in their relationship had reversed, and she had grown stronger, he weaker. She was no longer his wayward pupil but rather his protector and mother. 'When I grow depressed', he wrote, 'I think of you . . . till I become like a child'. Her faults were nothing now compared with her strength. Marianne, too, had learned something of his great need of her and the subsequent power it gave her, power that her natural shrewdness would enable her to use with advantage over the following years. In the future this would be a prime factor in the relationship.

In all his illnesses he persuaded himself that certain foods made him ill: 'a potato or a glass of milk', he told Tom Moore, 'would cause me more trouble than all the princes or attorney generals put together'. Now, against his better judgement, he tried a little 'milk from the cow'. Next day he blamed the milk for causing his mood to fall into 'such a dreadful depression of spirits' that he could bear to be away no longer. 'Do not be alarmed at finding me very thin', he warned as he prepared to depart. He travelled from Taunton to London at the start of September, reduced to 'skin-and-bone' and still in the 'Slough of despond'.

On September Quarter Day the Hunts moved to a cottage in 'the country, though scarcely out of town', at West End Lane, Hampstead: 'really and *bona fide* a cottage, with the most humble ceilings and unsophisticated staircases; but there is green about it, and a little garden with a laurel' and, on the gate, was his name on a brass plate. Loving Hampstead he looked to its green serenity for a miracle restoration. Despite his weakness, he bustled about arranging his 'little library of poets' and hanging his paintings, precious tasks, he confessed, he could let nobody else look after. Though the effort of moving exhausted him, he could nevertheless report he was 'gaining strength by small degrees and small portions of exercise'. He looked forward to entertaining his friends to a 'plain joint and pudding' and drinking a sociable glass of wine among his books and pictures. On 4 October, however, little Thornton was taken ill, 'having walked out on Saturday in shoes too thin for the country ground after these rains; he was also frightened afterwards by a dog'. Marianne dosed the child with magnesia and soaked his feet, and he improved slightly. Under the strain of this worry and the approaching trial, Hunt's precarious recovery ceased.

On 9 December 1812, at the Court of the King's Bench, the case of *The King* v. *John and Leigh Hunt* began. Presided over by Lord Ellenborough who had unsympathetically judged their previous trial, it aroused public excitement. The crowd outside so swelled that it was impossible to open the doors to the public and impossible to disperse the crowd. Henry Brougham, speaking for the defence, maintained that the Hunts were provoked to attack by the 'unworthy adulation' of the *Morning Post*, whose 'panegyric' had aroused the brothers to legitimate contempt. The vices of a prince and his courtiers, he told the jury, were not above reproof. What 'danger to morals' would arise if the press freely criticised the vices of the great? While he did not dare to contend openly that the *Examiner*'s attack on the Prince was true, he cunningly managed to suggest it by taking the particulars of an article, one by one, and indirectly making clear that they were founded in fact — a ruse not lost on Lord Ellenborough.

Brougham made much of Leigh Hunt's sterling character. He spoke eloquently of his integrity, his quiet and virtuous way of life and his disinterested zeal for sensible reforms:

He is a rigidly studious man; a man not advanced in life, being, I believe, considerably under thirty, but always surrounded by books rather than by men. His delight is to pursue his studies, which he does, incessantly, from Sunday to Sunday, in his retirement; while he also prepares his weekly journal, the topics in which are various, as those of a public journal ought to be, including the history of the events of the times in which we live, and among them, observations on general politics. He is devoted to no Political Party; he knows of none.

Brougham applauded Hunt's public-spirited writings on poverty, severe military punishment, and the abolition of the slave trade. He was unable, however, to quieten the hostility of Lord Ellenborough, or the specially selected jurors, five of whom were reputedly in the state's employ. Lord Ellenborough condemned both the Hunts and their counsel, and found they had published a 'foul, atrocious and malignant libel'. A quarter of an hour later the verdict was unanimous, the Hunts were guilty.

The sentencing was postponed for more than a month, and Leigh Hunt passed his time in the *Examiner*, attacking Lord Ellenborough, the state of England, the Prince's artistic taste, and the vices of the Court. His spirits varied. He was mostly sunk in depression but, as he had noticed at other times, his mood could veer disconcertingly in the opposite direction into 'a great flow of natural spirits'. Benjamin Haydon, whose mercurial temperament was not unlike Hunt's own, visited him at Hampstead a few days before the sentencing, and found him full of fun and wit. They 'walked out and in furiously after dinner' and discussed the forthcoming sentence. Hunt 'said it would be a great pleasure to him if he were certain of going to Newgate, because he should be in the midst of his Friends' — a reference to the proximity of Christ's Hospital. 'We both laughed heartily', Haydon recorded, 'at the idea of his being in the midst of all his Friends at Newgate!! and his being reduced to say it would be a great pleasure the idea of his going there!!!'

On 3 February 1813, Leigh Hunt dressed himself in his best suit, hat and gloves, and placed in his pocket a little copy of 'the *Comus* of Erycius Puteanus', a favourite work which might give him comfort in his ordeal. Steeling themselves the Hunts mounted the dock together, Leigh being determined not to disgrace his older brother. Lord Ellenborough read the libel, and Mr Justice le Blanc delivered the sentence. The defendants should be 'imprisoned for two years, one in Coldbath-fields, and the other in the Surrey county gaol in the Borough; and at the end of their imprisonment should pay a fine of £500 and find security of their behaviour for five years more'. Leigh Hunt would always remember that moment: 'At the sound of two year's imprisonment in separate gaols, my brother and myself instinctively pressed each other's arms.' He had been prepared for the possible loss of Marianne and his children through imprisonment. He had not bargained on losing John, nor on a sentence of such length. The brothers suddenly were speechless and unable to address the court or each other. 'It was', Leigh Hunt recalled with emotion, 'a heavy blow'.

6 THE WIT IN THE DUNGEON

Leigh Hunt's earliest recollections had been of prison and of the 'game of rackets' punctuated by rowdy songs and drunken oaths. Now at 28, seeing the high wall of Surrey Gaol, those memories must have returned vividly to join his new forebodings.

Immediately after the sentencing, he and John had been bundled into separate coaches and driven to their respective prisons. After waiting for an unnervingly long time in the prison yard, Leigh was finally admitted. The gaoler, dressed in a nightcap and supping a basin of broth, declared he would have given £100 rather than have Hunt come to this place. After bargaining, he allowed Hunt the privilege of sleeping in his own garret until the windows of the cell could be glazed. To disorientated Hunt this was a welcome beginning. He was more moved by the delicacy of the undergaoler's wife who turned the key in the lock each night so stealthily that he was scarcely aware of the nightly locking in. Nevertheless the constant clanking of chains and crying of prisoners was like a 'malignant insult' and the isolation pressed like a physical burden. His family and friends, realising the necessity of Marianne's presence and of a system of support, feared the worst. Alone, Hunt became uncontrollably depressed. When he felt his fits of nervousness coming on he would pace back and forth in his cell for as long as three hours to dissipate the tension and eventually fall into an exhausted sleep. There was one consolation: his 'spirit of martyrdom'. Prison was a symbol of achievement, a moral victory over tyranny achieved before the eyes of 8,000 *Examiner* readers. In prison he read the life of Walter Raleigh and felt a sense of kinship: like Raleigh, he was a prisoner making history.

In these early weeks the pulpit of the *Examiner* was of comfort, and the letters from sympathetic readers cheered him. Moreover, John and he, though separated in flesh, had never been closer in spirit. When a possibly jealous Marianne enquired about a quarrel between the brothers, Hunt furiously replied that it was just as likely that her two arms had fallen out. His separation from John was one of his chief complaints in the *Examiner*. Was it not enough to imprison them, he asked, without parting two brothers who were related as much by love as by blood? Such a punishment went well

61

beyond the bounds of justice. Otherwise he accepted his fate, and was also proud of Marianne's heroic acceptance. He described her to his *Examiner* readers as 'a true Englishwoman both in spirit and tenderness', who supported his cause unquestioningly. Certainly Marianne was dutiful, but one doubts whether she did share his feelings. Her intellect was 'childlike' and her nature more prosaic than his, and there were many times when her loyal acceptance wore thin and she reacted like an ordinary female. 'I am almost envious when I see women going along arm in arm with their husbands', she wrote to him. Then she remembered her duty and assumed her loyal posture: 'it is for the public good, my dear love, therefore we must bear it with composure'.

Hunt's parade of loneliness was no exaggeration. The warmth and security of Marianne and the children were now a prop of his existence. On 5 February 1813 he submitted a petition to the prison governor describing his 'violent attacks of illness accompanied with palpitations of the heart and other nervous afflictions'. He begged the presence of his family and the daytime society of his friends as necessities to his health. Field, now almost qualified as a lawyer, drew up the paper and sought medical certificates from Hunt's past physician, Sir William Knighton, who as doctor to the Prince of Wales had felt obliged to withdraw, and from his present physician, Robert Gooch, Field was unceasingly kind and useful; he had accompanied Hunt in the coach to prison, and now conducted much of his legal business. Brougham, too, called frequently and busied himself on Hunt's behalf, and the old Christ's Hospital coterie was as much in sympathetic evidence as ever. Haydon's words 'I feel for you to my soul', were echoed by many friends and acquaintances. Best of all, there was cheerful news from John Hunt, who was making the best of his imprisonment. Look on it as a long sea voyage, he advised Leigh, and keep in mind 'the higher honour you will obtain by the victory'. John had obtained clean rooms and the promise that his family could join him, and he urged his brother to demand similar privileges.

Early in March, Hunt's petition was granted. Two rooms in the prison infirmary were assigned to him, and a painter and carpenter summoned to decorate them to his taste. Sickly Thornton was obliged to remain with his maternal grandmother, but Marianne and baby John had already joined Hunt, and it was with enormous relief that he greeted them.

Filled with forebodings that he might not survive his imprisonment, he decided to keep a journal to review his past life and provide future instruction for his two sons. Sitting in his cell while Marianne prepared a frugal supper of gruel and the baby lay asleep, Hunt made a list of his prison reading to show them how 'a good conscience and innocent studies' might sustain a man in adversity. Each day he set aside a time to study, and already he had read books of essays, travel, biography and medieval, Elizabethan and Italian literature. Friends sent books and the bookseller James Cawthorne kept him generously supplied. He was also working on a poem which he had begun a year or so before, when on holiday in Hastings with Marianne, though poetry 'is very trying work', he confided, 'if your heart and spirits are in it, particularly with a weak body'. Soon he increased his regular journalistic activities, finding that the added work gave him less time to brood and reduced his sense of ineffectuality, and by May he had taken over 'the whole management of the paper'. With time to spare he could also probe the complicated issues of domestic and foreign politics, so vital in those Napoleonic years. His spirits rose, his facility increased, and he delegated to others only that work which his confinement utterly prevented. In artistic, theatrical and parliamentary reportage, he was helped by his brother Robert, by Charles Lamb and by Thomas Mitchell and Thomas Barnes. Barnes, his special assistant, was already a gifted reporter on the *Times* and in three years was to become its editor. Under their combined regime the *Examiner* flourished.

In the middle of March Hunt was moved to the two rooms on the ground floor of the prison infirmary. As philosopher of cheer, he knew the importance of life-enhancing surroundings and he transformed his rooms with paint and paper into a poetical bower. The barred windows were disguised with Venetian blinds, the walls papered with a trellis of roses, and the ceiling 'coloured with clouds and sky'. A carpenter constructed shelves for Hunt's books and for his bust of Homer. Furniture was brought in, a piano and a servant were hired, the portrait of his brother John was hung over the mantel, and the controversial portrait of Milton graced another wall. There was 'not a handsomer room on that side of the water', wrote Hunt; 'there was no other such room except in a fairy tale', wrote Lamb. Outside the window the small yard also was transformed. Walled with green palings, planted with a grassy plot bordered by flowers and transplanted trees, it became a magic garden. Never before had visitors seen the equal of its blossoms, or eaten a tastier apple tart than that culled from its young apple tree. Hunt made the most of every possibility of pleasure and diversion. In fine weather he would study out of doors, and through two summers he rejoiced in the lilac tree hung with delicate blue bunches, the snowy broom and the swelling daisies. He would send his brother John nosegays 'perfumed with sweet briar and sparkling with heartsease'. In his garden he could have been 'a hundred miles off'.

Hunt parcelled out his day in rituals and routines which kept him busy and secure. He wrote, he embarked on useful study at appointed times, and he went to his poetry writing as 'regular as clockwork'. Years later he would attribute his habit of solitary, concentrated study to these prison schedules and he would bless them for inculcating so valuable a habit. Each morning and sometimes at evening he would walk with gloves and book through the prison garden as though on a long London walk, with little Thornton who had joined his parents in April trotting at his side. Thornton was his constant comfort and they would play for hours at hide-and-seek and battledore, spin tops, roll marbles, and dig and water Thornton's favourite sunflower plant. Thornton loved these games, but the tension of prison life depressed him and Marianne watched anxiously as he grew pale and hollow eyed. By day he was given to nervous tricks of pulling faces and striking things. By night he sweated and suffered terrifying nightmares, which caused his sympathetic fellow sufferer, Charles Lamb, to marvel that this 'nurse-child of optimism' who had been brought up 'with the most scrupulous exclusion of every taint of superstition — who was never allowed to hear of a goblin or apparition' should 'start at shapes, unborrowed of tradition' and awake in 'sweats to which the reveries of cell-damned murderers are tranquility'. Hunt, remembering his own fear-ridden childhood, had erased all obvious terrors from Thornton's waking life but was no match for the sleeping unconscious. The physicians, Knighton and Gooch, were adamant that Thornton must leave the prison. Hunt was dismayed at the thought of losing his wife and son, but he could not bear to see Thornton decline before his eyes. Marianne, exhausted by the burden of supporting a nervous husband and a nervous child, also showed signs of illness. Consequently toward the end of April Marianne left prison with her two children and went to Brighton, the home of her girlhood.

An almost complete sequence of surviving letters describes that sea-side visit and the thoughts and activities of wife and husband. They are frank, detailed and expressive, recreating with striking immediacy the lonely months of April, May and June. Marianne had digested the lessons of her courtship. Though her spelling and expression were still shaky and her interests narrowly domestic, she had learned very well what her husband wanted to hear. 'Pray do not repress your dear, dear feelings', he told her, and she did not. Indeed there were times during their separation when the sexual longing of both burst forth into their letters and Marianne's became 'outrageous'. She saw their hearts and bodies united — 'you know what I mean . . . I must not think about it'. The 'pleasure of hearing about it', wrote Hunt, 'almost overbalances the pain. . . we shall mingle into one and be inseparable'. For an intimate baring of feelings a biographer must in particular bless Marianne, for in this her letters are often richer than those of her literate and cultivated husband.

Marianne and the children had intended to go to Brighton for a mere few weeks, but they did not return to Surrey Gaol until three months later. During the separation Hunt complained constantly of smothering depression and deprivation, but more often it is with Marianne's sufferings that the reader's sympathies lie. Hunt was certainly ill and missing his family painfully, but Marianne too was ill and anxious and her days were rigidly regulated by the needs of two small children. At Brighton she rose at five thirty, breakfasted at a quarter to eight, walked the children until eleven, then ate bread and rested. At half past twelve they were out again, and John and later Thornton had a daily bathe in the sea. This was very expensive as she had to tip the bathing woman sixpence and pay three shillings and sixpence for the bathing machine. At two they dined, they walked from four till six, then home to tea and bed for the boys. At nine, Marianne had beer and a crust of bread, and at ten she was in bed. It was no lively existence, and it also evoked unhappy memories of her Brighton girlhood: 'every step I take reminds me of persons and things I do all I can to forget'. The physician she was obliged to call was an estranged friend of her family, indeed godfather to her sister Bess, but he relieved her of embarrassment by behaving with 'delicate attention and respect'. By early May she was feeling faint and sick; she might be pregnant. 'Oh Henry!' she wrote bravely, 'if we should have a dear little girl'. Her private feelings were less cheerful. The necessity of quickly weaning baby John produced milk fever. One evening her temperature soared and she fell into a fit; she was in agony. But to Hunt, already lamenting their protracted parting and a resurgence of his own illness, she was protective. 'Don't let what I have told you distress you', she begged.

At least Thornton was much improved and able to do without his soothing powders. The tepid sea improved his appetite, and he rode donkeys and played like a normal three-year-old. He was also succeeding splendidly with the Greek words which his father sent him to learn and replied regularly, using the little inkpot proudly provided by his parent. Each night he prayed that God would make dear Papa well.

Hunt was overjoyed at Thornton's improvement and sent him many tender messages. It seemed the family might be reunited, but then Thornton caught chicken pox, and Marianne could not describe her 'state of alarm and suspense'. Thornton, 'patient as a lamb', was covered with itching pustules, 'so disfigured, you would hardly know him,' and running a raging fever. John, though he showed no signs of disease, was wakeful and fretful, cutting a tooth. 'Oh', Marianne cried, 'what miserable nights have I passed!' She was almost demented with the strain of nursing and the worry about the additional money they were spending on doctor's visits, barley water and jelly for Thornton, and the hire of a sick bed. She even lost her purse, was obliged to consider pawning her watch, and her urgent pleas to Hunt for money were not welcomed. Two weeks previously he had been forced to repay a loan and to meet the bills of the paperhanger and picture seller. 'I have been sadly buffetted by pecuniary demands', he sternly told her, and he 'sometimes felt as if my senses would almost topple over and be too much for me'. He had sold part of his library to the bookseller James Cawthorne, had signed more promissory notes, and had luckily arranged an advance of £50 for the poem he was writing.

With such debts and with the entire family ill, it was a time of pessimism. Then suddenly it was over. John recovered, Thornton was well, and husband and wife were reunited to walk in their magic garden and lie beneath their ceiling sky. Through September they rejoiced at their reunion. In October John became ill and Marianne, who may have suffered a miscarriage, showed signs of illness. Again the doctor advised a change of air, and mother and baby were sent to Sydenham for a few weeks which stretched into another wearisome month.

To relieve Hunt's loneliness, little Thornton spent some of the time in prison, and during these days his happy games of building bricks and his bedtime salutation of 'How do ye do, my dear Pa? Are you better than you was?' became dearer to Hunt than he had thought possible — his 'dear, dear boy, the very thought of whom makes the tears start in my eyes'. Meanwhile Hunt displayed his nervousness and loneliness with a child-like ingenuousness which called forth Marianne's maternal devotion. In the early days of their parting he needed all his strength to resist calling her back, and he tried many ways of curing his morbid moods, writing as much as possible, with intervals of pacing or skipping to fend off his nervous attacks. At night he slept fitfully and was often disturbed by the prison noises. Fortunately his self-management and philosophy of cheer began to win, especially when the complicated system of support devised by his family and friends began to take effect. Bess was installed as his resident housekeeper and John's sons, Marriott and Henry, frequently stayed with him. Writing for the *Examiner* lessened his sense of helplessness. He found diversion and satisfaction in his editorial duties which progressed 'with steadiness and gratification'; he found that he could now 'petrify' the compositors with his volume and punctuality, though the intense work troubled his eyes and made it difficult to look upon the daylight. Then, as later, he was too vain to wear spectacles though he sometimes compromised with a glass on a black ribbon. Such therapy improved his self-respect and health alike. He grew more capable of enjoyment, less prey to nausea, headaches and rheumatism. At the end of May he noticed a lightening in his mood. Longer intervals stretched between his more 'distressed fancies'.

Reversals came, and with them days when Hunt's head was full and when 'a smart fever' and influenza of the throat, uneased by rubbings with hartshorn and laudanum, rendered him low and irritable. A 'short and severe letter' at this moment from Marianne, herself ill and depressed at Brighton, brought from him an answer but it was not the explosion he would once have levelled and its mildness bore testimony to their changed relationship. 'Oh Marianne', he wrote, 'I do not mean to reproach you, nor do I feel the smallest shadow of anger — my feelings would rather make a child of me at present rather than produce anger; but do not write me such another letter: — I can bear worldly trouble, I can bear pain of body, I can bear as I have borne, the united attacks of sickness and persecution, but the reproaches of those who are nearest to my heart I cannot bear.' He was a supplicant child, so dependent upon Marianne that, when she failed him, he was in no position to dictate, only to plead. He needed her more than she needed him. She began in these months to realise that the marital power was hers.

By mid year Hunt, on his own admission, had begun to enjoy his imprisonment. His family came incessantly and numerously; the Hunts, Kents, Hunters, their relatives and friends and servants, laughing, talking, squabbling, eating meals, drinking wine, playing games, sleeping on the sofas as if this were a tolerant lodginghouse. It was nothing to have several staying the night and many more requiring the turnkey to unlock the doors and escort them out at the curfew time of ten o'clock. His old friends came with food and books and poems and accompanying processions of their friends and relatives. Mitchell, Field, Pitman, Barnes and Brougham all visited him. When they could not come they sent gossiping letters and black puddings, pheasants and hares. Field brought his sisters, and Barnes brought a fellow *Times* reporter who soon became a constant caller. This was Thomas Massa Alsager, a former manufacturer, now music and financial critic and a bachelor. Marianne rather fancied him. 'What a man he is!' she exclaimed. His musicality, love of games and financial sense made him a valuable companion, and in no time he was one of the family, playing marbles and shuttlecock with the children, answering Thornton's questions, and inviting Hunt's guests to his neighbouring house at curfew time.

Safe in his womb-like existence Hunt now held court. It became fashionable in progressive circles to be seen in his prison, and his gaolers were highly impressed. John Scott, now editor of the *Examiner*'s chief London rival, the *Champion*, became a regular caller. Henry Robertson brought a sonnet addressed to imprisoned Hunt. Jeremy Bentham called and played battledore in the garden, proposing to amend 'the constitution of shuttlecocks'. Benjamin Haydon 'blew in', ravenously hungry, 'calling for his breakfast and sending those laughs of his about the place that sound like the trumpets of Jericho'. Pitying him, Bess boiled him eggs, and Hunt, aware of his grinding poverty, lent him money, declining that quick repayment which his own lean purse required. Hunt was both attracted and repelled by Haydon's ardent, quarrelsome, manic-depressive nature. He may even have felt a measure of responsibility for his predicament, having encouraged Haydon in disastrous attacks on the Royal Academy through the *Examiner* the year before. Now, working with 'enthusiasm stimulated by despair', Haydon finished his vast 'Judgement of Solomon' and placed it on successful exhibition. To express his gratitude to his patrons, John and Leigh, he had the giant 12 foot canvas carted to their prisons so that each in turn could share in his success.

In contrast, Charles and Mary Lamb came quietly to Hunt in all weathers, 'hail or sunshine, in daylight and in darkness, even in the dreadful frost and snow'. Charles brought a charming poem to his favourite child Thornton:

    Gates that shut with iron roar
    Have been to thee thy nursery door;
    Chains that clank in cheerless cells
    Have been thy rattle and thy bells;

Lamb may also have brought radical William Hazlitt, a former artist turned journalist, the son of a Unitarian minister who had been a pastor in America. They had met the previous year at Haydon's studio; and Haydon, recalling the three men together, would record Hazlitt's croakings, Leigh Hunt's wit and Lamb's quaint incomprehensibilities — 'a rare scene'.

Those paying court multiplied. A young, musical and literary clerk in Coutts Bank named Charles Ollier, whom Hunt had met three years before over an *Examiner* review, became a frequent caller. Hampers of food began to arrive weekly from Charles Cowden Clarke, a country schoolmaster's son who had met Hunt briefly at a party and been bewitched by the 'spell of his manner' and by his 'small sweet baritone' raised in a sea song. Sir John Swinburne arrived, aristocratic, wealthy, artistic and literary, a French-educated Catholic and radical member of Parliament who sympathised with Hunt's cause and would in future times befriend him financially; years later his grandson, Algernon Charles Swinburne, would also sympathise with Hunt's life and work. Hunt revered Sir John, and longed to kneel before him like a son asking a father's blessing.

As Hunt had a fine of £500 hanging over his head and as he had to find a further £250 as surety before release, he was tempted to accept Swinburne's substantial offer of money. Already many other financial promises had been made, some anonymous. Shelley had written a passionate letter with a promise of money, and Brougham had passed on the offer from a guilt-stricken member of their own jury to contribute towards the fine. John and Leigh, however, rejected all proposals on principle: 'it becomes us not to be paid for performing our duty', they wrote in the *Examiner*. But as the bills poured in, Hunt confessed to Marianne that his heart was 'shaken'. Marianne, for her part, loyally accepted their decision, although she wondered if they might not take just sufficient for the fine, if 'not a farthing more'. In fact on his release Hunt was obliged to borrow from his publishers — 'those knaves in Paternoster Row' — against the sales of two of his books, to find the money.

There were merry days at Surrey Gaol, with much 'bustling talk and merriment' and 'music in the evenings, which always does me service', as Hunt told Marianne. They spoke on 'all sorts of subjects — politics, historics, poets, orators, languages, music, painting'. Across the table where he wrote his daily letter to Marianne at Brighton, he one afternoon noted Bess, the Misses Hunter, Marianne's cousin Virtue Kent, Mitchell and Barnes sitting over their wine; at tea time Alsager, Field and Miss Field were to join them, while Mrs Hunter and small Nancy Hunter sent apologies. Such company was necessary to offset Hunt's anxiety, but one cannot help feeling for Marianne, anxious and solitary, when she remarked tartly that she hoped he did not tire himself.

Among these callers who flocked to Hunt's rooms, one stood out from the familar crowd and provided Hunt with an intellectual and emotional charge. In the middle of May Thomas Moore, a warm friend of three years who considered Hunt 'one of the most honest and candid men I know', brought with him a handsome fellow poet whom Hunt had distantly seen bathing in the Thames near Westminster Bridge years before. He was Lord Byron, and he confided that he had read Hunt's early verses with reverence while still a schoolboy. The year of 1812 had marked Byron's apotheosis in fashionable London: he had published *Childe Harold's Pilgrimage* and become instantly a fashionable poet; he had entered society and become instantly a fashionable lover. In the House of Lords his success was less instant, but his two speeches supporting progressive issues had proclaimed him a liberal Whig. In his politics, as in his love of literature, he had much in common with Moore and with Hunt, and it was natural that Moore should bring this literary lion to pay court to Hunt in prison.

Like many of Hunt's friends, Moore hailed Hunt's imprisonment with verse, paying a happy tribute to the fresh spirit that can warble free 'Through prison bars, its hymn of liberty'. On 19 May 1813

Byron, anticipating his visit next day, sent Moore a verse letter:

> But now to my letter — to *yours* 'tis an answer —
> Tomorrow be with me, as soon as you can, sir,
> Already dress'd for proceeding to sponge on
> (According to compact) the wit in the dungeon.

Over the intervening years Byron's phrase, 'the wit in the dungeon', has come to immortalise Hunt's imprisonment.

On 20 May Byron duly came, and the afternoon passed quickly, with talk of books, school, Italy and poetry and in particular the long narrative poem Hunt was writing. Some of Hunt's friends called though Moore, knowing Byron's shyness, had requested no other guests. A slight coolness became perceptible but Hunt had no doubts about the success of the afternoon. There was enough of his father in him to love a lord, especially a literary one! 'It strikes me that he and I shall become *friends*', he enthused to Marianne. There was something in the texture of Byron's mind and feelings that seemed to resemble a thread in his own, 'only a different wear may have altered our respective naps a little'.

Byron called next time servantless and carrying books for Hunt to use in research for his long poem. That he carried them himself suggested social equality, a gesture not lost on Hunt who became enthusiastic and could not wait to tell Marianne. He had got a fancy into his head, he told her, that he might help Lord Byron. Marianne was dubious; she had heard rumours of a profligate life. Hunt reassured her that Bess liked him — in Marianne's eyes perhaps a reason not to like him. His heart and understanding, Hunt continued, were excellent, and early vagaries, the corruption of society and youth — he was but 24 — must be allowed for. Perhaps the friendship with a kindred spirit like Hunt, older and wiser and more disciplined, might 'be able to render his heart and understanding a service, and help to lead them off into enjoyment more congenial to them both'. He was sure Marianne would approve. But Marianne did not approve, nor was she at all mollified when Hunt depicted her society as a necessary part of Byron's reformation. Hunt had no doubt that Byron had never met a woman like Marianne: good, domestic, 'capable of loving one person sincerely and making sacrifices for him'. Poor Hunt! His comments showed how sadly he misread both Marianne's and Byron's natures.

Byron had not misread Hunt's psychology and his comments in

his diary and letters to friends depict Hunt shrewdly. In the following half year, apart from the gift by Byron of his two Turkish poems and an effusive letter from Hunt obviously hoping for further visits, they remained apart, yet these two brief early meetings were sufficient for Byron to see Hunt with considerable clarity. He liked and admired him. Above all he admired his 'goodness'; preoccupied with his own wickedness, Byron put much value on goodness. He saw Hunt as an extraordinary character, not of the present age, a Pym or a Hampden with spirit and independence. If Hunt went on as he had begun he would deserve much praise. Yet at the same time Byron saw his faults. He recognised his masochistic sense of martyrdom, calling him 'the bigot of virtue', he saw his ingenuous immaturity, calling him not 'deeply versed in life'; he recognised his irritating authoritarianism, calling him 'Sir Oracle'. Yet for all this he was still a 'valuable man', a 'good man'. Byron wrote, 'I must go and see him again'.

7   DAYS BY THE FIRE

Hunt's imprisonment was, publicly and personally, a triumph. Deriving maximum pleasure from his study and work, enjoying an ever enlarging group of friends and rejoicing in the support of his family, he escaped what had seemed an inevitable breakdown. Moreover, he emerged as the imprisoned champion of liberty.

The summer of 1814 brought more happiness. Hunt's third child and first daughter was born in a burst of brilliant weather, and convalescing Marianne lay at the door and enjoyed the blossoming garden. The actual birth had been quick, so quick that there had been no time to call Dr Gooch. Hunt himself assisted. He was always to find the birth of his children a moving experience and he was proud of Marianne's easy labours, likening her to a Neopolitan peasant who was healthy through exercise. The little girl was called Mary after her mother and grandmother, and Florimel — it means flowers from honey, Hunt told his readers — as tribute to her flowery arrival and to Edmund Spenser's *Faerie Queene*, one of his poetic models.

Poetry was on his mind. Prison had given him leisure to study poetry, and the society of interested friends had given him opportunity to discuss his study. Moreover, with payment of his fine still hanging over his head and his debts accumulating from his prison junketings, he needed the money a published poetic work might bring. His studies had dramatically changed his view of the living poets. In the past two years he had discovered the worth of the previously derided Lake poets, and had taken in the great Romantic manifesto, the Preface to the *Lyrical Ballads*. Coming to admire Wordsworth, he had begun to formulate a revolutionary system of poetic subject and diction that was to find expression in the narrative poem he had discussed with Byron. This required another year's labour at least. But he could not wait that long to tell his public the fruits of his study even though he was likely to be torn down by those very critics whose ranks he had lately deserted. Taking his courage in hand, in 1814 he embarked on a recital of his new ideas in an updated version of 'The Feast of the Poets', the poem that had appeared three years ago in the *Reflector*, following it in 1815 with an even newer version in which his latest ideas were placed before the public.

Many of Hunt's poetic friends, including Byron, appeared in these two new versions. The hero of both was Wordsworth. In the 1814 edition Hunt, applauding contemporary poets, greeted Wordsworth as a writer of great but unfulfilled promise; Hunt hoped that his talent would 'speedily' emerge. Wordsworth in fact did speedily emerge and, accompanied by Benjamin Haydon, he came in June 1815 to visit Hunt. Hunt spoke to Wordsworth, Haydon recalled, 'with burning feelings of homage'. A few weeks later, Hunt produced a new *The Feast of the Poets* where Wordsworth appeared as the 'Prince of Bards'.

Hunt appended prose notes of inordinate length — 124 pages of notes to 25 pages of poem — in order to set out his poetic philosophy. He agreed with Wordsworth that current poetic taste was extravagant and sickly, and needed simpler and more primitive subjects and a diction drawn from the beauties and 'unsophisticated impulses' of nature. The magnificent Wordsworth had written such poetry. It was with his choice of subject that Hunt disagreed: Wordsworth's idiot boys and mad mothers led the reader, on the pretext of interesting him in individuals, away from society. As a social reformer and a gregarious personality, Hunt could not support a move away from society. Rather he believed that poetry must make men good and happy by promoting a higher spiritual and hence a richer social life. So in the prose notes of both editions, he reiterated his view that the poet must be aware of social and political issues and lead his readers towards their solution. He must educate by spiritual seduction, and not by manifestos.

The Feast of the Poets was not the only long poetic work Hunt would complete in prison, nor the only one uniting poetry and reform. In the spring of 1814, inspired by 'public joy' at the defeat of the French, he temporarily came to terms with his ambivalence towards Napoleon — the libertarian turned tyrant whom he admired and abhorred. In such a mood he compsed a masque, celebrating Europe's release from the Bonapartian 'Arch Enchanter' and the rebirth of true liberty. He enjoyed using the seventeenth-century masque form, exulting in its tolerance of fantastic stage devices as he wafted Napoleon and the Allied Princes above the stage on clouds.

Hunt's friends were quick to praise the masque which he called *The Descent of Liberty,* and Byron even presented him with a lock of Napoleon's hair. Dr Gooch, Henry Robertson, Charles Ollier, the Bluecoat coterie, and even Wordsworth's family admired the 'abundant beauties' of their presentation copies. More copies went to Charles Cowden Clarke, who read the *Feast* and *The Descent of Liberty* in company with a young friend, John Keats. Inspired by Hunt's verse, Keats scribbled his own in imitation, and worshipped Hunt under the idealised name of Libertas.

Meanwhile Hunt was engaged on the long narrative poem which he had toyed with as far back as 1811 when he, Marianne and Thornton were on a sea-side holiday at Hastings. According to his later testimony, he had been fearful of his soaring happiness and tried to reduce it to more natural proportions by working on a melancholy subject. He was riveted by a passage in Dante's *Inferno*, telling of the adulterous and incestuous love of Paulo, Prince of Rimini, for Francesca, his brother's wife. The theme had so haunted him that he could not obtain 'comfort' until it had matured into a poem, *The Story of Rimini*. In Dante the guilty lovers are condemned to eternal punishment, but in Hunt's mind condemnation and suffering were not appropriate. Intent on showing the innocence and beauty of natural impulses, and the wickedness of many customs sanctioned by society, he reinterpreted the story. Attractive Paulo is sent by his less attractive brother to woo Francesca for him. Paulo succeeds too well so that, when she travels as a bride to Rimini, Francesca loves Paulo with a reciprocated 'fatal passion'. The pair try to resist, but soon yield; their sexual surrender brings remorse at once, and eventually discovery. In later years Hunt would give the story Dante's ending but in his original version the brothers fight a duel, and noble Paulo deliberately falls upon his brother's sword, and Francesca dies of a broken heart. In 1844, however, Hunt concluded the poem like Dante with the double murder of wife and lover by the enraged husband. For the rest of his life he would vacillate between the alternative endings, the one ennobling, the other punitive.

The Story of Rimini, especially in its earliest version, is a justification of incestuous adultery. In *Rimini* the nobility and innocence of such love emerges triumphant, to shame a society which sets 'authorised selfishness above the most natural impulses'. Its hero and heroine are idealised saint-like creatures, worshipped after death by youths and virgins: he 'lovely in form and mind', she the 'first of womankind'. Their lovemaking, though fatal to them, is shown as inevitably right.

As a reviewer in *Blackwood*'s argued, Hunt's choice of an immoral theme was curious — the more so in one normally safe and cosy — and must have expressed some strange personal compulsion. The reviewer was not slow in seeing, in Hunt's own household, parallels which certainly existed and were even closer than the critic could have known. Between Hunt and his sister-in-law Elizabeth Kent ran a strong if ambivalent thread of feeling. At the time of Hunt's courtship it was common knowledge in the family that Bess was bound to him by 'strong attachment' and he less strongly to her, and that if Marianne rejected him, as for a time she did, he wished to marry Bess. Nonetheless Bess self-effacingly promoted the marriage, even urging reconciliation at the time of their estrangement. Later, after Thornton was born, Bess frequently lived in the household; during Hunt's term in prison she was even his resident housekeeper in those weeks when Marianne took the children to the sea. Intellectual Bess, with her self-taught command of two languages and her knowledge of literature and history, her grounding in botany and her graceful prose, had that cultivated and sympathetic mind which Hunt craved and which Marianne could not provide. His letters to her, especially those written when he and Marianne were in Italy, stress that he considered her more than all other women together – Marianne excepted. Bess, he affirmed, was 'linked with all the interests and hopes of my life'.

Dante's story of two brothers loving the same woman struck a sympathetic cord in Hunt during the summer of 1811. He, with his love of two sisters, probably saw Dante's story as a mirror image of his own dilemma. Through the less personal medium of Dante's story he could explore and dramatise his own intense feelings.

In Dante the love is consummated. Was this true in Hunt's own case? The question aroused some conjecture amongst Hunt's friends and enemies — 'the talking world', as he and Bess dubbed it. Most of the gossip and conjecture was to appear later, when Hunt fell under the spell of Shelley's bold advocacy of free love. At this distance the complete truth is impossible to know. But certainly a domestic triangle existed, and it caused intense pain to Bess — who once reputedly tried to drown herself — and some pain to Marianne. And Hunt, to convince himself or the world of the essential innocence and nobility of such a relationship, transformed it into *The Story of Rimini*.

Rimini was important to Hunt on other grounds; it was a showpiece for his poetic 'system'. On the one hand he longed to follow in the footsteps of Dryden and revive the harmonies of the English heroic couplet, which had degenerated into the artificiality of Pope. On the other hand he longed to follow in the footsteps of Wordsworth, to explore a theme and develop a diction that expressed the unsophistiated impulses of nature. At the same time he desired to retain the imaginative richness of true poetry found in those great masters, Shakespeare, Chaucer, Spenser and Milton. He believed that language, while it should retain an idiomatic spirit, must avoid the 'vulgar idiom' of real speech and must be heightened by the 'strength and sentiment' of its utterance. In short he aimed to blend art and nature in a new way; and the attempt utterly absorbed him, as his surviving manuscript shows. *Rimini* was written and rewritten with agonising indecision. Alas, too few times did he achieve his aim of heightened naturalness, falling too often into the commonplace banality he deplored in Wordsworth or into a pretentious artfulness. But he was undoubtedly innovative. Though the poem lacks instinctive sureness of touch, it stands as a milestone in English literature.

In *Juvenilia* Hunt had shown a partiality for coining new words. In *Rimini* the tendency took flight. As celebrator of the philosophy of cheer he sought a new language and, as Haydon observed, he often used obscure words to express his feeling. He also used ordinary words in extraordinary ways — he spoke of 'flings' of sunshine — and he changed parts of speech, transforming nouns and verbs, adjectives and adverbs, like a jigsaw puzzle. He invented clumsy comparisons like 'franklier' and 'tastefuller', and numerous compound words, sometimes with happy ingenuity, sometimes with strained and overloaded meaning, as in 'house-warm lips', 'pin-drop silence', or the coquettish and archaic 'clip-some waist'.

The philosophy of cheer permeates the poem — cosy, sentimental, negating the ostensible aim of high tragedy, reducing the fatal passion to pleasurably safe proportions. At the start of the fourth Canto the narrator announces that

E'en tales like this, founded on real woe,
From bitter seed to balmy fruitage grow:

and that balmy fruitage saps the poem's vigour. Hunt's distaste of strong emotion is visible in his passionless adjectives: fond, amiable, cordial, gentle, cheerful, dainty. They pile one upon another like clean paper tissues. His touch is sure only when expressing his lovers' most intense emotions, particularly their ambivalent recognition of desire — testimony to the personal nearness of what he described. Hunt was most at home depicting the impersonal physical world and his rich tableaux, painted more to delight the eye than the mind, are still among the poem's glories. What is generally agreed to be the finest section, 'The Fatal Passion' in the third Canto, shows his strength and weaknesses. Francesca is reading in her summer-house:

> So sat she fixed; and so observed was she
> Of one, who at the door stood tenderly, —
> Paulo, — who from a window seeing her
> Go straight across the lawn, and guessing where,
> Had thought she was in tears, and found, that day,
> His usual efforts vain to keep away.
> 'May I come in?' said he: — it made her start, —
> That smiling voice; — she coloured, pressed her heart
> A moment, as for breath, and then with free
> And usual tone said, 'O yes, — certainly.'
> There's wont to be, at conscious times like these,
> An affectation of a bright-eyed ease,
> An air of something quite serene and sure,
> As if to seem so, were to be, secure:
> With this the lovers met, with this they spoke,
> With this they sat down to the self-same book,
> And Paulo, by degrees, gently embraced
> With one permitted arm her lovely waist;
> And both their cheeks, like peaches on a tree,
> Leaned with a touch together, thrillingly;
> And o'er the book they hung, and nothing said,
> And every lingering page grew longer as they read.

Hunt knew his difficulties and was anxious for reassurance and advice. In prison he had showed the manuscript to Byron, and today in the British Library one can see Byron's faded pencil asides: 'perfection', 'superlative' and 'excellent' are written in the margins. Byron saw the faults but was more aware of the virtues. 'You have excelled yourself if not all your Contemporaries in the Canto which I have just finished', he told Hunt as he read the account of the lovers' sexual surrender. There is more originality, he continued, 'than I recollect to have seen elsewhere within the same compass — and frequently great happiness of expression' with very few faults, and they 'being almost all *verbal*' and to do with 'quaintness — & obscurity — & a kind of harsh & yet colloquial compounding of epithets — as if to avoid saying common things in the common way'. Byron had no doubt that the poem would give its author 'a very high station'. To Thomas Moore he wrote that 'Leigh Hunt has written a real *good* and *very original Poem*, which I think will be a great hit. You can have no notion how well it is written, nor should I, had I not redde it'. Of the genuineness of Byron's enthusiasm in these letters of 1815 there can be no doubt, even though in three years' time he would see *Rimini* in a harsher perspective and castigate its 'compound barbarisms' and its disfiguring style: '*Nimini Pimini*', wrote Byron sarcastically. 'There never were so many fine things spoiled as in 'Rimini'.' Like the poem's dedication to Byron, which overflowed into familiarity and came to grate on Byron and his friends, *Rimini*'s faults eventually drowned its virtues. But in 1815 Byron accepted the dedication as it was meant — 'a public compliment and a private kindness' — and valued the poem as an important experiment.

So by the end of his imprisonment Hunt was author of four new works, three of them published, and the successful editor of the *Examiner*. The day of his release, 3 February 1815, was likely to be an anticlimax, and so it proved. He felt almost like running back to his cell, and indeed his agoraphobia was so acute that the crowds in the street seemed like an insult. In those first days of freedom, fearing he might fall down in a faint, he ventured no further than the neighbouring house of hospitable Thomas Alsager, whom he presented with a sonnet and a miniature of himself as token of his gratitude. Having hugged his brother John on that first morning of freedom, he soon moved to lodgings in the Edgware Road, a stone's throw from John's house. Here the family reassembled with Bess Kent in residence and her cousin Virtue Kent, a woman as upright as her name, making up that suite of attendant females which later acquaintances would note as a feature of the household. Here Hunt recreated something of the hothouse atmosphere of prison, draping his room with green and white, painting the furniture to match, so that he achieved the effect of a 'box of lillies'. He was still nervous and prone to accidents. One morning Virtue Kent saved him from burning when his dressing gown caught fire, an incident that was faithfully reported to *Examiner* readers. As time passed, his hopes of speedy readjustment faded, and from 'morbid' symptoms he passed into what he called the 'hideous impertinence' of living. He was unable to resume his theatrical reviews because he could not bear the enclosed atmosphere of the theatre, and he even refused Byron's offer of a box at Drury Lane.

The safe, simple pleasures became important and the society of old and trusted friends was a necessity: the Bluecoat coterie re-assembled. Brougham came also, and Tom Moore and Haydon, but Byron's visits provided Hunt with his biggest emotional boost. Hunt had advised Byron in *The Feast of the Poets* to moderate his passions, and to frequent the society of the disciplined, politically reformist middle classes, and now in seeming deference to this advice Byron called often. The 27-year-old poet, so elegant in his tight white trousers, would sit on Thornton's rocking horse and ride with a 'childish glee becoming a poet', while Hunt propounded his poetic 'system'. Byron in turn invited Hunt to his house in Picca-dilly, where he met the literary Whig banker, Samuel Rogers, Byron's friend John Hobhouse, and possibly Coleridge — who in an adjoining room is said to have recited 'Khubla Khan'. In February 1815 when London society was ablaze with the scandal of Byron's marital estrangement, Hunt wrote a tentative and tactful letter, to which Byron replied with candour, sensitivity and unmistakable respect. Hunt was moved by the letter, with every justification, for Byron's sincere admiration for Hunt and his 'goodness' pervades his letters of this period. Hunt took Byron to his heart, giving him generous support in the *Examiner*, reviewing his writing and his politics, and defending his marital reputation against the smears spread by other papers. Byron would later acknowledge that Hunt was one of the few literary men who dared offer even an anonymous word in his favour. It is sad to know that nearly a decade later, the over-vulnerable Hunt learnt that others had also stood close to Byron in 1815 and 1816 and had received similar confidences.

In autumn 1815 Hunt felt stronger, indeed so strong that he moved from the sheltering proximity of brother John at Maida Vale to a little cottage in the propitiously named Vale of Health, a cottage probably leased by his step-father-in-law, Rowland Hunter. It was one of a cluster of houses set in a peaceful undulation of Hampstead Heath with nearby ponds and trees. For two years it was crowded with Hunt's family, Bess, Marianne's cousins, servants and the hordes of visitors, and congested too with those essential artifacts of the pursuit of cheer: Hunt's engravings and paintings of literary and classical subjects, his busts of celebrated patriots and writers, copious books and manuscripts, locks of hair from famous people, the indispensable vases of flowers, a grand pianoforte, and the battered but comfortable sofas and chairs in which he observed the religious ritual of the fireside. This cottage and its cheering contents are forever famous in the annals of English literature, being celebrated in poetry by Hunt and his friends.

Throughout his prison sentence Hunt had dreamed of 'Lovely-brow'd' Hampstead, visualising in a series of sonnets its ever-changing beauties, its winter 'sky whitening through wiry trees', its 'brown dells' signalling autumn. 'Every spot from this place', he would write in 1823, 'is sacred to me for some recollection', and none more so than his mother's grave surrounded by green ascending meadows. He found the Vale of Health the epitome of 'all suburban ruralities', near enough for morning loungings in the London bookshops and evenings at a theatre or friend's house and yet far enough away to offer the fine prospects of the Heath. He returned that autumn with all the joy, as he himself said, of an ardent lover rediscovering a long-lost mistress.

In Hampstead his agoraphobia gave him less trouble. Sociability, his antidote for anxiety and depression, now found its full celebration. A free agent once more, a hero with more doors open to him than at any previous time, he gloried in his new freedom and friendships old and new. In the diaries of Benjamin Haydon and Henry Crabb Robinson, in the essays of Lamb and Hazlitt, in many literary memoirs and above all in his own essays and poems we see the post-prison Hunt impressing his personality on many topics and people.

London literary circles were inbred, the same set of acquaintances meeting at numerous houses. 'Well sir, shall we go and eat Haydon's mutton', Hazlitt would ask his small son on Sunday mornings, for Sunday dinners at Haydon's studio were fascinating gatherings of artists and writers. 'What would I not give for another Thursday evening', wrote Hunt about Charles Lamb's Thursday supper parties, where friends found hilarity and wisdom. On Tuesdays Thomas Alsager was at home for music and whist, and even diffident Hazlitt entertained guests. In company with these men, whether as host or guest, Hunt performed with charm and vivacity.

Haydon was close to Hunt in these years and depicted him vividly in prose and paint. In September 1816, acknowledging a sonnet addressed to him by Hunt, Haydon proudly recalled that Hunt 'saw my genius the first hour he was in my company, adhered to me from that first moment, predicted my success, defended me in oppression, assisted me in distress'. Haydon was susceptible to Hunt's charm, calling him 'one of the most delightful companions on Earth', and yet he had the perception to see his faults with unusually shrewd eyes. Aware of Hunt's independence, kindness, honesty and genuine goodness, he also saw the superficiality and weakness that were part of him. Above all he fathomed the apparent contradition, recognising the basic helplessness that made Hunt so negative a character and the basic vitality that made him so positive a one. He described Hunt as an anxiety ridden dictator who had to control every situation for his own safety, an angel when all was going well who did not hesitate to pledge 'his person, his property, his talent' to his friends, but who repudiated these friends with anger and irritability when under fire. He recognised the vulnerability that caused Hunt to expect that his slights to others would be forgiven but made him merciless when he himself felt offended; the lack of confidence that made him happiest in the society of 'inferior adorers'; and the sharp loneliness which made company so essential to him that he feared to be alone 'even *for an hour*'. His praise of Hunt is equally illuminating. He admired him as a verbal virtuoso, a brilliant role many would remark on — 'in wit and fun, quotation and impromptu' the foremost performer at every party. Alert, fluent and lightning quick, in Haydon's vivid metaphor Hunt was a three-pronged instrument, and no matter how you threw him he landed with a spike up at the ready. Craving approbation and attention to an absurd degree, Hunt pranced lightly over subjects 'on a little poney filled with the air of his own vanity'.

Perhaps Haydon was most discerning about Hunt's optimism. It was not, as his friends might think, a 'lovely fancy shooting out without effort the beauties of its superabundant brightness' but the 'product of a painful, hypochondriac Soul that struggles by dwelling on the *reverse* of its own *real* thoughts, perpetually to illumine its natural and forlorn dinginess'. Haydon exposed in one sentence the origin of Hunt's philosophy of cheer and his mechanism of emotional denial.

From his intellectual equals Hunt called forth an ambivalent response. He relied on charming others or being charmed himself; and an intellect as acute and wry as Hazlitt's or Lamb's was not easy to charm. Hunt for his part found it difficult to worship them, knowing that despite their talent, their inner struggles were as keen as his own. Hazlitt, Haydon and Lamb were, emotionally, tightrope walkers. Lamb was forever clouded by threats to his own and his beloved sister's sanity, and Hazlitt was so shy he could scarcely meet one's eye or firmly shake one's hand — a hand like a wet fish, said Hunt — and the look on his face said that he had faith in nobody. Between these men and Hunt, however, ran a mutual tolerance and even affection that withstood the shifts and shakes of their troubled natures, and an excitement that provided an impetus for a closer friendship. There can be no doubt that Hunt loved Charles Lamb, and had a 'sort of irrepressible love for Hazlitt' which would have been even deeper if Hazlitt had permitted it. Comparing the three men, Bryan Waller Procter, a young lawyer who first met Hazlitt at Hunt's in 1817, wrote that Hazlitt talked best, Lamb made the wittiest remarks, and Hunt had the most ingenuity. Common tastes and sympathies cemented the intimacy, and Procter noticed that when Hazlitt launched his political tirades, Lamb and Hunt kept a collusive silence. Procter also saw them as talkers rather than debaters, which suggests a lower level of tension than might have been expected.

Hazlitt was a constant visitor to the Vale of Health and a major contributor to the *Examiner*, where early in 1815 he wrote a series of experimental essays on human behaviour which he called 'Commonplaces': on miscellaneous subjects, these appeared informally with Hunt as a collaborator. Calling the final collection the *Round Table*, they published it separately under that name late in 1815. Just as Hunt in the *Reflector* had presided over the beginning of Lamb's career as essayist, he now presided for Hazlitt.

Hazlitt liked Hunt's prose for its raciness, sharpness and 'the sparkling effect of poetry'. Perhaps there was too much of 'a caprice, a levity, and a disposition to innovate in words and ideas'. Still 'the genuine master-spirit of the prose-writer is there'. Hazlitt had no illusions about Hunt as a writer, nor about Hunt as a man. He noted, as had Haydon, that Hunt required a circle of devotees to feel at home, and sat at the head of his table with gaiety, grace and nimble presence of mind. He 'has continual sportive sallies of wit or fancy; tells a story capitally; mimics an actor or acquaintance to admiration; laughs with great glee and good-humour at his own and other people's jokes . . . has a taste and knowledge of books, of music, of medals; manages an argument adroitly; is genteel and gallant, and has a set of bye-phrases and quaint allusions at hand to produce a laugh'. On the other hand, Hazlitt was quick to notice, Hunt did not always listen, obsessively demanded centre stage, and was impatient of interruption: the very qualities that made him king of the fireside dethroned him in the wider world. Hazlitt thought that Hunt's genial philosophy was stultifying and that reality demanded a sharper, more disciplined lifestyle. 'He is too versatile for a professional man, not dull enough for a political drudge, too gay to be happy, too thoughtless to be rich. He wants the enthusiasm of the poet, the severity of the prose-writer, and the application of the man of business.'

It was a tribute to the importance of such relationships that at the beginning of 1816 Hunt published in the *Examiner* a series of verse epistles to his friends — Moore, Field, Byron, Hazlitt and Lamb — in the familiar, colloquial style of his poetic 'system'. The epistle to Hazlitt celebrates cheer, describing the sensory and intellectual delights of a day spent browsing in bookshops:

> To tell you the truth, I could spend very well
> Whole mornings in this way 'twixt here and Pall Mall,
> And make my gloves' fingers as black as my hat,
> In pulling the books up from this stall and that: —
> Then turning home gently through field and o'er style,
> Partly reading a purchase, or rhyming the while,
> Take my dinner (to make a long evening) at two,
> With a few droppers-in, like my Cousin and you

His letter to Lamb, in a similar spirit, carried a hint of a temporary rift that he longed to heal:

> But *now*, Charles you never (so blissful you deem me)
> Come lounging, with twirl of umbrella to see me.
> In vain have we hoped to be set at our ease
> By the rains which you know used to bring Lamb and pease

The last line, containing one of Hunt's well known puns, was admired by those he had bewitched and eschewed by those he had not. Lamb responded generously to this compliment, affirming that no shadow of misunderstanding was left between them, but there was a residue of unease that betrayed the tension in the relationship.

The post-prison years were strong in celebrations of friendly and domestic subjects with poems to Marianne and the children and a charming one to Thornton during sickness:

> Sleep breathes at last from out thee,
>   My little, patient boy;
> And balmy rest about thee
>   Smooths off the day's annoy.
>   I sit me down, and think
>   Of all thy winning ways;
> Yet almost wish, with sudden shrink,
>   That I had less to praise.
>
> Thy sidelong pillowed meekness,
>   Thy thanks to all that aid,
> Thy heart, in pain and weakness,
>   Of fancied faults afraid;
>   The little trembling hand
>   That wipes thy quiet tears,
> These, these are things that may demand
>   Dread memories for years.
>
> Sorrows I've had, severe ones,
>   I will not think of now;
> And calmly, midst my dear ones,
>   Have wasted with dry brow;
>   But when thy fingers press
>   And pat my stooping head,
> I cannot bear the gentleness, —
>   The tears are in their bed.
>
> Ah, first-born of thy mother,
>   When life and hope were new,
> Kind playmate of thy brother,
>   Thy sister, father too;
>   My light, where'er I go,
>   My bird, when prison-bound,
> My hand in hand companion, — no,
>   My prayers shall hold thee round.

These poems meant much to Hunt and formed an integral part of his poetic and personal philosophy. Often lacking poetic and intellectual merit, they did little for his reputation; he was to discover this in September 1816 when, eager to earn money, he could not persuade Taylor and Hessey to publish them.

Hunt's equals viewed him sharply, but his unequals — the inferior adorers of Haydon's telling phrase — saw him through rose-coloured glasses. Cowden Clarke who met Hunt at an evening party shortly before the imprisonment, found him 'fascinating, animated, full of cordial amity and winning to a degree of which I have never seen the parallel'. A frequent visitor to Hunt's prison cell and then to the Vale of Health, where he ate gooseberries and drank wine amid the busts and vases, Clarke found himself in a group which met regularly in Hunt's presence. There was Henry Robertson, at one time the *Examiner*'s opera critic, 'always ready with his tenor, his joke, and his breathing nod of acquiescence'. There was Charles Ollier, the literary and flute-playing bank clerk who had met Hunt in the *Examiner* office in 1810, had visited him in prison, had now written a novel and was about to join his brother in publishing, where he would bolster Hunt and his literary friends. There was Tom Richards, 'a good comrade, a capital reader, a capital listener'; and there were the Gattie brothers, Frederick, William, Henry, Byng and John, the last with a fine tenor voice that slipped like a rill over sunny pebbles. Maria Gattie had married Charles Ollier in 1814.

The thread that held these friends together was love of music, and music was high on Hunt's list of therapies. From singing with his sister in childhood, his love of music had grown in earlier *Examiner* days when he had extended his dramatic criticism to the English musical stage and, from 1816 onwards, to the Italian opera which he considered a divine art form, combining painting, music and poetry. Hunt had no real technical understanding of music though he played the piano to amuse himself, had an 'exquisite ear' and sang in a ringing voice of 'extraordinary compass, power, flexibility and beauty'. In music as in politics he relied on intelligence and personal response, believing these outweighed other considerations. Transforming his drawbacks into assets he managed to reach an audience hitherto uninterested in musical drama.

In the musical centre of this group — for assuredly Hunt was the emotional centre — stood Vincent Novello, affectionate, unselfish and faithful, who had presumably met Hunt in prison and had commissioned a portrait of him by the artist Wagemen to commemorate his release. Novello was three years Hunt's senior, organist to the Portuguese Chapel in Grosvenor Square, and an amateur composer and populariser of classical music. He was part Italian and married to a partly German wife, and in the cosmopolitan setting of his home in Oxford Street he entertained lavishly. The rose-tinted walls of his drawing room were hung with his friends' pictures, the plain grey carpet was embroidered with vine leaves by Mrs Novello, the sofa table was strewn with books, and on a fine-toned chamber organ the host played for friends. Later Novello's daughter would remember 'Leigh Hunt with his jet black hair and expressive mouth . . . Lamb with his spare figure and earnest face; all seen by the glow and warmth and brightness of candlelight'.

To tone-deaf Charles Lamb, staggering 'under the weight of harmony', the evenings were somewhat pretentious, and in his famous *Elia* essay 'On Ears' he described his difficulties, also hilariously rhyming that he did not care a 'farthing candle' for Mozart and Haydn, nor for Handel. But to Hunt the recitals were bliss, from the first notes of the organ, through the games they played and the songs they sang, to the last crumbs of the supper of celery, bread and cheese — Italian cheese chosen especially for the author of *Rimini* — washed down with genuine Lutheran beer, the only part of the evening to please Charles Lamb. Most of Hunt's close friends, including Keats and Shelley, would become friends of Novello. The Novellos and their circle were assiduous celebrators: their own birthdays, Shakespeare's birthday, the composer Haydn's birthday — the story runs that artist Haydon thought it was *his* birthday — and New Year and Twelfth Night. Hunt's essay on Twelfth Night relates how they celebrated in traditional style, and the party ended with breakfast at dawn in the book-lined library.

Mary Sabilla Novello, nicknamed by Hunt 'Wilful Woman' and 'Ave Maria', was an admirable housekeeper, and her parties and picnics were gastronomic marvels of sizzling crab-apples, spicy elder wine, roast lamb, jellied meat pies, and the unheard of Italian exotic, a salad. The Novellos and their children came to Hampstead often for family games and picnics in the green fields, and on one such day Clarke first met young Victoria Mary Novello, who became his wife. While the children played, the adults sat and talked and read, Hunt sometimes reading aloud with dramatic gestures and much mutation of voice till the party rang with shouts of laughter: 'his dramatic reading was almost unequalled', Clarke recalled, and carried his listeners along 'in a trance of excitement'.

Hunt was fond of saying in these months that his only needs were his family, a leg of mutton, the run of the fields, the London bookshops, his old friends, and time to develop his poetic talent. His fireside was the hub of his universe, his 'sacred sunshine', and his feelings and habits were unashamedly domestic. Five out of seven days he devoted to poetry, which was winning its struggle against politics. In February 1816 the publication of *Rimini* proclaimed his poetic ambitions to the public and, despite censure for obscurity and quaintness, it won a generous measure of favour, especially from Hazlitt in the *Edinburgh Review*. The *Examiner* in 1816 contained more poetry by the editor than in any previous year. Hunt's change in direction from the real world of the reformer to the imaginative world of the poet has puzzled biographers. It has been seen variously as the discouraging effect of imprisonment or as a disenchantment with European politics following Waterloo, but if his heart had been in his work such relatively minor factors could not have tipped the balance. Certainly, prison had given Hunt leisure to study poetry but it had also given him leisure to study politics — and he had chosen poetry, thus reverting to those early ambitions that had been dampened in the course of his political career. The upsurge of poetry stemmed more, it would seem, from the positive factor of independence, and in particular independence from John Hunt, than from discouragement or disenchantment. At 32 he was emerging as his own man, and his own man was a poet.

Hunt had proclaimed that his needs were inexpensive, but his debts were not. To pay his £500 share of the legal fine he had been obliged to take publishers' advances, sign promissory notes and sell his books, being too proud to accept the assistance offered by sympathisers. In 1814, requiring £450, he had mortgaged to the publishers Gale and Fenner *The Descent of Liberty*, the next edition of the successful *The Feast of the Poets* and the uncompleted *The Story of Rimini*. Curiously he had already obtained money for an unfinished *Rimini* from James Cawthorne, who published the 1814 edition of the *Feast*. But as *Rimini* neared completion Gale and Fenner read the manuscript and rejected it as too short — they may also have been put off by its originality — and demanded their money back. In December 1815 Hunt began to badger other London publishers with *Rimini*, desperate to raise the £450, 'the largest and most disagreeable debt I have ever known'. On Byron's advice he went to Byron's publisher John Murray, a generous man whose politics and temperament were not Hunt's. Openly chary of such an innovative poem, Murray refused then and later to buy the copyright, but agreed to share the profits of the first edition, the share coming in 1816 to almost £50. Though Murray behaved reasonably, Hunt chose to take offence, feeling that he had laid himself open by asking for help. Still in trouble, he then borrowed in order to pay back Gale and Fenner, and lived for the rest of the year in anxiety, at times anticipating the inexorable day of reckoning, at other times refusing to face it. He begged from friends, borrowed from Ollier, persuaded Taylor and Hessey to make an advance on another unfinished poem, and hawked the *Rimini* copyright around various publishers, indulging in such complicated financial dealing that in the end no one really knew to whom it belonged.

With a fine sense of self pity, Hunt in November 1816 was dashing off notes, complaining that while booksellers lived in mansions, writers like himself lived in cottages 'as poor as the rats that infest them'. Feeling vulnerable he countered by blustering, or making over-involved negotiations which irritated his publishers: at other times he was the innocent and angry victim. The more useful course of attempting to understand the situation, or even to engage a wiser mind to negotiate for him was – even at this early stage of his life — discarded both emotionally and intellectually. He was 'never a manager of money', he told the publisher Constable complacently in 1816, and at the same time he filled pages of his letter to Constable with tortuous business proposals and invective against publishers who had, according to his version, tried to dupe him. His financial muddling would recur many times and earn him many enemies.

It must have been the debt of £450 that Haydon had in mind when in January 1817 he deplored Hunt's conduct in allowing his brother John to sign bills for £500 on his behalf, and then making little attempt to prevent John's arrest for debt. Haydon found Leigh Hunt reading a story of Boccaccio with an inferior adorer while John and he 'were fagging around all day in the dirt' to raise the money and so prevent John's imprisonment. Leigh added insult to injury by arriving three hours late — 'it was likely to rain' — to meet them. Is there anyone, raged Haydon, whom Hunt has not offended in financial matters? Even allowing for Haydon's exaggerated narration, the story has a ring of truth. He knew only too well that the green fields, bookshops and happy visiting in the Vale of Health allowed Hunt to escape into a sheltered world where debts and quarrels could be forgotten.

In the middle of 1816 Marianne gave birth to a son called Swinburne, named after Sir John Swinburne who had probably helped with money. The naming of the child, like the dedication of Hunt's next book of verse, may well have been a partial repayment as well as a token of Hunt's admiration and respect. For two 'heart-triggering' days both mother and child were in danger and Hunt was beside himself. Through the autumn Marianne was weak and dispirited, while Hunt, now that the active danger was over, distanced himself from her distress. It was an angry and determined Mrs Hunter who took matters into her own hands, consulted doctors and upbraided Hunt, and eventually saw that Marianne had 'the utmost care'. As the year drew to a close and Marianne continued feebly, Hunt's spirits rose. Exciting events lay ahead of him — the most exciting of his life — and already, like an eager horse, he had caught a whiff of them.

8 REALMS OF GOLD

Hunt saw himself increasingly as a serious poet. As 1816 progressed and *The Story of Rimini* graced many a table, numerous others began to see him with such eyes. Haydon wept at the poem, Hazlitt praised it in the *Edinburgh Review*. Byron's wife saw a resemblance between the thorny husband and her own, and the future writer William Howitt walked one summer's day in Sherwood Forest with a copy in his hand and was 'drunk with beauty'. While the *Quarterly Review* brutally condemned it, that was to be expected from a political enemy.

Nor was it only his poetry that absorbed Hunt. In the *Examiner* he published the work of other poets and was eager to help them. Some had not published before and were identified only by initials and pseudonyms; all were devotees of the author of *Rimini*. As Hunt crowded the *Examiner* columns with his verse letters, starting with a gushy tribute to Byron which pictured the noble exile's journey to Italy and Greece attended by sea nymphs, his words were devoured by young poets all over England who no sooner read than seized their pens in imitation. One such was JK, his real name John Keats, a young medical student and friend of Cowden Clarke, who had followed Hunt's career with hero-worshipping interest for some time, composing a poem to his idolised 'Libertas' on his leaving prison, and dwelling on every word of *Rimini*.

In Switzerland that summer Byron had joined forces with an eccentric English ménage, an aristocratic and radical 23-year-old English poet called Percy Shelley, his 19-year-old girlfriend, and her 18-year-old step-sister who was currently Byron's sexual companion. Hunt had some slight acquaintance with Shelley, having met him in 1811 through Rowland Hunter and having exchanged several letters since, and he knew the father and step-father of the two young girls, the novelist and political philosophist, William Godwin who was a frequent guest of both Hunter and Charles Lamb. In that humid summer of 1816 how amazed Hunt would have been to realise the configuration of forces that were preparing to descend on him in the Vale of Health. For a few months his simple cottage would contain some of the most creative gatherings in

English literary history, forming an emotional sun that would pour out its rays on Hunt for the rest of his life.

In August Shelley returned to England with his household and settled uneasily at Bath, waiting for Claire Clairemont, the stepsister, to give birth to Byron's child. Shelley was unsure of what lay ahead. His early poetry, like the revolutionary *Queen Mab,* was unnoticed in respectable circles but admired in the radical underground, and his later and more respectable *Alastor* was unnoticed by the critics. He felt depressed and poetically ineffective.

In London John Keats moved away from his medical studies, pursuing his enthusiasm for poetry. In hope he sent verses to Hunt at the *Examiner* and badgered Clarke for assistance. With each month his work improved and when in September Clarke brought along a page or two of Keat's latest manuscript, Hunt was astounded, as was his other guest, the wealthy lawyer, stockbroker and minor poet, Horace Smith. They responded with 'unhesitating and prompt admiration', amazed at Keats's maturity of expression. An instant invitation to Hampstead was issued and in relaying it Clarke passed on a favourite book in Hunt's circle, a copy of Chapman's translation of Homer. Under the stimulus of Hunt's praise and potential acquaintance, and the excitement of Hunt's favourite author, Keats was moved to new heights of poetic inspiration. After reading for most of one night he dashed off a sonnet which at 19 marked him as one of the most brilliant of the Romantic writers: 'On First Looking Into Chapman's Homer'. Thus, Hunt was literary midwife at the birth of one of the great works of English literature.

The first meeting between Hunt and Keats took place a little later at the Vale of Health. Clarke, accompanying Keats, remembered how the young poet's step quickened and his large expressive face glowed as they neared Hunt's house. They became, in Hunt's phrase, 'intimate on the spot'. The first morning stretched into two more, Keats by now a 'familiar of the household', and signalled many idyllic autumnal wanderings about the Heath and woods and other realms of gold. Every imaginative pleasure was shared and enjoyed, 'from the recollection of the bardf and patriots of old, to the luxury of rain at our window, or the clicking of the coal': thus spoke the philosopher of cheer. To avoid the long trip at night to his London lodgings, Keats accepted a sofa bed made up in Hunt's library and there, in a half-way reverie between sleep and wakefulness, he composed 'Sleep and Poetry', celebrating the busts of those 'bards and patriots of old' — Alfred, Sappho, Petrarch, Kosciusko — and engravings of Poussin and Raphael that he saw around him on the library shelves and walls. Hunt was enormously proud of his young protegé. He showed his poems to Hazlitt and Godwin and Haydon and the literary lawyer Basil Montagu, who pronounced them extraordinary. With typical generosity he introduced Keats to his circle, opening important friendships. Charles Ollier, a budding publisher alert for new authors, quickly commissioned Keats's first book of poems.

In the warming light of Hunt's praise, Keats grew in confidence and poetic power. Poems flew from his pen with a facility that astonished observers. One parlour game at Hunt's required the writing of a sonnet in a given time, with a timekeeper watching the clock. The competitions were so frequent that an unkind critic likened them to shooting matches, declaring facetiously that with all this sonnet-firing someone was bound to be injured. Keats's prowess at the instant sonnet was extraordinary and he thought nothing of dashing off a dedicatory poem to preface his new book, amid the bustle of an evening party, while a messenger stood waiting to take the copy. Within two months he had become a member of a glamorous literary circle. He was praised in the pages of the *Examiner* and was about to produce his first book. No wonder that one November evening he composed a poem to his three living gods, Wordsworth, Haydon and Hunt, 'Great Spirits Now on Earth Are Sojourning', greeting Hunt with the tender and touching words:

He of the rose, the violet, the spring,
The social smile, the chain for Freedom's sake.

A few weeks later the miraculous months came to their climax in the most famous of Hunt's literary articles. In the *Examiner*, he proclaimed three young poets, John Keats, John Hamilton Reynolds and Percy Shelley, as a new school of poetry to rival the Lake poets. For Keats, now at his emotional and professional crossroads, the article was the deciding factor in his resolve to abandon medical studies for full-time poetry; for Shelley, also at his crossroads, it proved just as decisive; for Hunt, his protegés' success would confirm his own journey on the path of literature and criticism.

Shelley had long admired Hunt. They shared a radicalism that went far beyond the outlook of the relatively conservative Keats. Shelley, too, had been delighted with *Rimini*, though being an instinctive poet he deplored Hunt's often maladroit adherence to his poetic 'system'. Shelley also saw in Hunt a potential guiding and inspiring spirit, in life as well as literature, and so he wrote to Hunt in that first week in December 1816, pouring out his heart with a freedom he had seldom used before, let alone to a virtual stranger. Geographically, he told Hunt, he wrote in the house of his friend, the poet and radical Thomas Love Peacock, at Great Marlow, but emotionally he wrote from a 'solitude of heart', trusting to Hunt's twinness of spirit and emotional and professional generosity. He admitted to intense longings to improve mankind but knew that his very zeal and ardour had negated his efforts, making his name execrated by those he most wanted to help and rendering him 'an outcast from human society'. Only in those like Hunt, sincere, gentle and self-devoted, could he hope to find sympathy, and on that sympathy he flung himself. He had already responded to a call in the *Examiner* by contributing £50 — whether to Hunt personally or to a charitable fund is not known — for which he had been remitted £5 in interest. With delicacy he now returned that £5, begging Hunt to indulge any 'literary luxury' he craved at Shelley's expense. It was no accident that Shelley, the most generous of all Hunt's benefactors, should begin their friendship with a loan. Hunt liked to receive, Shelley liked to give. An important and complementary principle in their natures had been established. As a crowning touch Shelley signed his letter in a phrase of unusual openness and commitment, 'affectionately yours'.

In reply to Hunt's prompt invitation Shelley appeared at the Vale of Health on 10 or 11 December 1816. The attachment which they quickly formed differed from that between Hunt and Keats. Whereas Keats was young and hesitant, Shelley was 24, confident, aggressive and capable of asking for what he wanted: he wanted Hunt. Almost at once Hunt fell in love: no other phrase can do justice to the speed and force of his feelings. It must be stressed, however, that Hunt's affections towards Shelley as to all other men were strictly, in his own words 'disembodied-, and 'unearthly'.

Hunt found in Shelley everyone he had ever loved and everything he had ever craved to find in one human being: the strong reformer, the sensitive poet, the loving friend, the eager scholar, the nonconformist, the lover of earthly living and the spiritual and ascetic being: father, mother, brother John, Marianne and Bess Kent all in one. Hunt would write that he and Shelley together encompassed 'a world of thought, feeling, fancy, imagination, pain, playfulness, subtlety, universality'. No wonder that Shelley came to Hunt like a flash of lightning. No wonder that Hunt's proudest title throughout his life would be 'friend of Shelley'. Years later, after Shelley's death, when Hunt came by chance across a picture of Shelley's house, he wrote beside it: 'I nestle to the memorials of him in this corner as a shivering soul to a fire left in the wilderness . . . how more alive art thou to me ever, than almost any living creature.' A few months after Shelley's death, Hunt wrote a poem 'The Choice', published in *The Liberal*. At the end of this hymn to the lifestyle of cheer, he set out the alternative places where he would like eventually to rest. 'One, in a gentle village, my old home' was his mother's grave in Hampstead. 'The other, by the softened walls of Rome' was Shelley's grave. In Hunt's mind, his mother and Shelley were powerfully linked.

Shelley was 'pleased' with Hunt that December, or so he wrote to Mary Godwin at Bath. Hunt was much more than 'pleased'. Seeing no reason to be anything but open, he pulled out all stops of conviviality. For those two days he paraded Shelley among his friends with generous pride. Keats was invited to meet him, and probably Cowden Clarke; Horace Smith, who certainly met Shelley about this time, described him as a 'fair, freckled, blue eyed, light-haired, delicate-looking' young man, modest in dress but clearly a gentleman, whose earnest and ardent mind revealed considerable 'psychological curiosity'. Shelley joined in the bantering within Hunt's circle, the 'jocio-serio-musico-pictorio-poetical' gatherings, the familiar jokes and recitations, impromptu concerts, sonnet competitions, the fireside ritual among the busts and vases, and the invigorating walks on the Heath. He fitted into the cosy atmosphere yet he tended to be aloof, being more inwardly than outwardly visioned, and the surroundings and companions were less important to him than to Hunt. Though Shelley would enjoy as keenly as his host the beauty of the sunset on the Heath, he created his own atmosphere and his own rules. For one thing he demanded a wholly vegetarian diet, which cannot have displeased the food faddist in Hunt but amused others. Haydon, who disliked the discordant note Shelley soon struck, recorded his own portrait of the newcomer: a spare, hectic, weakly looking fellow, carving cabbage and broccoli on a plate. Such was Shelley's influence that he soon converted Hunt to vegetarianism, and temporarily turned him into a veritable crusader.

In mid December Shelley returned to Bath where desperate news awaited him. His wife Harriet, estranged for some years and the mother of his two children, had drowned herself. In the severest emotional crisis of his life Shelley sought support. Though he scarcely knew Hunt in many ways, he knew that whatever he asked Hunt would give — more, he would be overjoyed to give, and would give without reserve. Shelley did not hesitate, leaving at once for London and Hampstead.

It is likely that Hunt knew little about Shelley's past life which had been, by conventional standards, wildly irregular. But now he backed him, comforted him, soothed and entertained him. Shelley arrived at Hunt's door ready to do battle with his long-time twin ogres of church and state in order to win custody of his two children from his wife's hostile family. Hunt not only agreed with him about church and state but with practical wisdom, as a respectably married father of four, offered at the Chancery Court to act as interim guardian of the Shelley boy and girl. He also supported the lawyers' pronouncement that Shelley and Mary Godwin must marry. In short he showed that he knew how to handle Shelley almost as well as Shelley knew how to handle him. Above all, he felt with burning compassion the burden of guilt and anger and grief that his new friend was carrying. Later he would write that those weeks tore Shelley's being 'to pieces'. Hunt's care and compassion astonished its recipient who, though he knew how to ask, could not have received often on this scale. 'I have found few such as he appears to be in the world', Shelley wrote to Byron. 'He was so kind as to listen to the story of persecution which I am now enduring . . . and to stand by me as yet by his counsel, and by his personal attentions to me.' To Mary he wrote that Hunt had been constantly with him and that 'his delicate and tender attentions to me, his kind speeches to you, have sustained me against the weight of the horror'.

Shelley stayed on at the Vale of Health, visiting lawyers and Mary's father, attending the Court of Chancery, always with Hunt supporting him. Mary came late in December to marry him and never forgot her first sight of Hunt in the flower-filled parlour, his dark eyes looking at her from under his wise brow. She returned briefly to Bath for her step-sister Claire's confinement, then back to the cottage late in January with her own son and nurse, arranging for Claire and her baby to take nearby lodgings in Hampstead. For three months the Shelley family took over the Hunt household. Though nine years younger than Marianne, Mary, nicknamed 'Marina' by Hunt, ordered her hostess about like a younger sister. She called her 'my good girl' and admonished her for fighting with Bess and thus annoying Hunt: 'cultivate his affection and cherish and enjoy his sagacity' she advised. Above all, she tried to reform Marianne's housekeeping, giving ceaseless instructions about servants, laundry and baby clothes which haphazard Marianne was slow to implement.

The cramped household tried to work out its upsets in activity and conviviality. Mary's journal eloquently depicts walks on the Heath, musical evenings, visits to the theatre and the opera, days of reading and flower arranging, numerous dinners and impromptu supper parties, and a stream of callers. Hazlitt, Basil Montagu, William Godwin, an encyclopaedic journalist named Walter Coulson, an old friend of the Shelleys called Thomas Jefferson Hogg, the Lambs, the Olliers, Cowden Clarke, Horace Smith, John Reynolds and his sisters, John Keats and his brother George were all to be seen at Hampstead that January and February.

Shelley dominated Hunt's dinner parties, his conversation alive with those atheistic and republican views which had made the Chancery Court designate him as an unfit parent. Once he argued against the monarchy till three in the morning, with Hazlitt insisting that he was not radical enough and Hunt affirming that he was far too radical. On the other hand Hunt sided with Shelley in religious arguments, mischievously abetting Shelley in the baiting of Haydon and his 'detestable' Christianity. Haydon was intensely irritated by Shelley's attitude to sex. Tormented by a sexuality that seemed to cause him much guilt — and his guilt possibly increased by the attraction he felt towards Bess Kent — he found himself tossed about, emotionally, by Shelley's loose morality. Haydon was also disturbed by Shelley's religious views and the way Hunt swallowed them. Hunt, who had oscillated from the Christianity of his courting days to a pious deism, now accepted Shelley's atheistic free love and parroted his ideas that wives 'should submit to the infidelities of their husbands without feeling insulted', and that he would not mind any young man, if he were agreeable, sleeping with his wife. An exasperated Hazlitt, commenting on Hunt's obsessive sexual discussions, is reported to have said: 'It's always coming out like a rash. Why doesn't he write a book about it and get rid of it.' In Haydon's view, Hunt's immature adoption of Shelley's principles caused indignity and pain to Bess and Marianne:

> His poor wife has led the life of a slave, by his smuggering fondness of her Sister, without the resolution or the desire to go to the full extent of a manly passion, however wicked. He likes and is satisfied to corrupt the girl's mind without seducing her person, to dawdle over her bosom, to inhale her breath, to lean against her thigh and play with her petticoats, and rather than go to the effort of relieving his mind by furious gratification, shuts his eyes to tickle the edge of her stockings that his feelings may be kept tingling by imagining the rest . . . is it not cruel to keep his wife on the perpetual rack of waning affection, to praise the Sister for qualities which his wife has not, and which he knew she had not when he married her?

Shelley courageously acted on his principles, said Haydon, but Hunt defended them without having the courage to practise them and was content with a smuggering fondle. The *Rimini*-like word 'smuggering', for Haydon summed up Hunt's titillating, play-acting approach to sex and Haydon may have been right. Certainly Haydon's interpretation fits what we now know of Hunt. But did Haydon take sufficiently into account the transformation Shelley had worked upon Hunt, or the power of Hunt's admiration for the active apostle of free love? Under all these pressures, perhaps his sexuality went further than Haydon realised.

Bess showed signs of the pressure with outbursts of temper, a reliance on the opium bottle, and quick reactions to Hunt's slights, whether real or imagined. From Haydon again comes an incident that reveals the burden she carried. Haydon was recuperating at Hampstead and he and Keats were invited one morning to Hunt's for breakfast. Keats set off early, but Haydon knowing Marianne's movable meal times did not arrive until eleven, having predicted to Keats that they would not yet have set out the breakfast cloth. When he came near the cottage he saw the guest sitting dolefully on the grass outside the door, and no food in sight. Keats told him that Bess 'who is in love with Hunt' had tried to drown herself in a nearby pond, but had lodged in the mud and been rescued by two cabmen.

Haydon suggested that this event took place in October 1816

when he was staying at Hampstead for his health, but that seems unlikely because then he and Keats barely knew each other. More likely it was sometime early in 1817 when their friendship had been established and the Shelleyan tides had engulfed the cottage. Hunt then was swimming in the seas of liberated love and Bess was struggling to remain afloat. In the light of the evidence one cannot automatically accept Haydon's view that they did not sleep together. Moreover, Thornton was sufficiently worried about the affair to delete many passages in his father's letters when a generation later he prepared them for publication.

The friends at the cottage came to resent Shelley. Haydon alternately fumed and melted, and shy John Keats wavered too. The centre of an enchanting situation in October and November 1814, Keats was soon nudged to the fringes. Hunt always tried to incorporate his friendships — he had scrupulously introduced Keats and Shelley to Novello's circle and he actively encouraged friendship between the two young poets — but Shelley grated on Keats's delicate nerves with his advice not to publish prematurely, his forceful radicalism, and his upper-class ways. Above all, he absorbed Hunt's attention. When Shelley was absent the old bewitchment reasserted itself. On Shelley's wedding night Keats and Hunt sat cosily at Hunt's fireside for a sonnet-writing competition, Cowden Clarke an onlooker, the grasshopper and the cricket the subject. Keats's poem is still remembered. Throughout February Keats tried to hold his own, ignored Haydon's fire and brimstone warnings of Shelley's corruption and his own misgivings about Hunt's insensitivity. On 1 March he took the advance copy of his precious poems in hand and walked to Hunt's at Hampstead, down the path beside the ponds. It was a magic evening. After dinner they sat outside and watched the stars, and Hunt leaped up and twined a wreath from a nearby laurel tree to crown this protegé of whom he felt so proud. Keats in turn picked trailing ivy and fashioned a crown for Hunt, and to preserve the moment of euphoria each wrote a sonnet. Then other guests arrived and Keats, in an act of devotion to his host, steadfastly kept the laurel crown on his head.

Next day, away from Hampstead, Keats's mood changed. Jealousy and harassment enabled him to see Hunt of the 'social smile' more sharply. He became angry and ashamed, and thereafter his attitude to Hunt see-sawed. A few weeks later he helped Hunt vacate the cottage in the Vale of Health, a 'chaos of packed trunks, lumber, litter, dust, dirty dry fingers': Keats was left to dispose of the debris. While the little cottage would symbolise Hunt's greatest days, it was a different symbol for Keats. In 1818 he wrote bitterly that Hunt had 'damned Hampstead' for him.

Shelley, full of optimism, had meanwhile taken a 21-year lease on Albion House at Great Marlow, and neither he nor Mary would rest until the Hunts joined them. Mary, lacking a female ally against her hostile step-mother and competing step-sister, and unwell with pregnancy, found that she needed Marianne — a mutual need when it transpired that Marianne too was pregnant and, barely recovered from her last delivery, sicker than Mary. Hunt likewise knew that wherever Shelley was, he too must be. He felt bereft without his friend's ebullience and kindness, and relived old memories. He remembered an incident on the Hampstead stage-coach, when Shelley hilariously broke the boredom with a dramatic recitation from Shakespeare, to the shock of an old lady passenger. He remembered how, returning one cold night from the opera, Shelley had found an old woman collapsed in the snow on the Heath and had knocked on all doors, horrifying the householders, until, unable to find a Samaritan, he had brought her back to Hunt's. In all senses he missed Shelley. Besides, to live rent-free at Great Marlow was a bargain, and he happily accepted.

At Albion House the Hunts threw off all traces of their graceless Hampstead departure. It was a large, damp house with numerous bedrooms, attics, a nursery and spacious communal rooms including a library stocked with books and an acre of walled garden, big enough for the Shelleys, their servants, the Hunts, Bess, and Claire Clairemont and her baby whom, in deference to convention, the Hunts brought with them as a 'cousin'. There was room besides for the numerous visitors whom Shelley invited. With this ménage it was perhaps no wonder that Shelley was locally suspected of keeping a seraglio. He worked compulsively on his new poem, 'Laon and Cythna', its theme incest, its symbolism strongly sexual, its sentiments a revolutionary manifesto of atheism, free love, sexual equality and the overthrow of oppression. Mary corrected proofs of her novel, *Frankenstein*, while Bess minded the children and Hunt — nicknamed 'Caccia' — wrote part of a play, edited the *Examiner* and began several poems on classical subjects. Carried away by Shelley's enthusiasm for the innocent eroticism of classical Greek writers, Hunt was also inspired by the modern Arcadia on his doorstep; he and Shelley and Hogg play-acted at a mock altar to Pan in the woods, Hunt hoping to see the nature god come down to convert the religious villagers to his heathen ways. Enthusiastically he wrote to Novello about his pleasure in the valleys, uplands, hedges, nooks and brooks, and the visits to sites famous in history and literature.

On the nearby Thames Shelley kept a skiff permanently moored, and many of their expeditions were on the river. About a mile across the water meadows was Bisham woods, where Shelley wrote or roamed with the children. Young Thornton, his companion from Hampstead Heath, was old enough to share his uninhibited horse-play, and Thornton remembered how Shelley would screw his long hair into the shape of an animal's horn, draw up his paws and approach with the growls of a wild animal, and how at other times he would tease with exasperating banter or with exquisite tenderness carry the tired boy home on his shoulders. Bess the amateur botanist recalled Shelley emerging from the wood with trails of green and white convolvulus falling from his straw sunhat and his hands full of flowers. At other times she remembered him lying face up in the sun in the drifting boat, while Thornton recalled him pulling a boat full of people along the bank like a tow horse.

Hunt's favourite haunt was neither woods nor water but a rustic seat in the garden, high upon a mound by the wall, with a prospect over sheep pastures, white cottages, and haymakers mowing and singing, while on the lawn below Marianne scraped clean the full-sized plaster statues of Venus and Apollo for Shelley's library as though 'revenging the cause of all uninspired fiddlers', or tried her hand at modelling a likeness of Mary until, she complained, the worms in the clay turned her pregnant stomach. Seeing her at work, Shelley wrote a revolutionary poem called 'Marianne's Dream', which Hunt later published. Shelley had bought the busts largely for Hunt's sake. Not so enamoured by these artifacts of cheer, he greeted their apostle's excesses with the exclamation, 'Oh, Hunt!'

At Hunt's insistence Shelley bought a piano, and on musical evenings Hunt would play and Claire sing. Shelley was even inspired to compose 'To Constantia Singing'. Hunt's political ardour was aroused too, because Shelley taught him how to balance the tensions between politics and literature. Politics in England were becoming more repressive, with secret government committees investigating reform movements. In March 1817 came the suspension of Habeas Corpus and the Seditious Meetings Act. Hunt fulminated in the *Examiner* against government repression and spoke out more openly than usual in favour of critics of religion.

Shelley meanwhile composed the first of two pamphlets pseudonymously signed the Hermit of Marlow, advocating a referendum on self-reform of the House of Commons and virtually recommending adult suffrage. Ollier published the pamphlet but dithered over 'Laon and Cythna' whose revolutionary message proved, despite Hunt's intercessions, too strong. He persuaded Shelley to recast it and it appeared in print the following year as *The Revolt of Islam*. Hunt was enthusiastic about the poem and gave it extensive publicity. It is probably the first poem of Shelley's maturity, and thus Hunt can be said to have presided over the poetic coming of age of both Shelley and Keats.

Hunt was almost mesmerised by Shelley. Though his junior by eight years, he treated Shelley like an 'ancient and wrinkled, but rather good natured grand-uncle'. Shelley tried to make him punctual and financially responsible. Though the son of a wealthy parent and recipient of a regular allowance, Shelley himself was in debt, and that summer he tried to put in order his own finances and those of Godwin, his father-in-law, by borrowing money. He also tried to help Hunt. Horace Smith, who had made much money out of stockbroking and lending, listened to Shelley's plea and sensibly proposed that Hunt should earn some money. Shy of venturing into print with 'poetical nonsense' Smith entrusted the editing of his own manuscript to Hunt for a fee of £100. Hunt accepted, apparently put the poems in a drawer, forgot about them and lost them. Smith was furious. Shelley, knowing that the stockbroker was too useful to be alienated, begged Hunt to heal the breach. Hunt did nothing and so in January 1818 Smith let off an 'amicable expostulation' that was in effect a thunderblast. Years of irritation mixed with affection came rushing out: his letter said what so many people must have felt about Hunt and his financial helplessness. While Smith worked all day for his living in a fetid atmosphere, adding mental anxiety to bodily fatigue, he saw Hunt enjoying himself, refusing to earn an honourable £100 but demanding as of right a loan of £200. It was all very well for Hunt to declare that in a real emergency he 'would not be found wanting'. These 'real and trying emergencies' seldom arose. True friendship, Smith concluded, 'you will perhaps again say, would overlook these offences; to which I reply that true friendship would not commit them'. Yet Hunt's friendship with Smith survived.

Shelley was an awkward middleman in these money transactions. He knew Hunt's habit of running from one debt to another, borrow-

Plate 1: Leigh Hunt, from a portrait by Jackson, at the time of publishing *Juvenilia. Special Collections, University of Iowa Libraries*

Plate 2: Leigh Hunt aged 36, from a portrait by Joseph Severn. According to Thornton Hunt, the best likeness of his father. *Special Collections, University of Iowa Libraries*

Plate 3: The Vale of Health, Hampstead by S. J. Sarjent. *Reproduced by permission of the London Borough of Camden from the collections at Keats House, Hampstead*

Plate 5: Leigh Hunt aged 66. *Special Collections, University of Iowa Libraries*

Plate 4: Leigh Hunt from a pencil drawing by Thomas Wageman in February 1815. *Special Collections, University of Iowa Libraries*

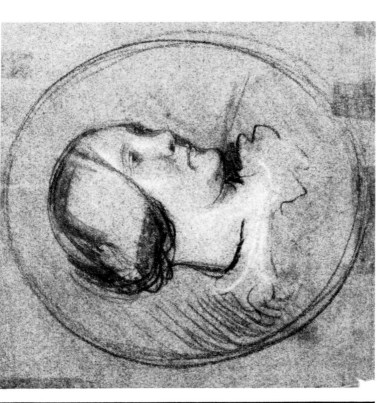

Plate 7: Marianne Hunt. *Special Collections, University of Iowa Libraries*

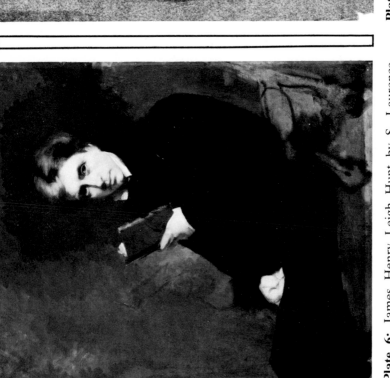

Plate 6: James Henry Leigh Hunt by S. Laurence (1837). *National Portrait Gallery, London*

Plate 9: Charles Lamb by W. Hazlitt (1804). *Courtesy of the National Portrait Gallery, London*

Plate 8: Robert Hunt by J. Linnell. *Courtesy of the National Portrait Gallery, London*

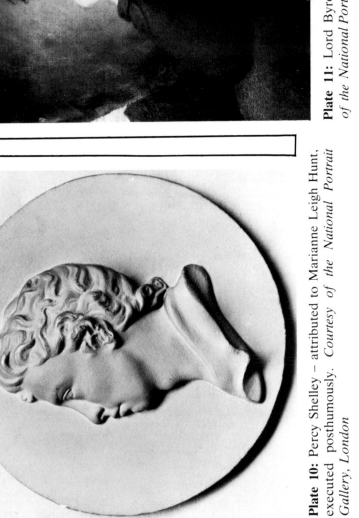

Plate 11: Lord Byron by R. Westall (1813). *Courtesy of the National Portrait Gallery, London*

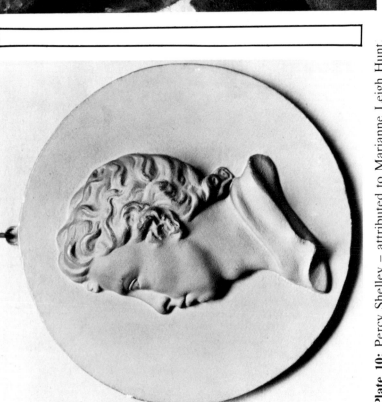

Plate 10: Percy Shelley – attributed to Marianne Leigh Hunt, executed posthumously. *Courtesy of the National Portrait Gallery, London*

Plate 13: William Hazlitt by William Bewick (1825). *Courtesy of the National Portrait Gallery, London*

Plate 12: Benjamin West by G. Stuart. *Courtesy of the National Portrait Gallery, London*

Plate 14: Benjamin R. Haydon by Sir David Wilkie (1815). *Courtesy of the National Portrait Gallery, London*

Plate 15: John Keats by Benjamin Robert Haydon. *Courtesy of the National Portrait Gallery, London*

ing from Peter to pay Paul. In August he was to write sternly, insisting that it would be 'a very horrid thing' if in borrowing £60 he did nothing towards a 'complete settlement' of his debts, and reminding him that his brother John had run out of patience. Such reminders Hunt blithely ignored.

Though he adored Great Marlow, Hunt missed the city. He thirsted for news like an exile, telling Novello how much he envied him a visit to *Don Giovanni*. In June when he went with Marianne and Thornton to spend a few days with John Hunt at Maida Vale he raced to the opera. The visit was also to rent a house, and he and pregnant Marianne moved to Lisson Grove, Paddington, at the end of July. In December Hunt's fourth son was born there and named Percy Bysshe Shelley Hunt: Shelley was still a magic name.

At Lisson Grove Haydon became a neighbour and haunted their parlour until an explosive quarrel, sparked by Marianne's failure to return borrowed knives and forks, drove him from their door. Shelley sometimes came to stay but he was irritable, unwell, restless, and looking for some form of escape. Hunt meanwhile was deep in his new book of poems, to be called *Foliage* and incorporating a new poem, 'The Nymphs', his 'Harry Brown' verse epistles, miscellaneous verses and a large section of translations called 'Evergreens'. Byron, out of temper with Hunt and uneasy about his colloquial poetic 'system', told Tom Moore that *Foliage* was an 'ineffable Centaur' begotten 'by Self love upon a Nightmare'. 'The Nymphs', however, may well be one of Hunt's best poems. Shelley called it 'original and intense, conceived with the clearest sense of ideal beauty and executed with the fullest and most lyrical power, and yet defined with the most intelligible outline of thought and language'. The poem has a sensitive joy in nature which owed much to Shelley's vigorous poetical and sexual outlook, and a sensuousness more open and genuine than Hunt would ever express again. His description of the Naiads still conveys this quality:

> They, towards the amorous noon, when some young poet,
> Strips him to bathe, and yet half thrills to do it,
> Hovering with his ripe locks, and fair light limbs,
> And trying with cold foot the banks and brims,
> Win him into the water with sweet fancies,
> Till in the girdling stream he pants and dances.
> There's a whole bevy there, in that recess,
> Rounding from the main stream: some sleep, some dress

Each other's locks, some swim about, some sit
Parting their own moist hair, or fingering it
Lightly to let the curling air go through:
Some make them green and lilied coronets new;
And one there from her tender instep shakes
The matted sedge; a second, as she swims,
Looks round with pride upon her easy limbs;
A third, just holding by a bough, lets float
Her slumberous body like an anchored boat,
Looking with level eye at the smooth flakes
And the strange crooked quivering which it makes,
Seen through the weltering of the watery glass:
Others (which make the rest look at them) pass,
Nodding and smiling in the middle tide,
And luring swans on, which like fondled things
Eye poutingly their hands; yet following, glide
With unsuperfluous lift of their proud wings.

Hunt's choice of classical subject — a characteristic, he explained, of the new school of poetry — owed much to his discussions with Shelley and Keats, but unlike them, he uses his mythology literally and not as a symbolic framework for his own thoughts. Unlike Shelley, too, his eroticism is cautious, tepid beside the pulsing poetry of Shelley's Marlow summer. Like *Rimini* the 'Nymphs' suffers from an affectation of language and sentiment which critics quickly detected. But it is a vital poem, and even the antagonistic *Quarterly* conceded Hunt's richness of language and imagination. Hunt suppressed most of the poem when later publishing his collected works, perhaps sensing that its spirit was out of harmony with his other verse. It belonged peculiarly to that heady, high Shelleyan summer.

Foliage was dedicated to Sir John Swinburne, whom Hunt described as a tender-hearted lover of art, music and flowers, who placed a statue of Jupiter on his organ, filled his vases with flowers, and did not depreciate this world because he believed in the next. The dedication and preface were the most explicit statements so far made on the philosophy of cheer, which was to be cultivated by a love of nature out of doors and 'sociality' indoors, and by imitating 'the fine imagination of the Greeks' whose sensuous appreciation promoted happiness and health. Beauty and unsophisticated nature, as in *Rimini*, were the aids to cheerfulness, joined now by 'imagination'. The profitable use of this trio was the secret of living. Those who denied enjoyment were 'involuntary blasphemers against nature's goodness'. Nobody required material riches to practise enjoyment, and three of the strongest aids to enjoyment — rural luxury, dancing and music — were inexpensive and within the reach of all. The true purpose of industry was not wealth but the ability to enjoy cheerful leisure.

Amongst those who knew Hunt's capacity for incurring debt, his injunctions on the virtues of inexpensive pleasure must have produced a wry smile. In others, like the spiteful and self-righteous *Quarterly Review*, Hunt's implied attack on the negative rigidity of Christianity, and his hedonistic praise of paganism, provoked fury. These religious sentiments Shelley, of course, endorsed, and Hunt's recipe for cheap living was equally attractive, for he continued to borrow money from Shelley.

More and more, Shelley had in mind to go to Italy where cheap living and sunshine and the diversion of travel would cure his illness, depression and lack of money; indeed some of Hunt's insistence in *Foliage* that cheap living could be as easily procured in England may well have reflected his dismay at Shelley's plans. Shelley did not wish to leave Hunt: he knew his friend's emotional and financial dependence. Money, from the beginning, had been their double currency of finance and affection, and with Shelley's firm decision to leave came also the resolution to make a magnificent financial gesture. It would be an apology for leaving, a commitment to the future, and a symbol of love. By means of insuring his life against an untimely death before his inheritance fell due, Shelley was able to borrow for Hunt the enormous sum of £1,400 — the equivalent of 22 years' wages for a skilled workingman of the period. It would wipe the slate clean and save Hunt from himself, or so Shelley thought.

The two friends shared one more burst of conviviality at Lisson Grove in February and March, and one sonnet competition on 11 February embraced Keats as well. On 11 March 1818 at Shelley's lodgings in London, the Hunts gave help in the final packing of their friends' possessions, and young Thornton was agog to be allowed to pack Shelley's pistols. The adults, exhausted and depressed, cheered themselves with hopes of a possible reunion in Italy. 'The thought of how long we may be divided', Shelley told Hunt, 'makes me very melancholy.' In the evening, unwilling perhaps to face the pain of parting, Shelley fell asleep on the sofa and did not wake in time to say goodbye. Next morning he left for Italy, never to return.

Looking back on their relationship years later, Hunt saw it as a
recurring pattern of meeting and parting:

> Wilt thou, whatever summer clime I gain,
> Be taken from me, thou winged heart?
> At every summit which I earn with pain,
> Shall we but clasp each other but to part?

9 FRIEND OF SHELLEY

With Shelley gone, Hunt sought solace in work. He settled down to his *Examiner* duties with vigour, going to the office on Saturdays and attempting to order his work and his finances with a new discipline. He bought fine clothes, presumably with some of Shelley's money, and declared himself very smart in his orange gloves, a blue frock coat and a splendid hat. The diarist Crabb Robinson, who had not seen him for several years, observed his social 'glee' one night at Charles Lamb's and found him much improved, though Mrs Hunt was a 'very disgusting woman'. Hunt went energetically into the social round and gave renewed attention to the theatre and reviewing.

To signify a new chapter, Hunt turned his work room at Lisson Grove into a 'bower', with geraniums, myrtle and heartsease — Hogg '*shrieked*' at the sight of the heartsease — and rearranged the bust of Raphael on his table underneath the print of Shakespeare, placed a picture of 'Jacques and the Stag' above the controversial portrait of Milton, added a rose tree, and covered the piano with two plaster casts (gifts of Hogg) and a statue of Mercury. There was hardly room for Hunt himself! He was pleased with the effect, declaring these were 'sights of beauty, genius, and morality'. Marianne, too, turned over a new leaf, conducting a school which for two hours a morning filled the house with blessed peace, though with her own illiteracy one wonders what she taught. They had engaged a drawing master for Thornton, a Mr Wildman, and the child advanced prodigiously. Wildman also sketched a head of Hunt, an astonishing likeness which Hunt sent to Shelley, hoping he would carry it with him like Boccaccio's story of the head in a pot of basil. When Hunt wrote at the end of April to his 'dear and illustrious vagabonds' he described the new arrangements, knowing they would draw forth a Shelleyan smile, and added the children's prattling messages, including one from delicate little Percy who sat in his nurse's arms, so 'grave and intent' as if he had 'all the ideas of his namesake in his head'.

Surprisingly, after these careful arrangements, the family moved in July to a new house in York Buildings, New Road, leased for seven years with an option to leave after four. It was larger and more elegant, with three rooms to a floor, and Hunt immediately employed painters, carpenters, paperhangers and a gardener to transform the house and replant the garden. He decorated his work table with a bust of the nature goddess, Isis, and over the study door he inscribed the lines from Davenant, 'To study quiet Nature's pleasant law'. He looked forward to fireside evenings over a 'little wine, less tea, and a few divine old books'.

From York Buildings Bess went to live with her brother Tom, the 'fast' medical student of doubtful company, now a surgeon and 'cupper' but soon to turn actor under Charles Kemble's management. Keats a few months earlier had noted Bess looked like 'a fury'; her departure could have been hastened by gossip. Had she been with them a few months later her position would have been barely tenable, for Hunt from the end of 1817 was the target in a journalistic war in which no detail of his private life escaped attention. His enemies were the conservative *Quarterly Review*, the most read journal of the time, and its editor, the satirist William Gifford, who was a personal enemy of Hunt and figured derisively in all versions of *The Feast of the Poets*. The magazine and its editor showed little mercy. The *Quarterly* had reviewed *Rimini* and *Foliage* with devastating recognition of their faults. The spiteful *Foliage* review was probably written by an old school fellow of Shelley's and ended with a scathing personal attack on Shelley.

In October 1817 the *Quarterly* was joined by a vigorous, less respectable young ally, *Blackwood's Edinburgh Magazine*, with a series on Hunt and his coterie using detailed information drawn from the literary pages of the *Examiner* and from *Foliage*. It christened the new school of poetry 'the Cockney School', a geographical designation, it claimed, like the Lake school, its adherents being essentially city dwellers of the lower classes who migrated to suburban Hampstead and pretended it was rural England. The entire philosophy of cheer was grist to *Blackwood's* grating mill: the firesides, the sonnet-writing, the crowning of one another with laurels, the puns, the busts and vases and musical evenings. Keats's salutation to Hunt — 'He of the rose, the violet, the spring' — became the Cockney theme song. For years the fantasy was elaborated, often clever, racy, piquant and funny, but always self-righteous, and elaborately cruel. The 'Round Table' of Hunt and Hazlitt added to the imagery: King Leigh of the Kingdom of Cockaigne, Prince John, champion knight William Hazlitt, infatuated bardling Johnny Keats, Cockney Raphael Haydon, court musician Novello, and court gazette the *Examiner*.

In more moderate articles, Hunt was accused of want of scholarship, anti-Christianity, Jacobinism, extravagant self-love, vulgarity and indecency. In less rational terms he was attacked for moral and political subversion and accused of immoral and unnatural crimes. *The Story of Rimini* was a 'genteel comedy of incest' that no woman desirous of keeping her chastity could read without flushings of shame. By mid 1818 Hunt was falsely accused by indirect suggestion of fathering Bess Kent's illegitimate child, and inartistically transforming the episode into a poem. Accustomed to attacks, though this was the worst, Hunt donned his hardest emotional shell and withdrew. Later he would claim that he did not see 'a twentieth part of what was said against us', though this is doubtful. On one point the Hunts were adamant. They despised a writer who, signing himself as Z, hid behind a mask of meanness and cowardice. In November 1817 John Hunt demanded the writer's name, but none was forthcoming until 1821 when John Scott, now editor of the *London Magazine*, ferreted out the truth. Z was a literary amalgam in which prominent elements were the young Scottish journalists John Gibson Lockhart and John Wilson. The exposure of their names and their malice had a tragic end. A few weeks later, on a foggy night in open fields near Chalk Farm, John Scott was mortally wounded in a duel with Lockhart's friend Jonathan Christie. Literary assassination had given way to real assassination.

From these attacks Hunt shut himself away. Since childhood he had had difficulty in defending himself — though no difficulty in defending others — and he had rationalised his incapacity in various ways. Now he thought that a 'loathing kind of pity' for Gifford held him back. It was not until the *Quarterly*'s attack on the *Revolt of Islam* that he was provoked to reply. 'I know you will *not* revenge yourself', he told Shelley. He did, however, take up his pen to write a clever stinging satire called *Ultra Crepidarius*. It describes the search by Mercury for one of his winged shoes, and how he finds a shoe which behaves most disrespectfully to everything beautiful: the shoe is William Gifford. In the end Hunt delayed publishing it, holding back, one presumes, for psychological reasons as well as the legal one that if he did sue a magazine such a satire would weaken his case.

Hunt had taken up the cudgels on behalf of Shelley, but he gave little support to Keats and Hazlitt. Keats suffered especially. Like Byron, he saw truth in the vitriol, and his own anxieties and inner conflicts rose to the surface. He hated himself for his complicity in the rites of cheer, and hated Hunt for involving him. His letters reflect his turmoil. One of December 1819 describes a musical evening at Novello's where he hit out, if not as virulently as *Blackwood's*, all the more tellingly since his shots were so close to the mark:

(Scene, a little Parlour — Enter Hunt — Gattie — Hazlitt — Mrs Novello — Ollier — Gattie) Ha! Hunt! got into you[r] new house? Ha! Mrs Novello seen Altam and his Wife? Mrs N.Yes (with a grin) *its* Mr Hunts isn't it? Gatie. Hunts' noha! Mr Ollier I congratulate you upon the highest compliment I ever heard paid to the book. Mr Haslit, I hope you are well (Hazlitt — yes Sir, no Sir — Mr Hunt (at the Music) La Biondina &c Hazlitt did you ever hear this — La Biondina &c — Hazlitt — O no Sir — I never — Ollier — Do Hunt give it us over again — divino.

Novello increasingly had Hunt's affections, being a source of both pleasure and money. At Novello's home Hunt made friends of importance. Thornton would describe one such friend, Arthur Gliddon, as 'as perfect a piece of affection as ever wore man's fleshly dress' and his kind, flirtatious wife as 'a specimen of beautiful womanhood'. Hunt called her 'peach face' and a woman of true feeling and breeding. Clearly he was susceptible. According to Hogg, he was on terms which could easily give rise to gossip. The Gliddons owned a superior snuff and tobacco shop in Covent Garden where one could enjoy a good cigar and excellent coffee in the comfort of a deep divan, two cheerful fires, and the glow of soft lamps in which the best newspapers could be read. On his frequent visits to the nearby *Examiner* offices Hunt visited the shop describing his visits to his readers in 1826. The two families of Hunts and Gliddons would in time be intertwined by marriage.

In 1818 and 1819 Hunt wrote infrequently to Shelley while Marianne was slow to despatch the essential household items which Mary begged her to procure. Throughout 1819 the letters of both Shelleys contained many queries concerning a promised box that took over six months to come, and on arrival proved to contain few of the items requested. Marianne's behaviour was in character but Hunt's was not. He seemed to be shutting Shelley out. His inner

defences and his withdrawal were never more noticeable than in
June 1819 when he heard of the death of Shelley's son William and
brushed it aside with 'not the worst loss a man can have', words that
ring hollow when one remembers his lines to Thornton on his sick
bed. Moreover, a year later he would write quickly and tenderly to
Novello when his son died and compose a charming essay on the
'Deaths of Little Children'. When eventually Hunt did rouse
himself and wrote to Shelley, he poured out not only his love but
also a gentle religiousness which his contact with Shelley had not
snuffed:

> I had received the news of your misfortune and thought of all
> which you and Mary must suffer. Marianne, I assure you, wept
> hearty tears of sympathy. He was a fine little fellow, — was
> William; and for my part, I cannot conceive, that the young
> intellectual spirit which sat thinking out of his eye, and seemed to
> comprehend so much in his smile, can perish like the house it
> inhabited. I do not know that a soul is born with us; but we seem,
> to me, to *attain* to a soul, some later, some earlier; and when we
> have got that, there is a look in our eye, a sympathy in our
> cheerfulness, and a yearning and grave beauty in our thought-
> fulness, that seems to say — our mortal dress may fall off when it
> will: — our trunk and leaves may go: — we have shot up our
> blossom into an immortal air. This is poetry, you will see, and not
> argument; but then there comes upon me another fancy, which
> would fain persuade me, that poetry is the argument of a higher
> sphere. So you smile at me? So you, too, Marina, smile at me?
> Well then, — I have done something at any rate. My dear
> friends, I affront your understandings and feelings with none of
> the ordinary topics of consolation. We must all weep on these
> occasions . . . may the calmest and most affectionate spirit that
> comes out of the contemplation of great things and the love of all,
> lay his most blessed hand upon you.

To Mary he wrote sweetly and divertingly: 'I wish in truth I knew
how to amuse you just now, and that I were in Italy to try. I would
walk about with Shelley, wherever he pleased, having resumed my
good old habits that way; and I would be merry or quiet, chat, read,
or impudently play and sing you Italian airs all evening.' He
pictured the Hunts and the Shelleys at the opera, and looked to
Shelley's old box 'almost hoping to see a thin patrician-looking

young cosmopolitan yearning out upon us, and a sedate-faced young lady bending in a similar direction with her great tablet of a forehead, and white shoulders unconscious of a crimson gown'. Shelley, with few friends in England and Hunt 'the best', was thirsty for news and did all in his power to maintain the lifeline, alternately exhorting and complaining as he tried to revive the correspondence. Mary, grieving the loss of her infant daughter Clara in 1818 and the loss of William in the following year, also wrote eagerly. Hunt, she seemed to feel, could offer at a safe distance the sympathy which Shelley did not provide.

Hunt's letters to Shelley in 1818 were chit chat of ordinary events, his reading and his new publication, 'a dressy almanack' called the *Literary Pocket Book or Companion for the Lover of Art and Nature*. Dear to Hunt's heart, it was an inoffensive calendar and memorandum book with original prose and poetry, fascinating anecdotes, and lists of practical or unusual facts to inspire and instruct his readers. It was such a success that Ollier brought out fresh editions annually. Even *Blackwood's* had kind words for it — 'a very clever and cunning contrivance' — though Keats called it 'most sickening stuff'. Even better, Hunt received all profits, until reverses in 1819 forced him to sell Ollier the copyright. In March 1819, after a gap of four months, Hunt wrote again describing the completion of his drama *Le Cid* which both Covent Garden and Drury Lane turned down, and the retirement of his brother John from the *Examiner*. John would move to Taunton near his wife's relations, to a Huntian parlour hung with prints of Raphael, Claude and Titian. His work was taken over by his eldest son Henry, one of Shelley's ardent supporters and 'a very nice ingenuous lad, who with his father's staider excellences, has more imagination'. More work now fell on Hunt himself, and there was less possibility of him visiting Italy. At the end of 1818 he had declared that if Shelley were ill or needed him he would come, but it took little reading between the lines to realise how half-hearted were his promises.

Shelley for his part was not half-hearted. The year of 1819 would be the year of his masterpieces — *Prometheus Unbound*, the *Mask of Anarchy* and the *Cenci* — and with each of them Hunt was linked. In Rome, with the portrait of Hunt before him, he composed his drama of incest, the *Cenci*, dedicated to Hunt 'after an absence whose months have seemed years':

Had I known a person more highly endowed than yourself with

all that it becomes a man to possess, I had solicited for this work the ornament of his name. One more gentle, honourable, innocent and brave; one of more exalted toleration for all who do and think evil, and yet himself more free of evil; one who knows better how to receive, and how to confer a benefit, though he must ever more confer than he can receive; one of the simpler, and, in the highest sense of the word, or purer life and manners I never knew . . . All happiness attend you! Your affectionate friend.

A year later, in his verse epistle to an expatriate English friend, Maria Gisborne, who was briefly revisiting England, he would write with lighthearted affection:

> You will see Hunt — one of those happy souls
> Who are the salt of the earth, and without whom
> This world would smell like what is is — a tomb;
> Who is, what others seem; his room no doubt
> Is still adorned with many a cast from Shout
> With graceful flowers tastefully hung about:
> And coronals of bay with ribbons hung,
> And brighter wreaths in neat disorder flung;
> The gifts of the most learned among some dozens
> Of female friends, sisters-in-law, and cousins.

In autumn 1819 Shelley read the accounts of the riots at St Peter's Fields near Manchester, the infamous 'Peterloo Massacre' where six died and nearly a hundred were wounded. Though living in Italy, his heart and political pulse were still in England. Now his anger erupted in a brilliant twelve-day stint of composition to produce a masterpiece, the *Mask of Anarchy*. Brilliant, colloquial — in a way that Hunt and his 'system' could never be — and shatteringly urgent, it synthesised his political philosophy and his poetic power. On 23 September he sent it to Hunt for publication in the *Examiner*. Speed, to ensure topicality, was of the essence. As one biographer has pointed out, a radical success in the *Examiner* at this point would have changed the course of Shelley's career. He would have become a cause, his *Cenci* might have been accepted by Covent Garden, and his *Prometheus Unbound* written in the same year might have had ready sales. The Hunt brothers conferred, knowing that publication would bring swift prosecution, for the government's attacks on the press had reached new heights. Indeed John did go to prison for seditious libel in 1821. One cannot imagine that if Shelley had been in England, Leigh Hunt would not have published it. He had supported the Hermit of Marlow pamphlets; what greater glory than to stand side by side with Shelley, fellow martyrs in the radical cause?

It seems that sometime in 1819 Leigh Hunt had relinquished his proprietorial share in the *Examiner* and was now merely employed as editor, so it was John as proprietor who risked prosecution. Presumably it was therefore primarily John's decision. Did Leigh press John in this? There are many questions one cannot answer, but Leigh's influence on his brother in such matters was strong, and if Leigh had insisted, John might have published it. One suspects that Leigh did not insist that Shelley be published. Did he feel a conflict between his love for Shelley and for his brother? Leigh Hunt explained none of this to Shelley in any surviving letter, and as the distinguished list of prosecutions for Peterloo grew, many of them friends and colleagues in the radical struggle, the Hunts' names were noticeably absent. What soul searching it must have cost Leigh can only be guessed at. When he finally did publish the poem in 1832, long after Shelley's death, it is obvious from the note he appended that he knew he had failed his beloved friend. He said, unconvincingly, that the time was not ripe in 1819 to inflame 'the people at large'.

Weeks passed and Hunt did not reply to Shelley's stream of queries about the poem's fate. Significantly in December 1819, on receiving two letters from the Shelleys, Hunt did write, making no mention of the *Mask of Anarchy* and then forgetting to mail the letter. On 23 December Shelley sent Hunt an angry and disjointed letter, making no mention of the poem but expressing disappointment and distrust:

> *Why* don't you write to us? I was preparing to send you something for your 'Indicator' . . . as you did not acknowledge any of my late inclosures, it would not be welcome to you — whatever I might send. We have just received all your *Examiners* up to October 27th . . . What a state England is in! But you will never write politics . . . Every word a man has to say is valuable to the public now . . . I have no spirits to write, what I do not know whether you will care much about — I know well, that if I were in great misery, poverty etc. you would think nothing else but

how to amuse and relieve me.— You omit me if I am prosperous. . . I could laugh if I found a joke in order to put you in a
good humour with me after my scolding — in good humour
enough to write to us.

Again Hunt sank into silence.

In the months of political unrest and agitation the moderately
radical *Examiner* temporarily gained in circulation. Hunt, who
despite Shelley's extraordinary generosity was again deeply in debt,
told Hogg in October that his prospects were 'never better' and he
hoped financially to fly free. But his family remained a financial
millstone, and Marianne was again pregnant and on 28 September
gave birth to her fifth son Henry Sylvan, named after his father
and presumably his father's passion for nature. Already, in search
of savings, the family had moved to a cheaper house, having
persuaded the landlord to allow them to sublet York Buildings.
They chose Mortimer Terrace, Kentish Town, a new outer suburb
between Hampstead and London. Hunt found it quiet and rural
with its woods and slopes, but Hogg, returning from a visit, said that
only Hunt could regard this depressing half-suburb as countrified.
Meanwhile Hunt was working on a translation of Tasso called
Amyntas which he would publish in the following year and dedicate
to Keats. Shelley disapproved of Hunt's translations and urged him
to keep to the 'perpetual creation' of original composition, although
it had good reviews and one reviewer declared the translations
better than Hunt's own poetry. The year before he had brought out
two new poems of his own on classical subjects, *Hero and Leander*
and *Bacchus and Ariadne*, also to a good reception and the *London
Magazine* wrote at length on his delicate verse, love of nature and
originality.

Although the *Examiner* really required all his efforts, Hunt
decided in October 1819 to launch a new journal. He called it the
Indicator, a name suggested not only by his famous *Examiner*
signature of the indicating hand but also by an idea of Mrs Novello,
who spoke of the Indicator bird of Africa which looked for honey
with 'a cheerful cry' in old woods and indicated its sweets to
whoever followed. It was a clever reference because Hunt performed this very function for his middle-class readers, pointing out
literary sweets old and new, including a few from his gifted friends,
thus becoming not only a guardian of literature of the past but also
the patron and populariser of literature of his time. Most of the

magazine he wrote himself: 'short disquisitions on men and things; the most interesting stories in history or fiction told over again, with an eye to proper appreciation by unvulgar minds; and now and then a few original verses'. He told his readers that whereas the *Examiner* was the tavern room for politics and theatre critics and living writers, his new paper was the private study where readers could learn the essence of whatever subject he chose to present in that intimate, innocently seductive, associational style that was becoming his favourite medium. Indeed the *Indicator*, he would say a few years later, 'enabled me perhaps to come to a true estimate of my station as an author'.

This journal of the philosophy of cheer, delivered every Wednesday morning to the breakfast table, contains much of Hunt's finest work. Bringing to fruition his attempts in the *Reflector* and *Examiner* to revive and refine the English familiar essay, it would have many imitators in popular educational literature, but few, as Thornton put it, showed the same finish, versatility or invention, or the same genius for communicating directly and affectionately with readers on those subjects that would arouse their sympathy, kindness, and natural pleasure. Many friends found the *Indicator* irresistible, and Charles Lamb expressed their pleasure in verse:

> Your easy Essays indicate a flow
> Dear Friend, of brain, which we may elsewhere seek;
> And to their pages, I, and hundreds, owe,
> That Wednesday is the sweetest of the week.

Crabb Robinson, normally no admirer of Hunt, found charm and a spirit of enjoyment in the magazine, and admired the way it 'catches the sunny side of everything'. Lamb summed it up:

> Wit, poet, prose-man, party-man, translator—
> H—, your best title yet is Indicator.

Meanwhile at Mortimer Terrace in 1820 the Hunts were neighbours of John Keats. Hunt, out of kindness, had found cheap lodgings for him within walking distance of Hampstead and of his new fiancée Fanny Brawne. Keats was ill and depressed with what would prove to be consumption, and Hunt sensed the need for a fatherly eye. Surprisingly, he had failed to realise Keats's antipathy to him, and this insensitivity was now a blessing as he was able to father him with confidence. As well as finding lodgings for the young man, he printed his work in the *Indicator* and reviewed at length his *Lamia*, a new poem from which Keats had quietly deleted any taint of Hunt for fear of earning yet another 'Cockney' label.

On 22 June Keats suffered a slight spitting of blood. The symptoms he had tried to ignore in February were now terrifyingly clear. That day, seeking solace, he went to drink tea with the Hunts and their guest Maria Gisborne, Mrs Gisborne recollected how quiet and withdrawn Keats was as they talked of Italian singers. That evening he had a severe haemorrhage, and his landlady in alarm sent for Hunt. Hunt at once had him removed to Mortimer Terrace and called a doctor. Throughout that unusually hot summer, until the middle of August, Keats stayed with the Hunts. Obsessed by the fears that are a symptom of tuberculosis, he alternately broke out in anger and weeping. He began to inveigh against *Blackwood's* (not, as is usually said, the *Quarterly*) whose cruelty had caused his mental anguish and hence, he thought, his present physical plight. Hunt half-believed this diagnosis and thought Keats should escape the reach of these evil spirits. He wrote to Shelley, who generously invited Keats to Italy as his guest, reassuring him, through Marianne, that he would be the physician of his body and soul. Keats, detecting patronage, thornily declined.

Through those sweltering days Keats lay like a prisoner and 'feared for his senses'. Hunt, observing his nervous as well as physical state, was full of dread. Though ill himself with fever and headache, he did his best to rouse Keats. He sat with him and together they composed for the *Indicator*, while the children quarrelled and Marianne did her slipshod housekeeping. One day they took a coach to Hampstead, and Keats rested near the house where his brother Tom had died and wept as though his heart would break. Inevitably the volcano of his emotions erupted, and a graphic account of the eruption is left in Maria Gisborne's journal. While Mrs Gisborne was observing that strange, sad household a letter arrived for Keats. Marianne, busy with the children, ordered the servant girl to take the letter to him. She did not deliver it and next day she gave notice and left. Sometime later Thornton found the letter and opened it — from Fanny Brawne but 'not a word of the least consequence' — and brashly gave it to his mother, who in turn handed it to Keats, with the seal broken. Keats, in his anger, was thrown into uncontrollable weeping. Rejecting Hunt's entreaties he insisted on leaving the house. In Hampstead he was seen sobbing, almost too weak to walk, and eventually he reached Mrs Brawne's in a state of collapse. Next day he wrote Hunt an apology: 'I feel really attached to you for your many sympathies with me, and patience at my lunes.' Hunt sent back one of his sweetest letters: 'I need not say how you gratify me by the impulse which led you to write a particular sentence in your letter, for you must have seen by this time how much I am attached to yourself.' He ended with a gentle pun: 'I am indicating at as dull a rate as a battered finger-post in wet weather . . . Your affectionate friend, Leigh Hunt.' Later Hunt would write, 'I could not love him as deeply as I did Shelley. That was impossible. But my affection was only second to the one which I entertained for that heart of hearts.'

In September 1820 Keats sailed for Italy in desperate hope of halting his consumption. Six months later Hunt wrote to his companion Joseph Severn, in Rome, knowing the pain a direct letter would cause the sensitive young poet:

Judge how often I thought of Keats, and with what feelings . . . If he can bear to hear of us, pray tell him; but he knows it already, and can put it in better language than any man. I hear that he does not like to be told that he may get better . . . He can only regard it as a puerile thing, and an insinuation that he shall die . . . if he can now put up with attempts to console him, of what I have said a thousand times, and what I still (upon my honour) think always, that I have seen too many instances of recovery from apparently desperate cases of consumption not to be in hope to the very last. If he cannot bear this, tell him — tell that great poet and noble hearted man — that we shall all bear his memory in the most precious part of our hearts, and that the world shall bow their heads to it, as our loves do. Or if this, again, will trouble his spirit, tell him that we shall never cease to remember and love him; and that Christian or infidel, the most sceptical of us has faith enough in the high things that nature puts into our heads, to think all who are of one accord in mind or heart are journeying to one and the same place, and shall unite somewhere or other again, face to face, mutually conscious, mutually delighted. Tell him he is only before us on the road, as he is in everything else . . . The tears are again in my eyes, and I must not afford to shed them.

By this time Keats was already dead.

That summer Hunt had suffered from migraine, biliousness and general weakness. As the year progressed his symptoms became stronger, their origin being clearly nervous. The precarious emotional balance, so carefully tended in the last few years, was tilting. In vain, he sought the remedy of cheer. 'Exercise, conversation, cheerful society, amusement of all sorts, or a kind, patient and gradual helping of the bodily health, till the mind be capable of amusement.' These were the only cures of nervous disorder, he wrote in the *Indicator*. Over the next two years he suffered a collapse which echoed that of 1812 in its severity. Far more than previously, real worries disturbed him; rarely had his anxiety so rational a base. Where had gone that noble gift from Shelley? Swallowed up, in a couple of years in improvident living. His income had fallen drastically also. The circulation of the *Examiner* had slipped, and he was no longer a proprietor. John, now both proprietor and printer, and legally the vulnerable one, was convicted for his attacks on the House of Commons, and sent for two years to Colbath-Fields Prison on 21 May 1821.

To help Hunt's nerves and pocket the family returned to the Vale of Health, to their former cottage — still, it would seem, leased by Rowland Hunter. Leigh's illness continued. As in the past he tried exercise and more dangerously he tried alcohol — anything to help him sustain his journalistic output. Even his beloved *Indicator* became too much for him; it failed in March 1821, he 'having almost died over the latter numbers'. By May he was writing nothing and the fat had vanished from his bones. 'Many do not know me at first sight, I am grown so thin and gaunt', he confessed. Meanwhile the children had measles and then scarlet fever, Mary Florimel was desperately sick with inflammatory fever and rheumatism, and baby Henry Sylvan had fits. Physician and friend William Knighton came at midnight on 11 July to save Mary Florimel: next day she was out of danger. 'It is seldom that I afford myself tears', Hunt told the Shelleys with unusual stoicism.

This wretchedness had one sensible effect. His barriers against Shelley came tumbling down. Hunt poured out his feelings in letters to Italy and to others. When Hazlitt attacked Shelley and Hunt in *Table Talk*, in a shrewd assessment of the self-centred side of Hunt's character and of Shelley's emotionalism. Hunt leaped to Shelley's defence. There followed an interchange in which the wounded feelings and affection of both Hunt and Hazlitt were exposed. 'My dear Hunt, I have no quarrel with you, nor can I have. You are one of those people that I like, do what they will', wrote Hazlitt. This mutual bearing of hurt restored the relationship and Hunt treasured the correspondence.

'My dearest Shelley, I would come to you instantly', wrote Hunt from Hampstead in August 1821, but he confessed that there were difficulties. He would come if his health did not mend — 'if I cannot write without driving the blood to my head'. Shelley and Italy were now 'my friend and my physician'. Hunt's hesitation came from the *Examiner*; his absence had lowered its circulation, and his return now boosted it by hundreds. As John's livelihood and his own depended on it, dare he leave it? As for his own family, they were too ill to travel at present.

Shelley sensed that Hunt was capitulating. He decided to press his point. He and Byron had already discussed two years before the possibility of Hunt's coming to Italy to write but Hunt had not accepted. Now he evolved a specific plan with Byron's help: 'you should come out and go shares with him and me, in a periodical work to be conducted here; in which each of the contracting parties should publish all their original compositions and share the profits'. Shelley predicted that any such profits would be large, and that Byron and Hunt alone should share them.

On 21 September 1821 Hunt replied emphatically to Shelley, 'We are coming.' He would give no time to second thoughts, and would leave a month hence, just after his thirty-seventh birthday. Though he praised Byron for his kindness, he would not hear of Shelley standing aloof from their profit sharing: a triumvirate, surely, with Shelley the sleeping partner. He would try to raise the passage money and he held the 'certainty' that Shelley would reimburse him. Now the Hunts were 'talking of nothing else but Italy, Italy, Italy' where they hoped 'to grasp the hands of the best friends in the world'.

10 THE WREN AND THE EAGLE

> The Kind Cockney Monarch, he bids us farewell
> Taking his place on the Leghorn-bound — smack —
> In the smack, in the smack, Ah! will he ne'er come back?

Thus *Blackwood's* celebrated Hunt's departure. Shelley had advised Hunt simply to put his music and books in a departing ship and he would have no trouble. 'I believe if he had recommended a balloon', said Hunt later, 'I should have been inclined to try it.' Despite his eagerness, his month of preparation dragged into two. The strain of packing, on top of the nervous and physical vicissitudes of the past months, were too much for Marianne. Two weeks before the sailing day she began to spit blood. Hunt by now was so determined to go that he made light ot it, declaring that 'such a voyage is the best thing in the world for her'.

Marianne's confinement to bed must have made preparations with the six children difficult. Moreover there was anxious debate whether Bess should accompany them. All sides had mixed feelings about such a plan, and in the end it was decided that the risk to reputation was too high. If all went well she might join them later, though rumours were soon rife that she had actually sailed with the household.

On 15 November 1821 friends came aboard the brig *Jane* at Blackwall to say goodbye, among them the Lambs and Novello. Hunt was in galloping spirits when he wrote next evening to Shelley, though his head already was giddy from seasickness. Marianne, sensing disaster, cut locks off the family's hair for keepsakes: they are still preserved at Hampstead. There were few joys, Hunt soon discovered, in a winter voyage, especially for those who had lived in reasonable comfort on dry land. The cabin was unbelievably small: just imagine, he wrote, 'the little back-parlour of one of the shops of Fleet Street or the Strand, attached or let into a great moving vehicle, and tumbling about the waves from side to side'. There was not even room for all to go to bed. The adults were obliged to sleep on the floor and the children wers crammed into narrow bunks along the walls. They had also brought a servant, who slept in an adjoining 'petty closet', and a goat — the gift of a kind friend — to

121

provide the children with milk. Marianne was further distressed by the sight of a cargo of gunpowder, which the drunken cook was fond of visiting with a lighted candle, and Hunt could not walk along the deck without fearing they would all be blasted into the air in the twinkling of an eye. In the face of such privation and danger he watched baby Henry Sylvan at play, and wondered what right he had to risk so much innocent flesh and blood. For four miserable days they endured rain and squalls off the English coast until the captain decided to shelter at Ramsgate. There for nearly three weeks they waited in lodgings, Hunt full of nervous impatience, tempered by meeting Cowden Clarke and his parents who lived there. Eventually Marianne, ill and weak, was carried in a sedan chair to the boat, and they were off again.

Now began a nightmare. The skies clouded and storms raged, their ferocity making 1821 memorable in shipping annals. All were sea-sick and the goat, milkless with fear, lay shivering in the canvas-covered longboat until Hunt lugged it, slipping and sliding, into the cabin and tempted it with biscuits. For ten days they thus endured, and it was testimony to the power of cheerful thinking that Hunt managed to control his 'constant dread'. Surrounded by a seasick, blood-spitting wife, six vomiting children and a vomiting goat, he managed to keep up the children's spirits and see beauty in the phantasmal appearance of the hanging garments that gestured mysteriously as the vessel rocked. When he struggled up to the slippery deck he could observe with awe the huge tormented sea-scape. He found it 'ennobling'.

On 22 December the *Jane* put in at Dartmouth. Exhausted and woebegone, the Hunts were again on English soil. Marianne was clearly too ill to continue and the passage money was forfeited. Hunt felt better but Marianne, considerably worse, was drastically bled by the local physician 'to prevent inflammatory fever on the lungs'. Thereafter she spent her time in bed, improving and relapsing. Meanwhile the winds raged and Hunt thanked heaven that they were ashore or they would certainly be dead. From Dartmouth they travelled to Plymouth and took lodgings in the suburb of Stonehouse, to give Marianne time to recover. Here Hunt forfeited a deposit of £30 on a passage, booked but then cancelled at the last moment, partly because Marianne distrusted the seaworthiness of the ship and the captain. 'What a disappointing, wearisome, vexatious, billowy, up-and-downy, unbearable, beautiful world it is', he exclaimed to Novello!

For five months Hunt enjoyed Plymouth, reading in the public library and accepting the homage of local 'Examinerians' when not watching at Marianne's sick bed: it was a strange time which he described as like Mahomet's coffin, suspended between the two attractions of England and Italy. With his hired pianoforte and the visits of friends from London, he began to wonder at the wisdom of going to Italy at all. Were it not for the prospect of cheap living, cheap education and Marianne's health he declared he might not bother.

Shelley, concerned about Marianne, alarmed by the delays, and appalled by Hunt's demands for money, wrote firmly and bracingly as to a wayward child, urging him to come. Had not Byron set aside rooms for the Hunts in his own palace and insisted with the Shelley's help on furnishing them? In January Shelley begged him not to wait until spring for fear that he would retreat to the circle of debt. Generously, he sent Hunt every penny he could scrape up in order to cover the expenses of the delay and a new passage. Hearing of Hunt's proposals to borrow from Byron, he warned Byron that Hunt's promises to pay in a given time were worthless and offering his own surety. Byron, remembering Hunt's championship of him in the past, willingly paid £250, a sum that could have sent the entire family around the world. It was just beginning to dawn on him that Hunt was arriving as a complete financial liability.

Byron was now having second thoughts about the forthcoming journal, especially as *Blackwood's* derided the proposed 'Pisan Alliance' and friends like Tom Moore were far from enthusiastic. Byron, too, found himself increasingly at loggerheads with Shelley who, in the hope of mending the situation, represented to each side with well-meant duplicity the other's eagerness and ability. Byron had the 'greatest anxiety for your arrival', he told Hunt, flatteringly suggesting that Hunt alone had the mental qualities necessary to manage the enterprise. But by June Shelley had become pessimistic. He wrote to Horace Smith that 'between ourselves I greatly fear that this alliance will not succeed, for I, who could never have been regarded as more than a link of the two thunderbolts, cannot now consent to be even that, — and how long the alliance between the wren and eagle may continue I will not prophesy'. He was devastatingly right.

Shelley wrote in April 1822 in the 'firm hope' that they had already sailed, but it was 13 May when Hunt's new vessel caught a fair wind and, amid farewells from Plymouth friends, set out for

Leghorn. Marianne was still ill, but Hunt was abrim with delight at the ever-diverting sea-scape. He kept repeating that magical word 'Mediterranean', the sea of Virgil and Homer. By 17 June they were in Genoa, a city truly 'la superba', a dozen Hampsteads. Hunt sat on deck dashing off elated letters home. He was triumphant that their original ship, the *Jane*, had foundered and he vowed — with reason — that a winter passage in the second ship would have killed Marianne. But here they were, all alive and exultant: 'The lucid Mediterranean sea washed against our vessel, like amber: a sky, blue indeed, was above our heads: inconveniences and dangers were left behind us; health, hope, and Italy, were before us.' At the beginning of July the ship sailed down the coast, past Lerici where Shelley was living for the summer, and into the harbour at Leghorn. Hunt was at once recognised by a dark handsome man standing in Lord Byron's boat. This was 'wild but good-hearted' Edward Trelawny, who found the voyagers in high spirits.

Trelawny took Hunt along the hot road to Byron's villa outside Leghorn, at Monte Nero. All was confusion: Byron's coachman had quarrelled with the cook, fighting had broken out in the garden, the poet had appeared brandishing pistols and the brother of Byron's mistress had been stabbed. Hunt arrived, panting in the Italian heat, and in the house found a much older, fatter, more languid Byron than he remembered — with his mistress, the Countess Guiccioli, and her brother who was bleeding in the shoulder from a knife wound inflicted by one of Byron's red-capped servants. So this was happy, balmy Italy!

In Leghorn the Hunts were installed in a hotel where they waited eagerly for the Shelleys to arrive. Mary Shelley, alas, had almost died of a miscarriage but sent a letter begging her dear friends not to come up the coast to depressing Lerici, a 'dungeon', but rather go with Shelley and Byron to their more permanent residence in Pisa. Shelley's own warm greeting preceded his arrival: 'A thousand welcomes my best friend to this divine country — many mountains and seas no longer divide those whose affections are united. We have much to think of and talk of when we meet at Leghorn — but the final result of our plans will be peace to you, and to me a greater degree of consolation than has been permitted to me since we met.'

At long last Shelley reached Leghorn: 'I will not dwell upon the moment', says Hunt with the reticence of pain in his *Auto-biography*. Fortunately Thornton has left a sharp account of

Shelley's arrival, recalling the shrill sound of Shelley's voice 'as he rushed into my father's arms, which he did with an impetuousness and a fervour scarcely to be imagined by any who did not know the intensity of his feelings and the deep nature of his affection'. As they came together Shelley cried out that he was 'so *inexpressibly* delighted! — you cannot think how *inexpressibly* happy it makes me'. Thornton observed how much healthier Shelley looked and sounded — stronger and more confident. Hunt found him the same as ever — how could he be different? Soon after Shelley's death Hunt was to make scattered jottings, and some referred to his prayer that the companionship of Shelley would 'restore the springs of life'. He looked to Shelley that day at Leghorn for a rebirth: a renewal of health, energy and purpose, and a sympathy that he could obtain from no other living person.

Shelley, for his part, looked to Hunt for 'consolation' and a measure of that deep support that Hunt had given in the aftermath of Harriet's suicide, a support equally vital as he faced a growing disenchantment with his marriage and his life: 'I only feel the want of those who can feel, and understand me', he had written to John Gisborne. 'Mary does not.' There can be little doubt that in the first few days at Leghorn and Pisa he poured out to Hunt's ears his disillusion with Byron, his distress at Mary's estrangement, and his acute wretchedness — a wretchedness that had erupted two weeks before in a series of terrifying hallucinations which had prevented him meeting Hunt in Genoa.

Shelley was appalled by Marianne's 'desperate state of health', and as soon as the Hunts had occupied the ground floor set aside for them in Byron's Palazzo Lanfranchi at Pisa, he sent for the celebrated Italian physician, Vacca. Vacca's diagnosis was fatal consumption: how long in termination he could not predict — maybe a year or less. He prescribed careful treatment. 'This intelligence has extinguished the last spark of poor Hunt's spirits', Shelley told Mary. The triumvirate was falling apart before his eyes, and the situation he had set up to help his dear friend Hunt was causing nothing but turmoil. Everybody was in despair, and everyone but Shelley complained. Byron declared he would leave Pisa and follow the Gambas, his mistress's aristocratic family, into exile because they had fallen foul of Tuscan law. He was decidedly unwelcoming, being dismayed by consumptive Marianne and the gypsy household. Angrily aware of the increasing criticism in many English periodicals of his membership of such a literary alliance, he was also, like Shelley, worried about Hunt's penury and his utter belief in their providence.

The Hunts were quick to sense the chilly atmosphere. Five beds were hastily procured because Byron had not expected the children. He distrusted them on sight, though Shelley found them 'much improved'. Marianne was, mercifully, too unwell to be required to acknowledge Teresa Guiccioli, of whom she did not approve.

Controlling his anxieties, Shelley endeavoured to iron out differences and put spirit into both sides. There were wrangles already over the projected journal and its name (possibly the *Hesperides*), its regularity, its format and its content of essays, stories and translations. Leigh had already arranged for his brother John to take over the printing and publishing, and Shelley had obtained from Byron a promise of his sensational poetic satire on Southey and George III, a 'Vision of Judgement', being a reply to Southey's year-old poem of the same name. Unfortunately the publisher John Murray already possessed a copy of the work and now had to surrender the manuscript to John Hunt for whom he had no love. Murray had his revenge, handing over — ostensibly by accident — an incomplete copy wich lacked the important preface in which Byron explained his reason for writing libellously. When in December 1822 John Hunt was prosecuted and tried for his calumny of the late King, the Pisan group maintained that Murray had intended his costly omission: Hunt was reluctant to forgive.

Shelley encouraged Hunt into believing he could manage Byron and Byron into believing he could manage Hunt. He was so central to the alliance that neither side wanted him to depart from Pisa. He lingered five days, calming Byron and trying to divert Hunt with pleasant excursions about the town, but at last he had to leave. Hunt gave him a copy of Keats' *Lamia* to read on the journey. 'I never', wrote Hunt with dreadful finality, 'beheld him more.'

Shelley took the post chaise to Leghorn and there a boat to Lerici. The afternoon of 8 June was oppressive and humid, and a storm broke before dusk. Days passed while Mary waited for him in the gloomy house on the beach outside Lerici, supposing he must have stayed on in Pisa. She was aghast when, a month later, a letter came from Hunt seeking news of Shelley's safe arrival. She jumped into a carriage with her friend, Jane Williams, whose husband had sailed with Shelley, and hurried to Pisa, awaking Byron on her arrival. For eight terrible days they waited while friends searched the coast for wreckage. Hunt wrote later:

> Our worst fears were confirmed. A body had been washed on shore, near the town of Via Reggio, which, by the dress and stature, was known to be our friend's. Keats's latest volume also (the *Lamia*, etc.), was found open in the jacket pocket. He had probably been reading it when surprised by the storm. It was my copy. I had told him to keep it till he gave it me with his own hands.

Years later he imagined Shelley returning the book to him in an afterlife. The death of Shelley was the end of that episode which had begun when new friends entered his life in England in 1817: Keats dead of consumption in Rome, Shelley drowned off Via Reggio while reading Hunt's copy of Keats's poems, and Hunt himself had only half of his life span accomplished.

To comply with health laws the washed-up bodies were buried temporarily on the beach where they lay. Mary Shelley and Jane Williams expressed a desire to have the bodies cremated so that the ashes could be buried elsewhere — Shelley's in Rome with his son, William — and Edward Trelawny made the arrangements. At least this is Hunt's earliest reading of a situation that altered with almost every version of the events which Trelawny later wrote. Trelawny interviewed authorities and arranged to use a furnace for the ceremony while Hunt remained in Pisa, helpless and 'tongue-tied with horror'. Then Byron and Hunt joined Trelawny and his assistants on the beach and watched as Williams's body was dug up and placed on the funeral pyre. There was nothing horrible or unfeeling, Hunt noticed, in those solemn rites. It was a ceremony both beautiful and distressing. Byron was so disturbed by the proceedings that he afterwards swam out to sea until, seized with cramp, he had to return.

Next morning they assembled again for Shelley's cremation. It was a perfect day. Hunt observed the forests of small pine edging the shore, and beyond them the snowy crests of the mountains:

> The Mediterranean, now soft and lucid, kissed the shore as if to make peace with it. The yellow sand and blue sky were intensely contrasted with one another: marble mountains touched the air

with coolness; and the flame of the fire bore away towards heaven in vigorous amplitude, wavering and quivering with a brightness of inconceivable beauty. It seemed as though it contained the glassy essence of vitality.

Most of the time Hunt was too distressed to watch. He sat in the carriage as they disinterred the decomposing body and placed it on the pyre with wine and spices and oil and salt, the copy of *Lamia* being thrown into the flames. Byron, as he saw the brains seethe and the corpse fall open, turned away in distress and swam to his boat. In the evening, in the carriage on the way back to Pisa, Byron and Hunt became drunk. They sang and shouted and laughed hysterically like 'men possessed'. Hunt was appalled at himself, for it was a genuine gaiety, 'real and relief'. His disorientation shook him.

Soon after Shelley's funeral, a bizarre action showed how far Hunt's spirits had been shattered. Trelawny had given him Shelley's heart, from the fire. Now Mary Shelley wanted it. She appealed to Byron who said that of course she must have it. Hunt, knowing from Shelley's own lips that Mary had estranged herself from him, could not give up the heart. He was filled with indignation, for Shelley was *his*. He wrote to Mary a letter revealing his extraordinary emotional confusion.

It is not that my self-love is hurt, for that I could have given up, as I have long learnt to do; but it is my love, — my love for my friend; and for this to make way for the claims of any other love, man's or woman's, I must have great reasons indeed brought me . . . In *his* case above all other human beings, no ordinary appearance of rights, even yours, can affect me . . . I begged it at the funeral pyre: I had it; and his Lordship. . . knew nothing of the matter until it was in my possession. . . and the heart that beat then with a melancholy rapture, beats as violently now, though with a different mixture of feelings.

In the end rationality prevailed and Hunt did give up the heart, though he retained a fragment of jawbone preserved in a little box for the rest of his life.

Hunt announced the news of Shelley's death in letters to John and Bess in England and Horace Smith in Paris and from these the early obituaries appeared, the very first in the *Examiner*. 'Good God!

how shall I say it', he wrote to Bess, 'My beloved friend Shelley, — my dear, my divine friend, the best of friends and of men — he is no more. I know not how to proceed for anguish.'

Few, if any, who have written on the ménage in the Palazzo Lanfranchi have adequately understood the nightmare in which Hunt was living. He had left England in the midst of a nervous breakdown hoping for escape and, with Shelley's help, for a rebirth. Instead, Marianne had been diagnosed as dying, and Shelley had died. He was in a foreign land with six small children. He was living in an environment which seemed hostile, with no money, and was largely dependent on the charity of a man who seemed to hate him. It was no wonder that emotion often took over and that he became highly irrational. It was no wonder that Shelley after death should be elevated to sainthood and everyone be judged alongside and found wanting. One can see this in Marianne's reverence of the little box containing the fragments of his jawbone, in Marianne's and Hunt's insistence, in their letters and journals, on the sense that Shelley was with them. 'God bless him! I cannot help thinking of him as if he were alive as much as ever, so unearthly he always appeared to me and so seraphical a thing of the elements', Hunt told Horace Smith. Marianne in her diary would record, as a presentiment of her death, how Shelley 'always seems to look placidly and steadfastly on me with an air of waiting'. In his poem 'The Choice', Hunt was soon to canonise Shelley into a type of saint.

Byron, however, was fast becoming a devil, and with that devil the Hunts had to live. Even without the shock of Shelley's death, the idea of living with Byron was an impossible proposition. Grief made Byron more withdrawn and edgy. Grief made Hunt more pettish, uneasy, and self-justificatory. The wren and the eagle had now to co-exist in a state of grief, without the help of their old peacemaker and intermediary. It was too much to expect.

The two households were separate, the Hunts on the ground floor, Byron and his household on the more select upper floors. Their routines were utterly different. Hunt arose early. At work in a small study overlooking the courtyard garden, he would hear with annoyance the sounds from above as Byron arose after a late night of writing and gin and water. Byron was a languid riser who breakfasted, read, lounged, sang Rossini — a composer whom Hunt despised — and had his bath. Dressed, oiled and curled, he then came down, still singing his Rossini airs in an unmusical way, to the garden below. There he would sit with his Countess among the orange trees before sauntering upstairs to his books and bed. He was handsome, blithe, prosperous and self-confident, always tossing some provocative pleasantry to Hunt, his literary pensioner, whom he presumptuously called by Shelley's pet name of Leontius.

In the cool of late afternoon they would ride together, either in Byron's coach or on horseback; sometimes Trelawny would join them, riding a spirited horse and smoking a cigar. Dressed in their blue frock coats, white waistcoats and velvet caps, they would stop at a vineyard where Byron was intimate with the pretty daughter, and amid loud and incomprehensible jokes Hunt would retreat disapprovingly into his shell. Even the Italian countryside that he had loved from afar and confronted with delighted recognition on the dusty road to Monte Nero now seemed tainted.

Everything was wrong for the women and children, too. Lacking a common language, Marianne and the Countess fortunately could not converse. Hunt liked Teresa Guiccioli, though he called her self-conscious, calculating, showy, full of Italian sentiment, and with bad legs. Byron, he thought, treated her with a shameful lack of respect and delicacy. Unfortunately Marianne and Byron had a common language, and they clashed. Marianne's uneasiness took the form of an aggressive inverted snobbery, which Hunt applauded, misinterpreting it as spirited independence. On one occasion Byron asked her: 'What do you think Mrs Hunt? Trelawny has been speaking against my morals! What do you think of that!' — 'It is the first time', said Mrs Hunt, 'I ever heard of them', and she probably added a sniff. When Hunt related this epsiode proudly to the world, *Blackwood's* was quick to describe Mrs Hunt as a 'pert abigail in a fifth rate farce'. Hunt also maliciously reported Marianne's *bon mot*, on seeing a portrait of Byron, that he 'resembled a great school-boy, who had had a plain bun given him, instead of a plum one'. Hunt was pleased to note that Byron deigned no response to these remarks and 'looked as blank as possible'. For his part Hunt was careful, on Shelley's instructions, to give Byron his full title, so much so that Byron became irritated and reciprocated with, 'my dear Lord Hunt', whereon Hunt reversed the address to one of complete familiarity which annoyed Byron even more. Somehow, they could not strike the right balance. When requesting money, Hunt was overfamiliar, or was sullen with embarrassment and defensiveness.

The relationship between Byron and the children was also impossible: he called them the 'Yahoos', 'Blackguards', 'Hottentots'. He

tied his bulldog across the marble staircase to keep the little Cockneys out of his apartments: the same bulldog savaged the ears of
Hunt's goat. Byron suspected the children were capable of mons-
trous acts of vandalism, for the Hunts were permissive parents at a
time when permissiveness was not fashionable. Hunt, influenced by
Rousseau's theories, was proud to report that his children 'lived in a
natural, not an artificial state of intercourse, and were equally
sprightly, respectful and self-possessed'. He was proud when
Thornton firmly spoke back to Byron, though less so when Byron in
a cynical joke told another little Hunt that too much truth and
sincerity hindered one from getting on in the world. Apart from the
steady Thornton, the Hunt children were unmanageable. Ring-
leader John would team up with Mary Florimel and the two would
tease their mother and incite their younger brothers to naughtiness.
Marianne, who admitted in moments of despondency that she was
neither a tender nor a competent mother, took out her anger on
Byron. She wrote in the pathetic journal that she kept in these
months:

> Mr Hunt was much annoyed by Lord Byron behaving so meanly
> about the Children disfiguring his house, which his nobleship
> chose to be very severe upon . . . Can anything be more absurd
> than a peer of the realm, and a *poet*, making such a fuss about
> three or four children disfiguring the walls of a few rooms — the
> very children would blush for him, fye, Lord B., fye.

Byron's comment was 'what they can't destroy with their filth they
will with their fingers'.

By September 1822, after trouble with the Tuscan authorities,
Byron decided to quit Pisa for Genoa, and in part at least to shake
off the Hunts. Mary Shelley, though her relationship with Hunt was
still strained, arranged to rent a house of 40 rooms at Albaro, about
a mile distant from Byron, and invite the Hunts to stay with her. On
18 September they went to Leghorn, with its harrowing memories
of Shelley and their own jubilant arrival. So distressed was
Marianne that she resumed spitting blood and wrote miserably in
her journal, 'How *can* I hope to be cured'. Eventually they set off by
road for Lerici, and Hunt had the melancholy pleasure of going with
Trelawny, who had arrived by sea, to Shelley's house to pace its
empty rooms and neglected garden. 'The sea fawned upon the
shore', he wrote, 'as though it could do no harm.'

From Lerici the Hunts sailed in a felucca to Sestri, where they were carried to the shore by a crowd of 'robust, clamorous, fishy fellows'. Arriving in Genoa by carriage over the maritime Appenines, they were soon at loggerheads with Mary. Though she had taken care in organising their quarters, even installing a piano, Hunt was critical of the palatial marble staircases, grand portico, numerous doors and windows: 'anything but snug' was his verdict. He was all for leaving. Marianne reported to her diary that her cough had violently returned, though 'to my comfort I have found an English washerwoman'. By November she was imagining her death and worrying about the wickedness of the children and how Hunt would cope when she was gone. There was also money to worry about, not forgetting that 'unkind relative' John Hunt, whose cruelty to her she felt, in her state of near mortality, she must now forgive. One suspects that from the early days of marriage she had been jealous of her husband's close relationship with his brother.

On 9 November Marianne reported again seeing the vision of the dead Shelley by her bed, waiting for her: 'I shall soon come my dear friends but how am I to leave my dear Henry and my children. Oh! this is bitter! but anything is better than living on in this way.' There is a theatrical flavour in Marianne's phrases but the mood rings true. Vacca gave her probably less than a year to live and she had just found herself to be pregnant, a condition generally considered fatal in seriously comsumptive women. Hunt did not dare to accept his double death sentence and reinterpreted the pregnancy. It was, he wrote to Horace Smith, 'the only way, according to the physician, to save her own health from a dreadful shattering', To Bess he wrote that 'childbirth is the only thing unquestionably that could have saved her life, so it will most probably not only do that much, but give her a new lease of it . . . The idea of losing her is so dreadful to me that I dare not look it in the face.'

Between Hunt and Bess passed a long and intimate correspondence that centred on Bess's welfare and her possible journey to Italy. Though he would have preferred to have her present at Marianne's confinement rather than a 'certain other person' — Mary Shelley — he knew that Marianne, in her 'present sick state', did not want Bess. There was, moreover, already false gossip in England about Bess's presence with them. If Marianne were to die, however, he would at once summon Bess. In one revealing paragraph in which Hunt can only be referring to Bess's possible place in his household in the event of Marianne's death, he wrote: 'you understand all my feelings on this subject, and know them all to the *core*. You know all which I would gain, and all, which for all the world, I would not lose. So no more of this. I should have never even alluded to such a possible ground of meeting, had I not, next to the hope of keeping her, been most anxious that you should not imagine I did not wish you over here.' Marianne came first in his life, then Bess. And if Marianne were to die, Bess must be in no doubt that he wanted her; this was a passage which, years later, Thornton and his censoring pencil seem to have missed.

The grand villa at Albaro was tense. Mary Shelley and Hunt were scarcely speaking: Hunt would roam about the stony alleys of Genoa and think miserably of Shelley. So wretched was Mary that she was forced to apply to Byron for money for a sofa, so she could sit in the evenings in her own room rather than with the Hunts. She longed to leave but could not bring herself to desert Marianne in 'so momentous a crisis'. Again, though so many years younger, she seemed the elder. Marianne suffered much pain, still intermittently spat blood, and was sure she would die. But she was in better health than they might have expected, as Hunt jubilantly told all, when on 9 June 1823 she gave birth to her sixth son. Hunt named him in honour of his best Italian friend — albeit only half Italian and living in England — Vincent Novello, who delightedly acknowledged the honour and sent blessings to little Vincent Leigh Hunt.

The crisis of the approaching birth had lessened the estrangement between Mary and Hunt. For one thing Hunt needed her, and Mary's affection for Marianne had increased enormously. Marianne was her 'best Polly' and her devotion to the wild children, 'her chicks', increased proportionately: Thorny, scapegrace Johnny, giggling Swinny, Percy the martyr, volatile Mary Florimel, and baby Henry Sylvan, who was her own son Percy's beloved playmate, to say nothing of the 'bimba nuova' Vincent, as much hers as Marianne's. Little Percy would prattle in Italian that since his friend 'signore Enrico' had brought a new baby, perhaps he would give away the old one, Henry Sylvan, to the Shelleys. Mary now declared to all that she was their 'grandmother'. She even took the Hunts' side in the quarrel with Byron. Whereas as late as May 1823 she had written that Byron had been 'very kind to me', Byron now became a villain of 'unconquerable avarice' whose 'remnant of shame caused him to avoid me' while Hunt's kindness 'is as active and warm as it was dormant before'. 'Dear Hunt', she would write, 'you know how to pour balm into the wounds . . . the wounds were there deep and incurable till you medicined them — Can one's own heart ever deceive one?' She told Jane Williams that Hunt now had her 'as much at heart' as she was out of it before. Evenings that had been painful were now playful, and once she even threw a glass of water over him; it became one of their favourite recollections.

When she did leave for England on 25 July 1823, Hunt and Thornton conducted her on the first 20 miles of her journey. At Turin she wrote longingly in fantasy that they would all pass the summer there in a simple cottage minus servants, with Marianne to make puddings and pies, Thorny to sweep, Mary to make beds, Johnny to clean kettles and pots, Swinny to be their 'Mercury', and Sylvan and her own Percy Florence their weeders, while baby Vincent should be their play-thing. They would all work, keeping time to Hunt's symphonies, and perhaps do the dusting to his favourite march in *Alceste*. Thus Mary imagined it. It was a far cry from the wretched winter at Albaro.

Now there was little to keep Hunt in Italy. Byron, who had resolved to fight with the Greeks against the Turks in their war of independence, had gone to Greece in company with Teresa's brother and Trelawny. And the magazine — the main reason for Hunt's journey — was no more.

Hunt had hoped to recoup his finances and his reputation with this magazine: its history encapsulates his own weaknesses and strengths, and the misfortunes to which he was so often susceptible. The first number was written quickly by Byron and Hunt, with some work from Shelley, but with Hunt providing more than 100 pages and four of the eight items. In September the manuscripts were shipped from Italy to London to obliging John Hunt, who arranged the printing and advertising. When the first issue appeared on 15 October 1822 the magazine was no longer entitled the *Hesperides*, Byron having thought of the inspired name of the *Liberal*. That was probably the first use of that word as a noun in the English language, it having been previously used as an adjective. 'Liberal' meant radical and unorthodox, and Byron showed that the magazine was correctly named because its main item was his unsigned 'Vision of Judgement'. The 'Vision' was poetic fireworks, mocking both Southey the laureate — who had called Byron lewd and impious — and the dead monarch whom Southey had so fawningly praised in his similarly named poem. Of that first issue, 7,000 copies were printed and more than 4,000 sold, a colossal figure by the standards of the time and the equivalent, by some ratios, of several hundred thousand copies today. There were large profits, of which Byron generously passed on his share to Hunt. Alas, they went to Hunt's English creditors, who now were so clamorous that John Hunt was obliged to appease them before remitting a small sum to Hunt in Italy.

The remarkable sales emboldened Hunt and even Byron. In his letters to John Hunt, Leigh insisted that 'affairs go on very well, and, as I said before, will do so'. He was still confident of his ability to manage his wavering lordship. The second number appeared on 1 January 1823 and was half as large again, virtually book size, bound in red-brown covers with correspondingly greater costs for printing and paper. Now they paid £1 a page — Byron's idea — to other contributors including Hazlitt, Mary Shelley, Horace Smith, Charles Armitage Brown and Hogg, though Hunt was still the most voluble author with eight out of 18 items. This second number, with higher costs and smaller sales, lost money. Leigh Hunt was depressed. Even the stoical John was pessimistic, and rightly so, for the third and fourth numbers barely covered costs.

In February Byron expressed his utter disillusion to his banker Kinnaird: 'I *opposed* it from the beginning, knowing how it would end, but that it answers little to them, and is highly injurious to me in every way. I wish to retire from it.' His attitude is understandable. Until he had given his money, verse and name to the *Liberal*, he had been relatively free from scurrilous and political attack: now there was 'continual declamation against the *Liberal* from all parties', and against Byron for his connection with it. While he cared little about his personal morality, he did care for his literary reputation. The warnings of Murray and Moorè had come to pass.

Byron was bailing out. Instead of writing an outstanding poem to raise the *Liberal*'s reputation, he withdrew *The Age of Bronze* from the third number and insisted that John Hunt print it and sell it separately. Told by Kinnaird of Byron's feelings, John Hunt behaved with tact and sense, suggesting that in the interests of all Byron should find another publisher. Byron, however, remained with John and saw through two more numbers of the *Liberal*. John also wrote to Leigh suggesting that if the *Liberal* should cease they should set up in its place a literary companion to the now solely political *Examiner*, to be called the *Literary Examiner*; and in July 1823 the *Literary Examiner* began its brief career. Meanwhile the third and fourth numbers of the *Liberal* appeared, Byron's only contributions being second-rate verse and translation. His poem

The Island, written expressly for the magazine, was again published separately by John Hunt. Like its predecessor it sold excellently, confirming Byron's belief that the *Liberal* lay on him like a dead hand. It is also fair to say that in the end it was Byron himself who helped to place a dead hand on the *Liberal*.

The fourth and final number in July finished Hunt's hope of fame and fortune in Italy. Shelley's dream of a magazine that would free Hunt from debt and crown his literary reputation had actually increased those debts. Hunt would later complain that Byron had behaved with detestable meanness to him and Mary Shelley, but one cannot know the exact story. Biographers of Byron have made intense efforts to clear his name of these allegations, and after reading all the evidence and noting the accusations, one has to conclude that Byron was essentially a generous and in many ways a forgiving man. In early 1822 when he loaned £250 to Hunt he wholeheartedly respected Hunt's integrity and loyalty and knew nothing about his reputation for improvidence. By April 1823, still lending money, he knew Hunt at first hand. To Moore he wrote that helping Hunt was like attempting to save a drowning man who persisted in throwing himself back into the water. He was generous enough to wish that Hunt would return to 'sensible, plain, sturdy, enduring' John Hunt and, with Byron's financial help, live in some comfort. When John was prosecuted for publishing the 'Vision of Judgement', Byron paid for counsel and volunteered to stand trial in his place. In Italy he gave Leigh Hunt at least £150 and the rent-free furnished apartment in Pisa, paid for the journey to Genoa, and went surety for John Hunt's bills which relieved his brother's debts. At last, he gave Hunt the choice of the return fare to England, where he feared arrest for debt, or the fare to Florence. Hunt chose Florence.

Hunt also had a case. For all his faults and his incompetence in handling money, he had come to Italy by invitation to edit a magazine, and he had edited it with ability under great difficulty and without the support he had been entitled to expect. Now stranded and disillusioned, with a sick wife and seven children, he saw in Byron his only hope — and Byron refused to rescue him.

It must have been a bitter feeling to be living in poverty in Italy and to receive occasionally news of how much he was missed by his friends in England. Thus he heard how the Novellos had moved from busy Oxford Street to the brick kilns, drab fields and isolation of Shacklewell Green, but in true Huntian spirit were finding and creating beauty in their new surroundings. There, on 19 October 1823, with vases jammed with flowers and the statues of the piping faun and Venus and Mercury carefully arranged near the painoforte, they were to celebrate Hunt's birthday *in absentia*, the guest list including Mary Shelley and Jane Williams. Novello and Mary Shelley both sent glowing accounts of the festivities and a tribute to Hunt who had taught them to 'enjoy the pleasures within our reach'. Indeed Hunt's 'spirit seemed to animate them all', and 'puns, good and bad — badinage, raillery, compliments' ran high: 'above all, music was triumphant'. At the singing of his favourite 'Ah Perdona', tears were shed from friendly eyes, and his health was drunk 'con amore'. Mary Sabilla, writing her letter in the early morning after the guests were gone, was so haunted by his image as to believe he was really with them.

Living in Florence since August, the Hunts could buy only the barest necessities. After a short and expensive stay in lodgings within the city at the Via delle Belle Donne — Hunt loved the name — and then in Piazza Santa Croce, he removed to nearby Maiano, two miles from the city, and rented part of an old farmhouse on a hillside well known to Boccaccio. It was cheap and comfortless and inconvenient, the furniture was of the sparest and shabbiest, the view of green lanes, vines and olive trees and mountains being the one asset. Hunt was beginning to loathe the aridity of the Italian countryside, and the cold of Florence's winters appalled him. Ice lay upon the ground for weeks. The rooms had smoking stoves, so there was not even the solace of the fireside ritual. Hunt sat wrapped in blankets from which his freezing hands emerged, until baby Vincent's succession of stiff backs called for the stove to be lit. He told Bess that 'the stiffness of age has come upon my joints' and the doctors told him it was sciatica. His eyesight also had deteriorated though it was helped by spectacles sent over by Marianne's brother.

Marianne was rather better, and Thornton was able to write that she 'had not spit blood for six days'. She was 'able to do a world of housework', necessary because they could no longer afford a female servant, but a miscarriage in the winter of 1824 left her weak and wretched. Altogether, their routine at the Villa Morandi was dreary. Hunt rose with the sun, wrote during the morning, walked for three hours at midday with the children, dined at three on one cheap dish and local wine, read until the children's supper, and then before an early bedtime he, Marianne and Thornton played chess. In compensation, Hunt had time to read widely, laying the foundation for much of his future journalism. He went regularly to the circulating library in Florence, taking Thornton with him and leaving him among the Walter Scott novels. On Saturdays he dined with Charles Brown, once of a counting house in St Petersburg, a friend of Keats and a former contributor to the *Examiner* and *Liberal*. Brown proved an indispensable friend. The doting father of an illegitimate three year old, for six months he took care of rascally, innocent-eyed little John Hunt in an attempt to teach him Latin, honesty and loving kindness. Even at a tender age John was far from tender and once had attacked a baby brother with a carving knife. Hunt hoped that separation from the family might effect a quicker reform but Brown was no match for manipulative John and largely confessed defeat. Brown could not 'bear to think of your disappointment', but did claim a small success 'in respect to truth, honesty, and cleanliness, and for that amendment he invites your praise'.

Hunt was at a low ebb in Florence. Craving news from home, he found a lifeline in Bess. He begged her to write and to send parcels and any affectionate knick knack that could be crammed into a corner — pen wipers, locks of hair, anything personal: 'Tell me if you can of every hair of your own head.' Eager to feel close to her, he begged her to recount to him exactly how she spent her day, and to designate special days — 2 May or 2 June — when they would continually think of one another in a communion of loving hearts. His tenderness to her was overflowing, and he vowed that had he not been 'a little afraid of exhibiting tenderness too much', he would shape sentences 'that would make your heart thrill you all over'. Above all, he begged her to come to him: '*When*, when WHEN do you come!' he wrote in June 1824.

Bess was unsure: there was 'calumny' in Florence. Hunt was disposed to disregard it, and to reassure her. He told her many times that next 'to your sister you are my great good'; 'my affection, as I have told you, a thousand times', is 'greater for you than for any other human being, next to my wife and family'. The biggest obstacle after the 'talking world' was Bess's temper. Could she control those 'wasteful harrassments' when she felt 'every appearance of slight, however trivial, and even to fancy them'? Proving herself to be clear-sighted, Bess was still inclined against coming. 'Believe me', she wrote, 'I can well bear it; for ardently as I long to behold you again, so great is my dread of injuring you (and so much have I suffered from that thought when you had little suspicion that I did so), that *I really do not know whether pain or pleasure predominates when I anticipate a journey to Italy*.' In September 1824 Hunt wrote accepting her view and then a week later, begging and pleading, he retracted. He could not persuade her.

Bess's decision must have been influenced by a new inner strength, gathered while the Hunts were away. In 1823, with Hunt's practical help and encouragement, she had published a book called *Flora Domestica, or the Portable Flower Garden: with Directions for the Treatment of Plants in Pots; and Illustrations from the Works of Poets*. It was practical and literary botany, dedicated to the Huntian principles of 'making dark days and close streets shine and be glad', and she was at present preparing another, *Sylvan Sketches, or a Companion to the Park and Shrubbery*, dedicated to Marianne. Self-reliance and success had obviously helped, though she was still addicted to opium. No longer so tempestuous, she was earning a reputation as a peace-maker in the family, and her characteristic expression of unhappiness was visibly altering before observers' eyes. Mary Shelley noted in her letters that Bess looked so much plumper and happier. Perhaps she sensed that to fall again under Hunt's spell would be her undoing. Meanwhile, Hunt longed for her on his country rambles, remembering how they had marvelled over the profusion and beauty of the weeds and trees of England.

Hunt was writing, as ever. Soon after arriving in Maiano he completed his amended manuscript of *Ultra Crepidarius*, the satire on Gifford which he had brought with him, but he was in two minds whether to publish for he was still inhibited at hitting back on his own behalf. In his anxiety 'whether my children would have bread to eat' he offered the publication to John. He regretted it at once. 'You should have tried to reconcile me to myself in it', he told Bess; moreover the satire did not even sell. He translated from Italian a rollicking poem, *Bacchus in Tuscany* by Redi, its setting visible from his windows and its first page carrying an affectionate dedication to John Hunt, its publisher. He also wrote articles for the *Literary Examiner* in his charming conversational style, putting on the magic cap of imagination. He conquered time and space to leap from Tuscany into York Street, 'like a rocket', and he walked around the London streets and his beloved Hampstead, recalling in loving detail their past history and those past and present friends associated with such places. The articles were a sort of literary tourist guide, of strong personal flavour and flair. Hunt's heart ached for Hampstead as never before — 'I longed to bathe myself in the grassy balm of my native fields'. Every particle of that ache went into those articles known as 'Wishing Cap Papers'.

So wretched were Hunt's health and spirits that his thoughts turned naturally to that spiritual support and solace of his mother's life, and his own childhood and adolescence. Despite Shelley's influence and his own questioning of accepted religious truths, he was no atheist — nor even a true deist, though young Thornton had been taught to say so when questioned. Hunt's God was a personal one, whose beneficence was intertwined with the cult of cheer. 'A natural piety no less than cheerfulness', he said, 'has ever pervaded my writings; the cheerfulness indeed was part of the piety.' In Maiano he composed his own meditations. Designed to strengthen courage and cheerfulness in himself and in others, they united the natural and supernatural. Religion, he wrote, is 'reverence without terror and humility without meanness. It is a sense of the unknown world without disparagement of the known.' In the hopelessness of Maiano he prayed: 'Come about me hopes; caress me, dear and tender recollections; give way, my weakness, and be gathered under the Shadow of the Undefinable.' Each morning he celebrated his rising with 'Morning is come . . . May I this day do what I can to diffuse a natural cheerfulness . . . May we all be comfortable and social, or go through the pains we cannot avoid, with hope and courage; and may our daily termination be a happy leisure.' His three commandments were 'be peaceable, be cheerful, be true'. He recommended the meditations to Bess: 'There is nothing in them but what ought to comfort and help you very much.' Written, Hunt explained, for those who had reverence for Christianity's Founder but no formal creed, they were a way of removing worldly distractions, refreshing a sense of right, and providing a 'devout and cheerful' light. John Hunt sensed 'a novelty in them which may strike', but wondered if there were really an audience for such a book. It was another ten years before they were published, and then privately.

Hunt, ashamed of his poverty, was chary of inviting acquaintances to his home, and there were few diversions in nearby Florence. Charles Brown was one, the writer Walter Savage Landor another. Despite Hunt's earlier criticism of Landor, they began a more amicable acquaintance over a strand of Lucretia Borgia's hair which Byron had given Hunt for his collection: hair, as Landor devoutly described, of 'pellucid gold'. Hazlitt came also to Florence with his new wife early in 1825, and was one of the few invited to sit down and enjoy the view from the Villa Morandi. To Hunt, conversing about friends in London, the clock was turned back and they could almost have been in his beloved Hampstead. Hazlitt found Hunt sadly depressed, 'moulting' and 'dull as a hen under a penthouse on a rainy day'. He was appalled that Hunt had not even the money to visit his much imagined Rimini.

Hunt in his poverty made few forays into Florence's colony of 200 English families but he did, according to anecdote, visit Florence on 19 April 1824 and converse out of doors with an English visitor Richard Westmacott. It was spring, a black butterfly of remarkable size and beauty hovered about them, and Hunt spoke of the Psyche of the Greeks. Later he would realise that it was the day and the hour when Byron died in Greece.

Hunt's spirits were also troubled by relations with his brother John. The seeds of the trouble had been sown back in 1819, a year of riots in England, of repressive government measures, and prosecutions for seditious libel. It was then, according to a later statement of the facts — and one accepts it because it makes more sense — that John Hunt had persuaded Leigh to retire as proprietor of the *Examiner*. As Leigh simply became the editor he could no longer be prosecuted. As John was the sole proprietor and the printer he alone could be prosecuted, and so only one brother instead of two was endangered. Meanwhile Leigh continued to receive his share of the profits and continued to edit the *Examiner* and write for it — except in 1821 when through illness he was obliged to hire an editor to do his work for some months. John Hunt was also lending large sums to Leigh. Eight years older, he had always felt parentally towards his youngest brother and had made or arranged many loans — not always wisely for Leigh was not always in dire need. Such over-indulgence tended to increase Leigh's irresponsible attitude to debt.

When Leigh Hunt left for Italy to accept a partnership in the *Liberal*, there was no formal arrangement about his position on the *Examiner*, though Shelley had cautioned him to obtain one. Clearly he could no longer edit it but he presumed that he would continue to receive his half-share of profits as the silent partner. He trusted utterly the brother who had propped him up for so long, and it was unthinkable to either of them that this emotional but unbusinesslike relationship would not continue. Meanwhile the new editor, John's son Henry Leigh Hunt, had ideas of his own on running the

Examiner and lifting its sagging circulation. It was to be solely political, with none of his uncle's literary flavour. Such was the delicate, tangled position when in April 1822 Leigh sailed away.

The new *Liberal* received John Hunt's support. Moreover he gained from the new connection, becoming publisher of Byron's highly successful poetry. When in July 1823 the *Liberal* died, Byron and Mary Shelley left Italy and Leigh decided to stay, that decision declared in John's eyes Leigh's abandonment of the *Examiner* and probably his abandonment of John himself. John felt very hurt. One is inclined to make this assumption because the ensuing argument was intense and personal and extended beyond business matters. Not only did Leigh fail to return to England but, desperate for money, he also demanded to know, through Mary Shelley, how much income he could expect from the now prosperous *Examiner*. In response to this pressure John at first prevaricated; he said quite erroneously that there had been no income in 1822 and 1823, thus betraying his own inner confusion. He followed by writing to Leigh in September 1823 a letter that proved a bombshell: Leigh was no longer a co-proprietor entitled to a half-share, but a contributor who would be paid two guineas an article and, in recognition of his past work for the paper, an annuity for life of £100. The annuity was not an experiment or a whim. Between 1809 and 1819 the *Examiner* had had a third partner, a Mr Whiting, who provided substantial capital before retiring with a life annuity of £200. But in Leigh's opinion — and on this rare occasion he did not see money as important — he had given far more to the paper than Whiting.

Novello, as go-between, urged Leigh to accept the annuity and for a time he did. Leigh also wrote diligently for the *Literary Examiner*, but not all his articles were accepted. He suspected that he was being choked out, and his debts were mounting so steeply that the annuity seemed insignificant. He meanwhile bombarded John with impractical schemes for a new co-proprietorship whereby he might show his reliability and good faith. John, pursuing a harder and harder line, in July 1824 refused to advance Leigh further money. It was a sad mess.

In Florence, destitute and bewildered, Leigh called in his friend Charles Brown. He painstakingly examined the records and called them 'the most perplexing papers ever laid before me'. John, like Leigh, was no businessman, and Brown found the accounts full of errors. He also detected the illogicalities in John's argument, but he was cautious and demanded more evidence. The more he read, the more appalled he was by the injustice done to Leigh through John's lending of money to him on such a grand scale. Late in 1824 Leigh owed John more than £18,000. John was accusing Leigh of irresponsibility and even ingratitude and yet, Brown enquired, whose fault was it that Leigh had not faced up to the compulsive nature of his spending? By lending so persistently, John had done him a serious disservice. Knowing Leigh, Brown had begun the inquiry by prejudging him as wrong and John as right; now he veered the other way. Sensing how deep was this disagreement, Brown consulted Hazlitt and Seymour Kirkup, an English artist in Florence, and they endorsed his findings. In their opinion John was denying Leigh a just claim for half the profits.

At this point tempers flared. In England Henry Leigh Hunt, who had none of his father's patience or tenderness for Leigh, sprang to attack, threatening foreclosure on the debts. In Florence, Brown responded to his bluster with calm aplomb. Whatever right lay on Hunt's side, it was clear that neither John nor his son wanted Leigh to serve on the *Examiner*. That denial was the real source of Leigh's complaint.

> They have thrust and kept me out of the paper, by force; I have in vain begged and prayed to be allowed to retain a share for my children, even by dint of writing for nothing during my life: — I have in vain proved to them that I can be regular, and that I have not lost my powers of writing: — my illness has doubtless been alleged to some as a reason for there being no hopes of my returning, my improvidence to others, the impossibility of getting my fortune up again to all . . . He thinks that for every offence done against *him*, one is to answer on every point, and pay soundly for every mistake; whereas if you bring never so many arguments for him to answer, his extraordinary self-satisfaction enables him to be content with telling you they are ridiculous, or with not answering at all, or for going to some friend of your *own*, making a partial statement, and getting his opinion to throw in your teeth.

He no longer requested half the profits as of old: only 'the *security* of *something* by way of amends for being thrown out, and the power of again contributing to the paper'. John the rescuer had suddenly become the persecutor.

In mid 1825 Leigh decided to return to England. 'We talk of

nothing but England, dream of nothing but England, desire nothing but England', he told Bess miserably. When John heard of the plans to return he reacted 'violently'. He cited 'angry creditors' who might order Leigh's arrest for debt, he spoke of 'degrading and soul-subduing difficulties' and Marianne's contribution as a 'bad manager'. The grievances of years came rolling out. Hunt was cut to the heart. His love and hurt fought within him, and he tried to retain his old notions of John's 'goodheartedness'. In the end he was so angered that he forgot his inhibitions at defending himself and wrote John an 'excessively angry' letter outlining 'some of his faults', but he regretted it at once and was obliged to write again and tell him some of his virtues: 'I cannot bear to vex a brother, a brother-reformer, and the son of my mother; but he should have thought of this with me a little too.'

One sympathises with Leigh but one also feels for John in his predicament. As Brown maintained he had been foolish, and yet his desire to save Leigh from financial drowning during all these years was understandable. Understandable, too, were John's exhausted love and patience, as he saw his efforts and his newspaper seemingly rejected by this ungrateful brother. As Leigh had elected to go to Italy, let him remain there and cause no more trouble.

Meanwhile Leigh Hunt was bubbling with schemes to return to England. He had already put to Bess the notion of setting up an English community of the Hunts, the Hunters and Bess, with 'the females to nurse and comfort one another, and myself to sing and play Italian airs to you . . . My Hunter coming down to his basons [sic] of tea, and books from London, and myself a fine flourishing writer in the Magazines. The scandalmongers would *certainly* be disappointed.' Now with creditors baying at his heels like 'Cadmus's teeth', he wondered if Boulogne would be a safer solution than England. Then on 30 August 1825 came reprieve. The year before, at the height of the argument, John Hunt had persuaded him to write for Colburn's *New Monthly*, and now Colburn sent them £200. There was no hesitating or waiting. They were off on the overland route: Shelley's death had warned them from the sea forever. Leaving the ever indispensible Charles Brown to sell the furniture and send on the boxes of possessions and pay the debts, the Hunts joyfully quitted Florence and Italy forever.

11   A POETICAL TINKERDOM

'I am not a fool at forty', Leigh Hunt told Vincent Novello. The next few years were to challenge the truth of his assertion. After a long and exhausting trip in jolting coaches and comfortless inns, made anxious by children's illnesses and Marianne's advanced pregnancy, they at last in mid October reached the green fields and mud of England, a blessed scene which Hunt did not propose to leave again. Novello welcomed them warmly. He had engaged lodgings for them in Hadlow Street, Bloomsbury and, thanks to Colburn's advance, there was enough money to send the boys to school, and to give Hunt a rest from work so that his health might mend. At Hadlow Street early the following year Marianne gave birth to her eighth child and second daughter, Julia Trelawny Hunt, named after John Trelawny.

If Hunt found his friends unchanged, they did not so find him. He was visibly older and thinner, though his magic was undimmed. Young Victoria Mary Novello, now a sensitive 17, soon to be married to Cowden Clarke, recalled many years later her first sight of Hunt on his return. She was captivated by his 'extraordinary grace of manner, his exceptionally poetic appearance', his conversation which was 'simply perfection . . . melodious in tone, alluring in accent, eloquent in choice of words'. He sang one of Moore's Irish melodies and she wept. Neither age nor illness could dim such powers.

The following year, presumably on the strength of Colburn's munificence, the Hunts moved to a pleasant house on the top of Highgate Hill, 'green with tall trees, and shrub grown gardens, and near adjoining meadows', and close to the Gliddons, the actor Charles Matthews, and the poet Coleridge with whom Hunt became better acquainted through Charles Lamb. Hazlitt and his wife were frequent visitors, Hunt declaring his exceptional ease in their society, reassured by Hazlitt's generous notice of him in *The Spirit of the Age* in 1825. 'Mr Hunt ought to have been a gentleman born', wrote Hazlitt, 'and to have patronized men of letters. He might then have played, and sung, and laughed, and talked his life away; have written manly prose, elegant verse; and his "Story of Rimini" would have been praised by Mr Blackwood.' Alas, the

145

happy ease with Hazlitt did not last; the following year a thinly disguised attack on him and Shelley from Hazlitt's pen in the *New Monthly* caused Hunt to complain to Thomas Campbell, the editor. Hazlitt's defence of Hunt's next book, however, atoned for the lapse. At Hazlitt's untimely death in 1830, any of Hunt's remaining anger crumbled on the recollection of their 17-year friendship, and he wrote an eloquent and loving tribute to 'one of the profoundest writers of the day . . . the best general critic, the greatest critic on art that ever appeared . . . an untameable lover of liberty'.

Victoria Mary Novello remembered staying with the Hunts at Highgate: the idyllic walks, sometimes as far as Hampstead, 'with home in its churchyard as well as in its meadows' and Hunt's conversations in the carefully arranged study after breakfast when he 'shone brilliantly' as he paced up and down. 'Clad in the flowered wrapping-gown he was fond of wearing when at home, he would continue the lively subject broached during breakfast, or launch forth into some fresh one.' Even at the first social meal of the day, she remembered, he was brilliant. In the following year the Novellos left 'dreary, unfriendly, unheard-of, melancholy, moping, unsocial, unmusical, un-meeting, uneveningy, un-Hunt-helping' Shacklewell for the greater civilization of Covent Garden where their home continued to be a focus for Hunt's old circle. But enlivening as such relationships were, they could not completely compensate for Hunt's sorrows which came thick and fast.

The quarrel over the *Examiner* dragged on through 1826. Charles Brown, writing charming, gossipy letters from Florence, enclosed his statement for arbitration and Hunt named their joint friend from Keats's circle, Charles Wentworth Dilke, as his representative in the dispute, and Arthur Gliddon and the literary lawyer Bryan Waller Procter as his assistants. Charles Ollier, reading Brown's statement, was 'filled with wonder' at John's behaviour and begged Leigh, 'for heaven's sake do not consent to sell your birth-right for a mess of pottage'. 'Your brother', he went on, 'never succeeded in any other speculation than *The Examiner*, and that would, in all probability have failed, but for your Editorship, which threw so much originality and amusement into its pages.' In Ollier's opinion, the claims that Leigh had 'injured the property' by neglect of duty were vain, as without Leigh there would have been no property. It was November 1827 before the trouble was finally cleared up and Leigh and John signed a mutual release, in Leigh's favour. He and John would avoid one another for the next few years, with painful feelings on both sides, until their affection broke through again.

Painful as his quarrel was with John, it paled before another event in 1827. Hunt's relationship with his mother-in-law, Mrs Hunter, had always been difficult, his radicalism challenging her stiff conventionality. Rumours concerning himself and Bess now caused more indignation. On returning from Italy he had taken Bess's part in a family argument, and the old rancour and suspicion had risen. The estrangement of 1826 became a complete break in the following year. At the same time there were anxieties over the children's health. Baby Julia was constantly ailing and 'giggling Swinny', now eleven years old and the 'most amiable, generous-hearted little fellow', was stricken with 'lung disease and hectic fever and great emaciation'. In July 1827 Hunt spent his days sitting beside the child as he lay on the sofa; he would alternately nurse and write, attempting to push aside his fears, knowing the case was 'perilous' and also that, true to the philosophy of cheer, it 'was useful as well as desirable to entertain' hope as long as possible. But as September drew to a close, little Swinburne grew weaker and hope collapsed. At the end of the month he died. When Novello's son had died, and Shelley's too, Hunt had counselled a therapeutic release of grief. Now facing the ordeal himself, he found it easy counsel to follow. It was not only for himself he grieved: his thoughts turned also to the distressed grandmother, Mrs Hunter, and to her he wrote one of his most moving letters:

> I think, if you could see his little gentle dead body, calm as an angel, and, looking wise in his innocence beyond all the troubles of this earth, you would agree with me . . . that there is nothing worth contesting here below, except who shall be kindest to one another. There seems to be something in these moments, by which life recommences with the survivors: — I mean, we seem to be beginning, in a manner, the world again, with calmer, if with sadder thoughts: and wiping our eyes, and readjusting the burden on our backs, to set out anew on our roads, with a greater wish to help and console one another. Pray, let us be very much so, and prove it by drowning all disputes of the past in the affectionate tears of this moment.

Worn down since his return by ill health and worry, Hunt was writing less than at any time of his career and had sent only sporadic articles to Colburn's *New Monthly*; his indebtedness to the publisher increased with almost every day. He had several projects in mind. He had always seen the novel as an important literary form, revealing as it did the human heart, and in Italy his study of history had given him a setting for an historical novel; he fancied the reign of King Charles II with a nobleman for hero. He had also begun autobiographical sketches, proposing to use them as foreword for a collection of his work. Colburn, however, was lukewarm, having in mind something more sensational. Since Byron's death a flow of books had given intimate revelations of the noble poet. Byron was the first of the pop stars with a huge fan following, and the sales of some of these books delighted their publishers. Colburn was interested in Hunt's autobiographical sketches only if they included one substantial and revealing article on Byron. Hunt, angrily reading the effusions on the new national hero, realised that he could write that article. Indeed he wrote a book, in 500 large pages.

Hunt believed in intimate biography. In *Classic Tales* he had written that 'in the knowledge of private life is the foundation of wisdom, that of public life is superstructure; let us study ourselves first as *men*'. His *Lord Byron and Some of His Contemporaries* was designed as a study of Byron the *man*. Once his pen was in hand he wrote quickly — generalisations, examples and anecdotes, his rancorous memories running away with him as he described in detail the arrangements at the Palazzo Lanfranchi and Byron's relationship with the Hunt family. Before he was a quarter through his sketch, he had discounted any generous or disinterested motives in his subject. He avowed that Byron knew only animal passions, that he could only write well or be pleasant when he was drunk, that he was naturally ill-tempered and superstitious, that he was ill-educated and lacked taste in literature and the fine arts, that he loved notoriety even more than he loved money, that he was ungenerous and incapable of logical argument, that he lacked moral courage and was no Christian. Marianne's virtuous *bon mots* about Byron's morals, Thornton's childishly wise answers and Hunt's self-righteous retorts all found their way into the narrative, until *Blackwood's* exclaimed with malicious relish and a touch of justice that Hunt was 'perpetually poking and perking his own face into yours, when you are desirous of looking only at Lord Byron's'.

To understand this rancour one must remember the depths of humiliation Hunt had suffered. In 1815 and 1816 he had thrilled to Byron, enjoying his intimacy and affection. In April 1816 he had

written an ecstatic 'Epistle to Lord Byron', proclaiming his friendship proudly to the world:

> And so adieu dear Byron — dear to me
> For many a cause, disinterestedly, —
>
> . . . . For a stretched hand, ever the same to me
> And total, glorious want of vile hypocrisy.

At the Palazzo Lanfranchi, feeling unwanted, helpless and harrassed, Hunt could only think how much he had been deceived, and
how hateful was his humiliator. His recipe was to believe in his own
moral superiority. That Byron may have acted from a totally
different and valid viewpoint, and been equally disillusioned, was
beyond Hunt's emotional understanding. Like a preacher, he saw
this truth as absolute and not relative, and he longed to deliver a
sermon in which Byron the world's hero was exposed as Byron the
shoddy and heartless poseur. Sitting beside the dying Swinny, the
humiliation of those Pisan months welled up inside him, and it was a
revelation of indignant self justification that he gave on every page.
Unintentionally his book exposed less the tyrannical landlord in
Italy than the hyper-sensitive, over-dependent and pathetically vin-
dictive lodger. The ostensible virtue, manliness and wisdom of the
Hunts were swallowed up by the anger of the narration. The other
sketches were milder and more predictable. Shelley's was adulatory
but also real and immediate; even *Blackwood's* found grudging
merit in it. Keats's was just a little patronising and possessive —
Keats's friends disliked it — while Lamb and lesser lights were
sketched sympathetically but effusively. But it was Byron whom
Colburn placed first in the table of contents, Byron whose name
alone appeared on the title of his book, and Byron's name which
sold the book.

Hunt's commonsense, absent during the revengeful orgy of recollection, eventually warned him that this book would be explosive.
He justified its publication by saying that he had the right to tell it as
it was; moreover it contained nothing he would not have said to
Byron's face and 'no shadow of untruth'. And one must believe that
this was the truth as he saw it. Hazlitt understood, insisting that
Hunt 'has merely described what he saw and felt, with vividness and
pathos'. Hunt of course sensed that his book ran contrary to his cult

of cheerful thinking, that it could provoke a scandal and should perhaps be tossed in the fire. He knew, too, how much he owed Colburn and how this book would repay his debt. He had often criticised money-grubbing and here he was publishing such a book for money. His uneasy and equivocal preface expresses these conflicting ideas.

The book sold like wild fire. Appearing in January 1828, its second edition came out within three months, and pirated editions appeared in other lands. Colburn, exulting in his hot commodity, had sent selected pages to the press even before the fat volumes came from the printer. *Blackwood's* had a field day of 30 vitriolic pages. So did Thomas Moore in the *Times*. For almost ten years Moore had felt cool in Hunt's company and more than cool behind his back. He had not forgiven Byron for allying himself with Hunt over the *Liberal*, the more so because Moore had originally been named by Byron as his possible collaborator in a European magazine. To make matters worse, he was severely mauled in Hunt's book on Byron. Everything thus combined to fuel his pseudonymous review signed T. Tidcock. Entitled 'The Living Dog and the Dead Lion', the review was enlivened with piquant verse:

> How that animal eats, how he moves, how he drinks,
> Is all noted down by this Boswell so small;
> And 'tis plain, from each sentence, the puppy-dog thinks
> That the lion was no such great thing after all
>
> However, the book's a good book, being rich in
> Examples and warnings to lions high-bred,
> How they suffer small mongrelly curs in their kitchen
> Wha'll feed on them living, and foul them when dead.

A few reviewers praised Hunt for telling the truth — the *Monthly Magazine* among them — but most deplored his anger. Hunt's literary reputation, slipping before he went to Italy, had declined further with the *Liberal's* failure and now it touched rock bottom. The furore helped to sell the book, but the triumph was shrewd Colburn's, not naive Hunt's. His child-like attempts to defend himself with some candour in letters to the *Morning Chronicle* only highlighted his original mistake.

Some friends defended him. Charles Lamb said he made a disagreeable subject as agreeable as possible, but Charles Brown in

Florence declared that he wished he had been stood at Hunt's elbow as he wrote and several old friends joined the baying hounds. Haydon composed for the jubilant Lockhart of *Blackwood*'s a parody called 'Leigh Hunt and His Companions', including in his anecdotes Marianne and Bess picking their noses and Hunt's subversive theories of sexual morality. His excuse was his belief that Hunt had 'used Byron shamefully'. His conscience, however, worried him so much that on the eve of publication he raced to the printer and retrieved it. Altogether *Lord Byron and Some of His Contemporaries* was a boon to Hunt's Tory critics, and it would be at least four years before his reputation began to recover.

Hunt remained an optimist. At the start of 1828 he produced, impulsively and less controversially, a weekly magazine in the style of his beloved *Indicator*. It was called the *Companion*, a reference to Hunt's relationship with his readers. 'The first quality in a Companion is Truth', was its motto. The *Companion* ran from 9 January to 23 July 1828. In the very week that his Byron book appeared Hunt informed his 'companions' that there would be no need for calumny: 'Chatting comfortably and in good faith with our companion the reader, we shall not think it requisite for his amusement to get up occasionally and thrust out a neighbour's eye.' The magazine was to be devoted to literature, and to politics that concerned mankind at large and might be called 'humane literature'. Hunt was aware that during his time away from journalism the audiences had changed, and that the new power of the press and the new wave of popular education had let loose a sovereign force of opinion. As a counter-balance he proposed to contribute calmness: 'The winds have blown enough. Let the sun shine forth, warming and irresistable [sic].' Cheer was the new order of the day.

This mood went with him to the theatre. It was seven years since he had been to an English theatre and he confessed himself excited as a child to be sitting reading the play bill and listening to the delicious discord of the orchestra tuning. In such a mood he heard the superb singing of Madame Pasta, falling in love with her at first sight: 'she makes the ground firm under my feet, and the sky blue above my head'. His pages were crammed with her excellence. Thus he chatted in his easy, associational style about simple, safe pleasures, as he had done in the *Indicator*. He wrote most of the material himself, from the small first issues to over 15 pages an issue by March. He did it well — though the inspired *Indicator* had more vigour — and he saw it as a labour of love. He consequently felt

saddened when in July, for financial reasons, he shook his readers'
hands in farewell, confiding that their rapport had supported him
over a painful period of his life, and that love of nature and pursuit
of truth provided their own consolation.

The *Companion* had failed but his urge to conduct another such
paper was still strong. He needed the money, he needed the mental
and emotional stimulus and satisfaction, and he knew he was an
excellent journalist. From June to August in 1830 he edited and
largely wrote another weekly, *Chat of the Week, or Compendium of
all topics of public interest, original and select*. When this failed he
began the *Tatler*, 'a half reviewing, half theatrical' daily, with
literary extracts and commentaries, criticism and light essays, much
of it charming, and most of it written by himself. When John Hunt
heard that Leigh proposed a daily paper he, like many, had believed
it beyond his strength. When it succeeded he wrote generously to
his brother, obviously longing for rapprochement, declaring that he
sincerely hoped that 'its success will procure you some reward for
the talent and industry displayed in it'. Mary Shelley told Trelawny
that this little twopenny paper kept Hunt above water but 'when
you consider that his sons, now young men — do not contribute a
penny towards their own support you may guess that the burden on
him is very heavy'. She seldom saw the Hunts, for they 'live a good
way off', but Hunt was 'the same as ever', she concluded, 'a person
whom all must love'.

The Hunts now lived in the country at Epsom, poverty having
forced them to abandon the pleasant Highgate house in 1828. Illness
compounded the poverty. Hunt was chronically ill but still able to
work. Marianne, though less consumptive, was ill in other ways. On
26 June 1828 'in the time of hyacinths and new hopes' her third
daughter had been born, named Jacintha Shelley Hunt, and in
November 1829 her fourth daughter and eleventh and last child,
Arabella. A year later placid, fair-haired Arabella died. 'If a
Mother's love could have saved her she would have been with me
now', wrote Marianne forlornly. 'She was taken from me: and my
arms were left empty . . . Dear Sainted Child *how* I loved thee,
Heaven and my own heart only know!' Ill, poor and grief-stricken,
Marianne became desperate. Always more forcefully active than
Hunt, her desperation made her aggressive. Her begging notes
became more frequent. She badgered her husband's influential
friends for money behind his back and spent it as fast as she received
it. In the surviving Hunt letters are numerous mentions of her

'consolation'. In Florence, Hunt had confessed to drinking as much wine to lift his spirits as he felt his health would bear. One suspects Marianne did too, and the habit did not stop in England where wine gave way to spirits. While Hunt floated in his cloud of cheer, Marianne found her consolation in the gin bottle.

The shoddy cottage at Epsom called for some consolation. Hunt spent the autumn of 1829 there in nervous crisis, writing *Sir Ralph Esher*, a fictitious autobiography of a nobleman in the time of Charles II, promised to Colburn in regular monthly parts. He was to be paid 20 guineas an instalment and it was eventually published anonymously in three volumes in 1832. Hunt, however, was not used to such sustained writing. Immersed in the characters — one of whom was based on Shelley — he suffered with them, finding himself flushing and shaking and holding his breath. Despite the torture, he plodded on. Each morning he dreaded the idea of recommencing work, but if he did not work he worried because they needed the money urgently.

At least he had oases. He could escape to London to stay with the Hunters, his excuse being to arrange finance for *Chat of the Week* with the Whiting brothers — the former financiers of the *Examiner* — and to deliver his monthly instalments to Colburn. Days in London were comfortable with dinner parties and a parade of visiting relatives and friends. Moreover his absence from Marianne led to a series of letters — now in the University of Iowa — which give revealing glimpses of their relationship. In their frankness and their domestic detail they rival the prison letters, and again a biographer must bless Marianne. She poured out her predicament without inhibition, as if she were sitting on her husband's knee and being consoled as his own dear Molly — for by that homely name he now called her, a revealing transition from the poetic sounding Marianne.

At Epsom without Hunt, the cottage was forlorn. The whole family was obliged often to call the doctor. Marianne had pain in her side and rheumatism in her legs and hands. Vincent was constantly weak and ailing, Jacintha was listless and ricketty, John and Percy unmanageable, Thornton ill with what appears to have been pneumonia, while the servant girl was not in 'mental health'. Financially they remained in a crisis. The boys had no shoes; they could not even go out to the garden, let alone visit London. The laundress, 'like a fury' at her arrears of wages, confiscated their linen and refused to leave the house until she received payment. After paying the rent, Marianne had no money for food and was already out of butter, cheese and tea. 'I shall not have *sixpence* in the house, or a *coal*, or in fact ANYTHING', she told Hunt. The landlord was "obdurate and says he must and will have his house. I tell you this because I think you had better not *come* down *yourself* as in his pet he might arrest you.' Thornton, who was her chief support, reassured her that the landlord could not throw them out. She knew that she must remain patient and cheerful and she confided to Leigh that she possessed one special solace: 'the dear delight of your being the *author*: and if you could know what *that* is to a woman you would not wonder at what I say'.

Through her letters — and his in return — runs an urgent physical longing. 'What a difference to go to bed alone', she would sigh. He would long to sleep in her dear arms as soon as possible and again feel her genial ample bottom against his stomach. After 20 years of marriage their sexual excitement was undimmed, a testimony perhaps to a philosophy in which sex ranked high upon the ladder of cheer. In London Hunt did his best to help her. He despatched what money and food he could; he wrote to the dunning tradesmen; above all he listened and consoled with infinite tenderness, recounting gossip of the Hunters. Mrs Hunter had got into a frenzy of outraged morality because Bess had come to stay while he was with them and threatened to 'write to us again all round'. While Leigh and Marianne had one another — poverty, alcohol, illness and Bess notwithstanding — they could not be destroyed. The marriage that had seemed so ill fated was, touchingly, alive.

Hunt at last managed to rescue the family from Epsom, renting a cottage in Cromwell Lane, Old Brompton, from the generous author and bookseller, Charles Knight. Miraculously he found a tailor willing to make them all a set of clothes on one year's credit. Bess obtained a cheap servant from the Asylum — 'a girl ' who had difficulty in obtaining posts because of her Unitarian religion. For a brief time conditions improved, but infant Arabella's death in 1830 saddened Hunt almost as much as Marianne. He wrote to Novello declining an invitation to Mozart's *Requiem* for fear it would put him into a 'state unsuitable both to the dignity of my philosophy and the cheerfulness of my hopes . . . I should have felt the Requiem too much as Mozart did himself.' In June 1831, as the *Tatler* floundered financially and his own health cracked, they moved from Brompton to Elm Tree Road, St John's Wood, not far from his beloved Hampstead. In November he solicited offers of a share in

the *Tatler*, writing to political radical Francis Place that the paper
was now precisely at that point when 'a spirited eye to the business'
would set it on its feet. He was contributing most of the *Tatler*
himself, going almost every night to the theatre — for his theatrical
reviews had an important following — and writing the review late
that same night at the printing office. 'When I came home at night,
often at morning', Hunt would recollect, 'I used to feel as if I could
hardly speak; and for a year and a half afterwards, a certain grain of
fatigue seemed to pervade my limbs.' He felt himself becoming
'weaker and poorer every day'. Moreover, his efforts were fruitless,
and the *Tatler* died in February 1832.

At least there was comfort in his new friends. In 1829 at Colburn's
house he met a 17-year-old law student of the Inner Temple called
John Forster, who was obsessed with the theatre. Within a year
Forster was much in literary society and embarking on journalism, a
year later he was dramatic critic, sub-editor and then editor of the
Examiner. Forster cultivated friends carefully, and he had the
knack of making himself indispensable by a genuine and vigorous
concern in their affairs. Alert, energetic, and an organiser, he owed
his rapid rise as much to his carefully acquired friends as to his own
merits. An acquaintance would call it 'an opossum-like, bough by
bough ascent'. Surprisingly for one so dependent on friendship, he
was often insensitive and rather arrogant, yet he was a valued friend
and business adviser to many distinguished writers. Hunt 'was the
first man of letters' Forster met, and 'the charm of his conversation'
and the hopefulness of his philosophy quite carried Forster away.
Both the fame of Hunt and the chaos of his financial affairs must
have challenged Forster's keenest instinct. By 1834 Hunt was
talking of their 'large friendship' and Forster of his 'very affectionate friend'.

Forster soon proved his usefulness. Late in 1831 he organised a
small private printing of *Christianism*, the prayers and meditations
which Hunt had written in Italy. Since these meditations were the
practical distillation of his deepest philosophy, Hunt longed to give
them to the world, and Forster's action gave him the greatest
satisfaction. In 1832 Forster again proved his loyalty. He believed
that the persecution of Hunt was almost unparalleled in the history
of letters. He recognised Hunt's genius and lamented that he could
not live in the station befitting it. One solution was a scheme to raise
money without hurting Hunt's feelings. Forster seized on the idea of
a public subscription for the publication of Hunt's selected poetic

works, to be underwritten by a committee of close friends. Such a scheme should ward off the pressing creditors, restore Hunt's reputation, and raise a sizeable sum. Forster was happy to implement it and Hunt, not shy of parading his needs, was more than happy to give consent. Publicising the new volume, the *Athenaeum* called attention to his plight: 'Mr Leigh Hunt, a labourer in the fields of literature, who has toiled on cheerfully and with good heart and hope under all the changing influences of a quarter of a century, is now, in "the sere and yellow" time of life, struggling against great difficulties with failing health.'

From all over the country the subscriptions rolled in, some from utter strangers, some from old friends and, curiously, some from old enemies. Thomas Moore, writing to Mary Shelley on 3 March 1832, declared his 'sincere regret' that Hunt was in distress: 'It would be very great satisfaction to me to contribute my mite, if you think my doing so would not be offensive to *him*.' Thomas Macaulay declared that 'I dissent from many of his opinions; but I admire his talents – I pity his misfortunes', and ordered his copy. So did Wordsworth, trusting that his action would not be taken as a 'test of opinion' and that 'the benevolent purpose will be promoted by men of all parties'. Even Robert Southey, criticised by Hunt for conservatism since *The Feast of the Poets*, subscribed his name and gave his money, while Haydon, in a bath of emotion, wrote at once to his 'dear old Friend' that he felt utterly for him.

Though the revenue from the book took only a few buckets from the ocean of Hunt's debts, the publicity was wonderful. Hunt had learned his lesson from the Byron book, and with tact he had deleted anything that seemed controversial. People thus remembered him with affection and respect. The leading literary magazines carried favourable reviews of the poems and assessments of his place in English literature. 'Perhaps', wrote *Atlas*, 'there are few men — even in this age of universal authorship — who have written more, and written so much in so pleasant and amiable a spirit . . . even those who most strongly object to the peculiarities of his style, are not unwilling to grant him a kind of consideration for the versatility, grace and pictorial felicity that distinguish his writings.' The *Athenaeum*, while admitting that he had sometimes judged hastily and written rashly, affirmed that 'in all that he wrote there was the presence of genius'. Above all, Hunt's work could now be re-assessed because a new taste was at work in the English reading public, a taste for softer, educative and more sentimental literature. This taste Hunt, the missionary of the cult of cheer, had promulgated for two decades. At last, he and the public were recognisably one.

The turning of the literary tide floated new friends towards Hunt. It was not until they arrived that he understood how lonely he had been: 'entirely out of the pale of intellectual acquaintance, — a toiling solitary'. In February he left St John's Wood and moved to number 5, York Buildings, Marylebone, hoping perhaps to beckon back the happier times of 1818, and looking with nostalgia at the plane trees he had planted so long before in the garden of number 8. But there was no going back.

Throughout 1832 Hunt's health was alarming; 'a bad head, often a bad side, always a leg swollen and inflamed'. He was melancholy, daily fearing arrest for debt: 'I never hear a knock at the door . . . but I think somebody is coming to take me away from my family.' Sometimes bailiffs were sitting in the house. As well there were the 'great *family* sufferings . . . One or two of my children, in temper and understanding unlike the rest, perplex me to a degree . . . and often make me ill and incompetent.' His son John, now in his twenties, appeared 'devoid of any faculty of self-restraint' and exhibited 'very remarkable violence and irregularity'. Like Marianne he drank intemperately. The wild young Percy Shelley Hunt, so unlike his namesake, believed like his brother John that Marianne hated him. Looking at Thornton, Hunt realised with a pang that he had passed on to his eldest son that same anxiety he had inherited from his mother. And yet Hunt was aware that his mother — and Shelley — continued to sustain him: 'If you ask me how it is that I bear all this, I answer, that I love nature and books, and think well of the capabilities of human kind. I have known Shelley, I have known my mother.'

Hunt's other sustainer was cheer. He valued it not only for himself 'but for the sake of making the happier atmosphere for others, and of rendering the more perfect homage to the Author of all good and happiness'. To strengthen his resolution he drew up a 'Bond of Health and Honour', ten golden rules to be practised daily. Signed solemnly by the Hunt and Gliddon families, the rules ranged from simple vows of early rising and personal cleanliness to contempt for petty vexations and sufferings, abhorrence of sullenness, deceit and procrastination, and the cultivation of unselfishness, openness and the perception of pleasure. Thus he coped with the miseries and disappointments, the ominous knockings at the door, and his children in rags.

In the summer of 1833, to escape landlords and tradesmen, the family moved to the cheap and unfashionable locality of Chelsea, to an old, wainscoted, decently sized house reminiscent of Hunt's childhood. It was close to the River Thames 'with huge shady trees; boats lying moored, and a smell of shipping and tar; Battersea Bridge (of wood) a few yards off; the broad River, with white-trousered, white-shirted Cockneys dashing by like arrows in their long Canoes of Boats; beyond, the green beautiful knolls of Surrey, with their villages: on the whole a most artificial, green-painted, yet lively, fresh, almost opera-looking business'. Thus Hunt's neighbour, Thomas Carlyle, would describe it. Hunt loved it at once for its quietness and its fragrant lime trees, and it would become a favourite home.

Thomas Carlyle helped make Chelsea happy for Hunt. They had first met in February 1832, the young Scottish historian and translator having admired Hunt from afar during the *Examiner* years. Familiar, like Hunt, with poverty, illness, melancholia and religious doubts, Carlyle had abandoned the ministry, been unhappy as a schoolteacher, and won scant success as a young writer. Walking gloomily along Edinburgh's Leith Walk in midsummer 1822, he had a curious spiritual experience that transformed his religious views and gave him common ground with Hunt. Like Hunt he saw mankind's progress furthered by heroes, recipients of divine revelation, 'a perpetual priesthood from age to age'. But Carlyle's hero was not normally the poet; indeed as he grew old Carlyle would 'utter his anathema against poetry' and despise Keats, Shelley and Hazlitt.

In 1832 the mind of Carlyle, though naturally pessimistic, was more open to the sunny influences of Hunt's romanticism, and they found much in common. Hunt read Carlyle's essay 'Characteristics' and, sensing a twin spirit, despatched a copy of *Christianism*. An intimacy at once embraced them. To Carlyle's stern but warm and tolerant eyes, Hunt was a 'pleasant, innocent, ingenious man; filled with *Epicurean Philosophy*, and steeped in it to the very heart. . . is even now bankrupt (in purse and repute), sick, and enslaved to daily toil: yet will nothing persuade him that man is born for another object than *to be happy* . . . A man copious and cheerfully sparkling in conversation; of grave aspect, never laughs, hardly smiles.'

Like Forster, Carlyle was fascinated by Hunt as living history, a literary hero surviving from the Napoleonic era.

Though eleven years younger and childless, Carlyle felt fatherly and protective towards Hunt. He and his wife Jane Welsh Carlyle longed to escort Hunt to their old house in the wilds of Scotland and nourish him on milk and porridge. They issued plentiful invitations and travelling directions, but Hunt was less interested for himself than for ailing Thornton, whose nerves and physical health had degenerated. Hunt had hoped Thornton would be an artist, but the paint seemed to be poisoning his system and the doctor, perhaps seeing psychological reasons for the illness, prescribed a spell away from home. Hunt begged that Thornton might go to Scotland in his place; he is 'a *good fellow*', he told Carlyle, intelligent enough to contribute knowledge to his hosts, loves music, is tactful and good tempered, and — a strange bonus — would make a portrait of Carlyle. The Carlyles were eager, and arrangements were made for Thornton to travel to Edinburgh, stay briefly with friends, and then go on to the Carlyles. In July 1833, 22-year-old Thornton wrote to Carlyle from Edinburgh, where he had just arrived, confessing that his letter was not decently rational. Absent from home for the first time in his life, his nerves were so jittery, his homesickness so intense, his bodily weakness so extreme that he had only one thought — to return home at once. Carlyle was somewhat 'vexed', but his own tendency to anxiety caused him to respond generously, reassuring Hunt that the son would surely rise to be 'a Man and Painter' in spite of all hindrances: 'there looks thro' him that fair openness of soul which, besides its intrinsic price and pricelessness, I have ever found the surest presage of all other gifts'.

Ten months after this episode, Hunt heard that the Carlyles contemplated moving to London. In high excitement he wrote away, proposing a house for them at Chelsea, for if 'you lived here, I should have somebody to walk with and talk with, and you should be some gainer too'. Carlyle was shrewd enough to have no illusions. He knew he was to be designated by Hunt as 'the new Shelley'; however, he accepted. In May he came to London and inspected houses as far flung as Hampstead and Brompton before accepting Cheyne Row, a few doors along the street from Hunt. Henceforth they were soul mates and neighbours.

Carlyle's description to his wife of his first sight of the Hunt ménage in Chelsea is vivid:

At length came Chelsea and Cheyne Row; a set of young bronze coloured gypsey faces were idly looking thro' a window; I asked them with a half-presentiment where Hunt lived; they answered Here, and that he was from home. I enter: O ask me not for a description till we meet! The Frau Hunt lay drowsing on cushions 'sick sick' with [a]thousand temporary ailments; the young imps all agog to see me jumped hither and thither, one strange goblin-looking fellow, about 16, ran ministering about tea-kettles for us: it was all a mingled lazaretto and tinkers camp, yet with a certain joy and nobleness at heart of it; faintly resembling some of the maddest scenes . . . They gave me tea, would fain have given me the Husband's shoes (a la Shelley, for I was to be the new Shelley): finally the goblin 'Percy Hunt', a very good sort of fellow, I think, enquired me out an omnibus . . .

A week later in his notebook Carlyle called the scene 'Nondescript! Unutterable . . . a sallow, black-haired youth of sixteen, with a kind of dark cotton night-gown on, went whirling about like a familiar providing everything: an indescribable dreamlike house-hold.'

Fortunately, once installed in his house nearby, Carlyle found that Hunt came only when invited. Hunt was always ready for a walk or to sit by the fire and talk, or even sing, till supper when he ate, with praise, a cup of porridge. Despite his reliance on pleasure and harmonious surroundings, Hunt's life now was almost stoical. His house was unbelievably dirty, the broken chairs, dusty table and ragged carpet being covered with bits of bread and egg shell and paper. The inhabitants always seemed in a state of undress, while Marianne who had grown grossly fat and seldom appeared in company 'looked devilish and was drunkish'. The 'poetical Tinkerdom!', Hunt's own room upstairs, was predictably arranged with care: 'no perturbation was to enter, except to calm itself with religious and cheerful thoughts'. Here, with two decent chairs, a bookcase and writing table, the 'noble Hunt' received guests 'in the spirit of a king'. Sitting on the window sill, 'folding closer his loose-flowing "muslin-cloud" of a printed nightgown in which he always writes', Hunt would commence 'the liveliest dialogue on philosophy, and the prospects of man . . . a most interesting, pitiable, lovable man, to be used kindly but with discretion'. And Carlyle added: 'I pity Hunt and love him.' The gloomy Scottish realism in Carlyle also roused Hunt's concern and pity, but he found

that Carlyle's 'darkest speculations always came out to the light by
reason of the human heart which he carries along with him'. Carlyle
will 'at last end in glory and gladness', he wrote, 'that's what makes
us all love him'.

Mrs Carlyle had need of even wider tolerance of Mrs Hunt: 'She
is every other day reduced to borrow my tumblers, my teacups,
even a cup full of porridge.' The servant was constantly knocking
and asking for a few spoonfuls of this and that because 'Missus has
got company and happens to be out of the article'. 'Missus is the
most wretched of managers', snorted Scottishly thrifty Jane, fuming
as she saw the waste at the Hunt house, with platefuls of crusts
thrown into the ash pit. As the weeks passed, Jane's indignation
grew: 'She actually borrowed one of the brass fenders the other day,
and I had difficulty getting it out of her hands; irons, glasses,
teacups, silver spoons are in constant requisition, and when one
sends for them the whole number can never be found.'

With Hunt her relationship was more civilised, and they carried
on a flirtation which cerebral Jane regarded with amusement and
even a little jealousy. Hunt made no bones about his Shelleyan
disapproval of the institution of marriage, though he quickly made
an exception of his own. He was, at 50, still susceptible to women,
and maybe increasingly so. Thornton was all too aware of his
father's sexual attraction: 'his striking appearance, his manly voice,
its sweetness and flexibility, the exhaustless fancy to which it gave
utterance, his almost breathlessly tender manner in saying tender
things, his eyes deep, bright and genial, with a dash of cunning, his
delicate yet emphatic homage, — all made him a "dangerous" man
among women; — and he shrank back from the danger, the quickest
to take alarm.' He possibly did shrink, at the point of danger, but
before that point was reached he clearly enjoyed himself. The
Novello women, 'Peach-face' Alistatia Gliddon, and now Jane
Carlyle, were amongst his emotional conquests. In 1835 Jane
Carlyle's feelings were sufficiently roused to take exception to
Hunt's attentions to her friend Susan Hunter. The episode is so
amusing and revealing that it is worth observing in detail:

Between ourselves it gave me a poorish opinion of him to see
how uplifted to the third Heaven he seemed to be by Susan's
compliments and sympathizing talk . . . He sang, talked like a
pen gun, ever to Susan who drank it all in like nectar . . . *'God
Bless You Miss Hunter'* was repeated by Hunt three several times

in tones of everincreasing pathos and tenderness as he handed her downstairs behind me. Susan for once in her life seemed of apt speech. At the bottom of the stairs a demur took place: I saw nothing but I heard with my wonted glegness — what think you? a couple of handsome *smacks*! and then an almost inaudibly soft God bless you Miss Hunter! Now just remember what sort of looking woman is Susan Hunter and figure this transaction! If he had kissed me it would have been intelligible, but Susan Hunter of all people!

One is glad to report that three years later Hunt celebrated his kissing of Mrs Carlyle with an immortal poem. 'Jenny Kissed Me When We Met'. which is found in nearly all anthologies of his work and well worth quoting:

Jenny kissed me when we met,
Jumping from the chair she sat in;
Time, you thief, who love to get
Sweets into your list, put that in:
Say I'm weary, say I'm sad,
Say that health and wealth have missed me,
Say I'm growing old, but add,
Jenny kissed me.

He so admired Jane Carlyle's sharp-witted, bantering conversation that he playfully christened her 'Dear, clever and querulous' and spread her reputation as a 'Scotch Madame de Stael'. To which Wordsworth unkindly responded, 'a *very* Scotch one'.

The orderly, thrifty Carlyles saw the Hunt household with disapproving but amused detachment; to live in it was another matter. In October 1834 Thornton married his childhood sweetheart, Catherine, the daughter of John Gliddon. The young couple continued to live with the Hunts and in 1835 Catherine gave birth to her first child, Margaret. John Hunt, 22 years old, wild and drunken, also still lived at home. In January 1835, on a bleak afternoon, Carlyle had a note from John saying that he had broken out of his father's house, could not get back, and was 'starving'. Carlyle fed him and listened to the story: 'a creature grown up to manhood without the slightest nurture or admonition, with wild, hungry wishes . . . they have had to keep for the last 20 months or more up in a garret, none of them speaking to him from which state he is at last broken out'. Carlyle advised him not to go back to the garret from which he would again break out, but to change his 'inner man' with perhaps, as a last resort, the army.

Carlyle was not surprised about the bizarre confinement in the garret, a 'common method of correction here'. Seeking a solution he wrote to his friend, the political economist John Stuart Mill, about 'Ishmael Hunt' asking that he be given work copying manuscripts, to which Mill agreed. Carlyle had hoped to keep the affair from Hunt, but he could not. To Hunt's agonised enquiries he wrote reassuringly that 'he seems to me to love you as a son should, to be in short a wild untamed creature with considerable stuff in him — whom the world will tame'. With insight he wrote frankly to Mill, pinpointing the failing of the Hunt family — helplessness. It was true but false, for Leigh Hunt, in all his wallowings and near-drownings, was a positive and dynamic survivor.

The children were one cause for worry, and the emotional storms with Bess were another. In the preceding months Rowland Hunter had gone bankrupt, Mrs Hunter had died, and Bess was now living with her half-sister Nancy and with Hunter. Her temper had broken loose in virulent and possibly menopausal tirades: the immediate cause was the necessity to live as a dependent of her stepfather and the underlying cause was probably her relationship with Hunt. Hunt was still her emotional lodestone, and she had even gone so far as to break with him, her motive — according to the family — being to provoke him to greater caring. Now, as Nancy looked for lodgings, Bess, with but £2 to her name, declared that she would find her own, giving Nancy 'to understand that she only wanted a convenient opportunity of destroying herself'. Nancy felt sure that the threats were directed at Hunt:

> She finds that her breaking with Mr Hunt had produced no great sensation. It would be a certain means of gaining a kind of power over him, which she has at present lost. She would be sure of exercising a strong influence or rather, I mean she would know that she would frequently be in his thoughts, and in a very intense manner, and as to the pain it would give him and everyone else, I think she would be glad of that with respect to him, and indifferent as to us. She is a very strange person.

Bess did not commit suicide. She obtained a post as a governess and in a few years would be living with Thornton and his wife. Moreover, she appears to have made peace with Hunt, though their bickering would continue until his death.

In the wretched years after Hunt's return to England, cheer had become an addictive drug that made his life bearable. Floating about in his muslin dressing-gown at Chelsea, with the philosophy of positive enjoyment in full flight, he mercifully lost touch with most of the troubles of his life. Instead he could enjoy what he called an 'indestructible love of my calm, same-faced old friends, Nature and books'. It was the only way he could survive.

12 IN HEART AND HOPE

In the early 1830s, Hunt's main occupation was to edit, successively, the *Chat of the Week* and the *Tatler*, both of which died young. He then edited the *Plain Dealer*, but its owners killed the paper after a mere three weeks 'because it did not *flourish*' in that short time. Hunt would describe it as an extemporaneous orchard, too romantic to last. That description captures much of his later journalism.

In April 1834, almost maniac in his energy, he began another magazine called *Leigh Hunt's London Journal*. 'Pleasure is the business of this Journal', he announced in the first number. 'Pleasure for all who can receive pleasure . . . We would make adversity hopeful, prosperity sympathetic, all kinder, richer, and happier.' On his own testimony, he more than possessed the credentials: 'there is scarcely a single joy or sorrow within the experience of our fellow-creatures, which we have not tasted; and the belief in the good and beautiful has never forsaken us.' Five months later he described the publication to his readers as a 'cheerful and most Christian journal', a periodical in which men might be sure of hope and cheerfulness. The use of the word Christian was characteristic of these years; like the title *Christianism* which he had given to his unorthodox meditations, the manifesto of this new jounal showed him beneath the umbrella of Christianity. *Leigh Hunt's London Journal* contained many reprints of past essays, enthusiastic mentions of past friends and examples of their work, the work of present friends like Carlyle and Landor, and a heartfelt obituary, on 7 January 1835, to Charles Lamb. They had met 24 years before, in Hunt's first periodical of literature and cheer, the *Reflector*.

Hunt now was acknowledged as 'the father of the present penny and three half penny literature'; his beloved *Indicator* had success-fully revived 'something like the periodical literature of former days', a formula repeated in the *Companion* and *Tatler*. As Charles Ollier put it, 'He is Hunt and nobody else . . . the inventor and head of a fine school. Of how few men, living or dead, can this be affirmed.' Even *Blackwood's* acknowledged him as a man of letters. Z's infamous co-persecutor Christopher North, alias John Wilson, wrote that *Leigh Hunt's London Journal* was 'not only beyond all comparison, but out of all sight, the most entertaining and constructive of all the cheap periodicals . . . like a spot of sunshine dazzling the snow'. At 50, Hunt was coasting home to an acknowledged place in literary history.

Leigh Hunt's London Journal met troubles. When Hunt and his co-proprietor disagreed, kind and courteous Charles Knight, author-publisher-populariser, took over, keeping Hunt as editor and paying his salary of eight guineas a week. This was a smoother arrangement, but the journal lacked funds and came to an end on Christmas Day 1835.

In 1835 Hunt composed his first long poem for some time. Thanks to cheap steam printing and the ever-increasing audience of literate middle classes, he was aware that more power than ever before resided in the writer. 'Cheaply diffused knowledge' in palatable form might so educate the masses that evil — which he saw largely as ignorance — might be eliminated.

Such ideas found allegorical utterance in *Captain Sword and Captain Pen*, an indictment of violence in a simple poetic form with heavy emotive rhythm, strikingly vivid scenes of slaughter and a passionate conviction that drew on his deepest feeling. This was not a poem of cheer but a denunciation of war and a hymn to beneficient, educative literary power. In this he threw off his airy dressing gown and resumed his reformer role with an intensity that recalled his *Examiner* days.

> Death for death! The storm begins;
> Rush the drums in a torrent of dins;
> Crash the muskets, gash the swords;
> Shoes grow red in a thousand fords;
> Now for the flint, and the cartridge bite;
> Darkly gathers the breath of the fight;
> Salt to the palate, and stinging to sight,
> Muskets are pointed they scarce know where;
> No matter: Murder is cluttering there.

The reviews were disappointing but the poem was applauded by his friends.

Though he often complained that ill health prevented his visiting his friends, Hunt was — largely through the convivial efforts of Forster and Carlyle — re-entering literary society. It was a society of young, rising writers, amongst whom he was a grand old man, a living link with the glamorous world of high romanticism, guardian of the memories of brilliant friends. Though Keats and Shelley were not yet publicly acknowledged as giants of English literature, a following of young writers was keen to acclaim them, and to worship Hunt as their high priest. Such a group Hunt met in the mid 1830s at the home of a radical Unitarian minister, William Johnson Fox. In 1834 Fox was a little thick-set bushy-locked man of 45 with a love of poetry. Indeed he had been the 'first public advocate' of the then neglected Alfred Tennyson, whom Hunt regarded next to Wordsworth as the greatest living poet. Fox had been a poor weaver's boy and he would still, as an amusing parlour trick, assume the stance of a weaver throwing an imaginary shuttle. His intelligence and magnificent oratory led him to the influential pulpit of South Place Unitarian chapel, but at the height of his career he sacrificed all for the love of his ward, gentle Eliza Flower. Leaving his shrewish wife he and Eliza went to live next door to Vincent Novello in an idyllic cottage at Craven Hill in Bayswater, where, cut off from conventional society, they set up a minor salon. Fox was a political, religious and moral radical, devoted to literature, and so he had much in common with Hunt. He now edited a formerly Unitarian journal, the *Monthly Repository*, which was deserting its religious flavour in favour of literature; and some of its contributors — minor writers like feminist Mary Leman Grimstone and political radical William Bridges Adams — had already contributed to Hunt's past periodicals.

Most of those who wrote for the *Monthly Repository* are forgotten. There was Egerton Webbe, a young poet and musician, a friend of Holmes and the Novello circle who was to become deaf and to die tragically in 1840. Hunt had particular affection for him, while he reciprocally embraced Hunt's cult of cheer as an antidote to the wretchedness of his deafness, and hailed Hunt in verse as 'the friend to whom I turn' like 'the scared dreamer to the morning light'. There was Thomas Wade, another young poet, and his future brother-in-law, William James Linton, poet, wood-engraver and later Chartist, who would recall Hunt playing and singing Purcell and Mrs Hunt peeling walnuts. There was John Stuart Mill, the precocious and brilliant philosopher whose friendship with Carlyle had indirectly led Hunt to these circles.

Benthamites were in prominence, and a distinguished older visitor was Thomas Southwood Smith, medical reformer, and friend and physician of Bentham, who had ritually and rationally dissected the philosopher's body on a thundery June afternoon in the presence of his friends — an incident eagerly discussed by Hunt and Carlyle. Smith's book *The Philosophy of Health*, in temper not unlike the philosophy of cheer, received enthusiastic review in *Leigh Hunt's London Journal*. Gentle, absent-minded Smith became physician to all manner of notable nineteenth-century writers. Invariably sent for in moments of crisis, he was therefore a familiar figure to the Hunt household, and Hunt composed for him an immortal couplet:

Ages will honour, in their hearts enshrined,
Thee, Southwood Smith, physician of mankind.

Often present was a short, Shakespearian-faced young poet, Richard Henry Horne, a revolutionary of the Mexican war of independence and ardent admirer of Hazlitt, Keats and Shelley and of Hunt's *Christianism*, who at once assumed the role of acolyte and soul mate. Equally congenial were the female friends of Fox, headed by Eliza Flower and her literary sister Sarah, married to William Bridges Adams. These women were as artistically gifted as they were unconventional, and noted for their quiet feminism. Their friends included the political philosopher, Harriet Martineau, John Stuart Mill's beloved poetess Harriet Taylor, Southwood Smith's radical daughter Caroline Hill, the Quaker authoress and poet Mary Howitt, and two Scottish sisters, Mary and Margaret Gillies, the one a writer, the other a painter and Hunt's future portraitist. In the next years Hunt would be often in their company.

Through John Forster, Hunt joined other friends in amusing parties and excursions. They included rising young lawyers and journalists, such as Thomas Noon Talfourd, amiable, intelligent and determined, a successful dramatist as well as lawyer, who had come as a poor country lad to rooms in Inner Temple Lane near Charles Lamb's and become his friend and first biographer. Just as Southwood Smith was the physician to many literary families, Talfourd was their legal adviser, the one to whom Hunt turned when arrested for debt, sued by his landlord or merely signing contracts. Talfourd continued to serve Hunt and literature privately and professionally until 1854, when death claimed him while sitting in his scarlet judge's robes.

Other friends were Lytton Bulwer, novelist, dramatist and parliamentarian, Douglas Jerrold, small, ugly and energetic, a former midshipman turned writer and reporter, and Laman Blanchard, editor of the *True Sun*, cordial, earnest, discerning and vivacious, a helpful friend whose suicide ten years later would greatly sadden Hunt. At Forster's, too, Hunt met a shrewd-eyed, dark-haired young journalist and novelist: 'what a face to meet in a drawing room', Hunt exclaimed to Forster. 'It has the life and soul of fifty human beings.' This young man's writings, *Sketches by Boz* and *Pickwick Papers*, were then considered similar to Hunt's: the word 'Dickensian' was still unknown. There was also Robert Bell, tall and capable and radical, once convicted for seditious libel, editor of the *Atlas* and host at Sunday dinners at his house near London. Such friends, old and new, were genuinely concerned for Hunt's welfare, whenever a crisis came to this crisis-prone man.

Christmas Day 1835 saw the last number of *Leigh Hunt's London Journal*. Hunt was plunged again into poverty, complicated by a writ for £43 borrowed in the previous year. One way out of the chaos of debt was a government pension. Carlyle drew up a stirring memorandum on Hunt's many merits; and Lord Holland, favourably disposed to Hunt, was solicited to use his influence with the Prime Minister, Lord Melbourne. John Bowring, a literary politician, and Lord Jeffrey, formerly of the *Edinburgh Review*, also assisted, Bowring arranging a petition with '50 to 60 of the best names' to lend their weight. Alas, Lord Melbourne considered that Hunt's subversive past disqualified him so, with no help forthcoming, the sheriff's officer continued to live in the Hunts' house, presumably to prevent any attempt to sell the furniture. Eventually in a combined operation between Forster, Carlyle, Talfourd and Lord Melbourne, the debt was paid from the Royal Bounty, enabling Hunt to sit at home 'in an easy chair under the cheerful belief that he should always ride over his troubles somehow'. The lily of the field was his favourite biblical text. He accepted 'poverty as the normal condition' and despised the 'mean virtue' of thrift as he blithely squandered his meagre means.

The sons whom Mary Shelley had castigated for idleness at last went to work. Through the influence of Hunt's friends, Henry Sylvan and Percy obtained jobs as clerks in the Treasury and in Somerset House. Thornton, through the offices of Laman Blanchard in 1836, became political editor of the *Constitutional* for a year, and, thanks again to Blanchard, moved north with his wife and family to the *North Cheshire Reformer* in Stockport, to be followed by the *Glasgow Argus*. To these newspapers his politics were not acceptable, and in 1840 he came back to London, to the *Colonial Gazette* and then the *Spectator*. Hunt missed his secretarial help, though his youngest son Vincent briefly took Thornton's place before going to school in Boulogne in 1837. Pretty, spirited Julia, who sometimes sang with Henry in the streets for money, began to give promise of a fine soprano voice, and singing teachers were hired. It was a bottomless pit.

The Hunts were growing even more irresponsible — if such were possible — in handling money. George Smith, the publisher, told an amusing and illuminating anecdote about Hunt's attitude to money in these later years. On being presented with a cheque for almost £100, he asked mischievously what should he do with this bit of paper. Smith explained that it could be cashed at a bank. Hunt did so, but arrived two days later in a panic saying that Marianne had mistakenly burned the new bank notes. His agitation had not prevented him, however, from buying a statuette of naked Psyche, and he held it in his hands, unwrapped, for all the world to see. Smith sensibly took action to retrieve the lost money. He obtained the numbers of the notes and they set off together for the Bank of England, where they were shown into a room in which three old gentlemen worked at tables. Hunt accosted the staid officials in wondering tones. 'And is this the Bank of England?' he asked. 'And do you sit here all day, and never see the green woods, and trees, and flowers, and the charming country?' In a tone of stern remonstrance he asked, 'Are you contented with such a life?' He held the naked Psyche in his hands and with his dark hair and flashing eyes he made a captivating picture. An embarrassed Smith had difficulty dragging him away.

For a decade or more, such authors as Isaac D'Israeli, Bulwer and R.H. Horne had proposed pensions for ageing authors. Now as the 1830s drew to a close a new concern broke out among authors regarding their status. Cheaper printing, the rising generation of ambitious authors from humbler backgrounds, a reformed Parliament where writers like Bulwer and Talfourd and Isaac D'Israeli's son Benjamin could reform the copyright law and the theatrical monopoly — all contributed to this sporadic crusade. In this movement Hunt was an early guinea pig, he was perfect for the purpose, his genius being unquestioned at a time that was producing few literary geniuses and his reputation now respectable. He was delighted to see his present poverty and past renown paraded as his friends thought fit. So emerged the Leigh Hunt Private List, its aim to give a weekly allowance of £3 a week, lump sums being fatal to him. Late in 1838 Horne joined Talfourd and Forster as the third trustee.

The trustees were soon noticed by Marianne. Horne, when he began his duties, was flattered by her coy notes, her concern for her husband's health, and her invitations to call and discuss financial matters when Hunt was not at home. As the months passed he decided that she was manipulating and utterly spendthrift. Falsely accused of keeping back her allowance, he had to reprimand her: 'I received a letter from a Subscriber to the "Private List" *some weeks ago,* who asked if it were true you had received nothing from "Private List" fund for the *last eight months.*' Her mischievous tales were disturbing because noted politicians and writers — and even Queen Victoria herself — were subscribers.

In the middle of 1837 Hunt was offered the proprietorship of yet another magazine, the *Monthly Repository*. At first a Unitarian paper, it had been under W.J. Fox a vigorous political journal of radical tinge, and under its last editor, Horne, a mediocre literary magazine with a dwindling circulation. Only Hunt, it seemed, would be brave enough or desperate enough to take it over. Friends from his Italian days, Savage Landor and the literary hostess Lady Blessington, rallied to his support, knowing that he would pour all his energy and imagination into the enterprise. Soon he reported that the paper grew 'imperceptibly, almost as a flower growing', but it was dead within a year. At least he had been able to publish there a female version of *The Feast of the Poets* known as 'Blue Stocking Revels, or, the Feast of the Violets', a tribute perhaps to the feminist climate of Fox's circle. Its pages had provided that psychological necessity for him, a voice to the public, but it brought no income: the Private List was more important than ever.

Hunt now had another iron in his ever-blazing fire: he had begun to write plays. The 1830s had seen a revival in pseudo-Elizabethan verse drama. A coterie of young dramatists, including Talfourd, Bulwer, Horne and the rising young poet Robert Browning, were pouring talent into page upon page of playscripts quite unrelated to real life, and mostly unactable without drastic alteration. Horne had just published such a play, *The Death of Marlowe*, which he respectfully dedicated to Hunt as one who had 'long assisted largely and most successfully to educate the hearts and heads of both old and young'. Hunt and Horne were now close and Horne would call

Hunt 'one of the most amiable and widely-sympathising men that ever lived', possessed of 'boundless charity' and with a 'religious passion in his soul' and the integrity to proclaim uncompromisingly his political and religious beliefs regardless of danger to himself.

During many discussions with Horne, Talfourd, Mary Shelley and other literary friends, Hunt shaped his plays. In 1838 he wrote *The Legend of Florence* in a mere six weeks of 'delightful absorption'. Though William Charles Macready, the actor-producer on whom the unacted dramatists centred their hopes and 'the finest living tragedian since the death of Kean', was not encouraging, deeming the play a dramatic failure, Forster was enthusiastic. He saw it as Hunt's declaration to the world. 'You have done something', he told Hunt, 'whatever the immediate fate of it on the stage may be. You have told the world that you are alive — and in heart and hope — and stronger in genius than ever — and not at all prepared to quit a scene, to whose hopes and prospects, such as they are, your past toils and sufferings have contributed so much.' During 1838 and 1839 Hunt reshaped his script and gave memorable playreadings to large and distinguished groups. At one reading of *The Legend of Florence* Cowden Clarke remembered the 'hushed room, its general low light . . . the scarcely-seen faces around, all bent in fixed attention upon the perusing figure; the breathless presence of so many eager listeners'. Jane Carlyle privately thought *The Legend of Florence* 'mortal dull', but others were enraptured by the beauties of the poetry and by Hunt's own magic as a dramatic performer, some whispering that the play itself paled beside Hunt's own performance. Not content with one play he began at least four others, one of which, *The Prince's Marriage*, was retained by Covent Garden.

In October 1839 *The Legend of Florence* was read to the Covent Garden Theatre's management. It was a powerful and highly successful reading, and the play was accepted. On 7 February 1840 at a grand opening night it took the stage at Covent Garden Theatre. Novello and Egerton Webbe, fatally ill but still cheerful and industrious, composed solemn and affecting music. All literary London was there, and those who were not, wished they were. At Rydal Mount, Wordsworth told Margaret Gillies he longed to be there to make his hands burn in welcoming the play. At the finale many in the audience were in tears, and when Hunt with his grizzled head and slight figure appeared on stage, his face pale, calm and resolute, the audience went wild. Their shouts of 'Hunt' rang through the walls of the theatre. 'Are you aware that when you came on', wrote Blanchard humorously the next day, 'you stood on your head instead of your heels?' It was a night of 'dazzle and tumult', and the reviews by Hunt's old friends caught the euphoria. Even *Blackwood's* saluted it. The Queen came twice. Haydon, resurrecting his friendship once again, insisted that parts of it surpassed Shakespeare. But it was not a play for the box office and after a short run it was finished.

During the brief run of his play, Hunt had taken another house with the usual scramble of borrowings to finance the move. Carlyle implied that success had gone to Hunt's head, and certainly Hunt told his actress-heroine, Ellen Tree, that he was ready to throw his normal literary work 'fifty thousand miles into the region of nothingness', and do nothing but write plays. Meanwhile, Carlyle growled that 'our intercourse lately had reduced itself altogether to the *lending of sovereigns*'. According to one story, probably apocryphal, Carlyle would quietly leave the gold coins on the mantelpiece for Hunt to collect, and so save both the embarrassment of asking and being asked. 'He is a born fool', thundered Carlyle. 'They are a generation of fools. They are better in Edwardes Square.' One senses that, nonetheless, he missed the Hunts.

The house in Kensington was small and two-storeyed, with a pretty little garden in front and access to an attractive garden in the middle of the square. It was a finer house and more central than Chelsea, and Hunt rejoiced in the grandeur of his study. Despite the inevitable quarrels with the landlord, Hunt would live here for eleven years, the longest of any of his residences. Along the square lived Mary Florimel and her husband John Gliddon — Arthur's nephew and Thornton's wife's brother. For a short time in 1840 Thornton and his family lived with this double brother-in-law before they moved to a house of their own in nearby Church Street. Hunt was thus surrounded by children and grandchildren. A doting grandfather, he loved the way Thornton's son, who hoped to be a doctor, felt his collar bone and dispensed imaginary pills to him. Remembering many long-forgotten incidents in his own childhood, he told his children and grandchildren about his own childhood games, and spoke often of his mother.

He spoke less often of some of his children. Henry Sylvan, a clerk earning £100 a year and the family's chief breadwinner, decided in 1842 to marry. Financially this was a blow to the Hunts but his choice of wife was a heavier blow. Like his sister Julia, whom Hunt

was grandly thinking of sending to the Naples Conservatoire, Henry
had a fine singing voice and often sang duets with his Italian playmate of long ago, Percy Shelley. It was through the Shelleys that
Henry had come to know Jane Williams and her wild, self-willed
daughter Dina. Jane liked men: she had had one legal husband, and
two de facto husbands, the latest being Shelley's old friend Jefferson Hogg. She also had adoring admirers, including Henry. Indeed
Jane's violent resentment when Henry turned his suit to Dina made
Mary Shelley wonder if he and Jane had not been lovers. Jane was
absolutely against the marriage and Hunt was also against it: that
was the one thing on which the two families agreed. A separation
was organised. Then Henry went into a decline and declared that his
'life was at stake'. At this Hunt relented, Dina was summoned, an
ultimatum was sent to Jane, and on 21 October 1842 Henry and
Dina were married and took up house at the Hunts'. Mary Shelley
watched the drama with interest. She was paying half of Hunt's rent
during these years and Lord Leigh, the son of Hunt's namesake,
was paying the other, so she felt disinclined to give more help to the
young couple, but even she had to admit that the birth of Dina's
sickly son made their poverty 'very painful'. That 'Hunt should have
allowed that marriage', Mary wrote angrily to Claire Clairemont,
'seems to me absolute and frightful insanity.' Few were surprised
when it turned out unhappily.

Marianne was crippled with rheumatism, her drinking was
steady, and she kept to her room, but sometimes Hunt was obliged
to write to friends and apologise that his wife was 'upset'. Vincent,
his best-loved son, and Mary Florimel his beautiful eldest daughter,
had tuberculosis, but Southwood Smith was consoling. Declaring
that with proper treatment Vincent would recover, he sent him
away to the seaside. Through the summer of 1843 Vincent worried
about his family. For in his emotions and empathy he was like the
young Leigh Hunt. 'My dear Boy', wrote Leigh. 'No two persons, I
think, in the world understand one another's feelings better than
you and I.' He had been his father's messenger and amanuensis,
indeed his manager, and he sent home a stream of love and advice:
what work Hunt should do, whom he should trust, what bills must
be paid and, above all, how he missed him. His only justification for
his holiday was that he should grow strong and take the burden of
petty care from his father's shoulders. When he received a buoyant
letter from Hunt he was all elation; when he received no letter he
was uneasy.

Mary Florimel, whom Procter had once called 'the fairest of earth's creatures', was given no hope. In July 1844 she died. Hunt wrote to Talfourd: 'She was indeed my handsome, and remained so all her life; and her life upon the whole was a very happy one, for she had great spirits and an excellent husband. So the consolation is great that way. But loss is loss.' Nor was this the only sadness. John Hunt, junior, had drifted along since escaping from his confinement in the Hunts' garret. Soon after leaving home he married and at the end of 1839 supported two children, one of them blind. He himself suffered from 'a stricture of the gut' and an 'incipient stone'. He worked at short-lived journalistic jobs from his father's friends, wrote a briefly acted farce, and published a few slight pieces. He appears to have lived partly by scavenging from his father's friends, and as his family increased so did his ingenuous applications. The story rarely differed: his own illness, a pregnant wife and starving children without fire or food or clothes. The bulging file of his letters at the Royal Literary Fund testifies to his unsuccessful applications over the ten years from 1836, and his casebook compiled in 1840 carries the comment that he was 'one of the most Persistent Begging Writers in London' who went through the Court Guide for prospective benefactors, a letter at a time. His wife', it concluded drily, for a many years had been always 'on the point of being confined'. Hunt's friends quickly turned their backs on this articulate beggar, and Wordsworth in 1843 consulted Moxom who advised him to do nothing or at most give a sovereign. John's credit had run out, and in the mid 1840s he was begging an odd half-crown or an old coat — anything would serve. In 1846, 'little ranting Johnny' died, aged 34. It was Thornton who looked after the starving wife and children and possibly sent them to Australia.

Leigh Hunt's brothers had also fallen on evil days. Robert was poor and ill, and eventually found haven in the charity of the Charterhouse. John Hunt, frail and a little deranged in the mind, spent much of his time weeping. In September 1848 he died, and was deservedly eulogised in the *Examiner*. In the midst of these woes Leigh was clear-headed and courageous but sometimes forlorn. 'I have, myself, a world of troubles to go through, daily', he wrote to his nephew Marriott, 'and my brain, partly by anxiety and partly by work, is kept in such constant state of ultra-sensitiveness, that where any additional strain upon it can do no good, I am thankful at having it spared me.' There were some credits. Thornton, who had grown into an ugly but magnetic man, was in

1844 a successful journalist, though he had inherited a touch of his father's improvidence. To his house in Bayswater he had invited the dying Mary Florimel and her husband and four children, along with artist Samuel Laurence and his Gliddon wife, several Gliddon spinsters, and Bess Kent and two other friends. Thornton Hunt's household ran on the principles of the French philosopher Fourrier who, not unlike Shelley, believed that all ownership should be abolished, including the marriage tie. Thornton's views on marriage and community living were unsurprising. His father in theory did not believe in marriage, and Thornton had grown up with the visible example of his father and Bess. In Italy his_father had even broached the idea of a commune of Hunts, Kents and Hunters. In his Phalanstery — Thornton's anglicisation of Fourrier's word — work and expenses were shared and all lived 'in peace and amity'. In 1849 the community moved to Hammersmith where it survived another two years.

Scandal awaited this suburban commune of peace and amity. In the mid 1830s Hunt had been approached for information on Shelley by a talented young man who had been clerk, actor and medical student, now turned philosopher and journalist. His name was George Henry Lewes. He became friendly with Leigh, and in moral and political tune with the family. Early in 1850 he and W.J. Linton and Thornton began a newspaper, the *Leader*, for free-thinking reformists like themselves. That same year Lewes's attractive wife Agnes, already the mother of four legitimate children, bore Thornton a child, and the next year another, and in 1853 a third, with Kate Hunt also producing children by her husband in these same years. The two families remained friendly; though they did not live in the same house, as some have claimed, they shared many outings and were constant visitors. At first the free-thinking husbands seem to have approved of the arrangement, and sweet natured Kate Hunt made no known demur. Kate after all had been brought up in the Gliddon household, infected by the cult of cheer. By 1853 Lewes was making his own nest, having formed a relationship with Mary Anne Evans, the young Coventry girl better known as the novelist George Eliot: in 1854 they flew away to Germany.

Hunt was close to Thornton and his friends, but it is doubtful if their problems worried him. He did not allow them to. Throughout the 1840s he visited, he held court, he survived and was grateful. During his ascetic, overworked days there was one consolation that did not fail to support him — the affectionate letters from friends and admirers. Few writers can have had such a band of devoted correspondents, all of whom paid genuine tribute to the gentle optimism of his philosophy. Thankfully Hunt had found fulfilment and his true place in the Victorian temper, and when he thought of his admirers the 'tears of gratitude and pleasure' sometimes came into his eyes.

13 THE LAST SURVIVOR

Hunt was now a literary tourist attraction, and many young writers called to see him, to shake the hand that had once touched Byron, Keats and Shelley. Once more he was a chief actor on the literary stage, and he adored it. He dressed 'fantastically' in a 'sacerdotal looking garment' — the flowered dressing-gown in summer or a monk-like brown one in winter — and when he went out he wore a velvet jacket and cloak that swirled about his spare and stooping figure. His metallic grey-white hair curled dramatically to his shoulders and he had a boyish impulsiveness and youthful dash which all his visitors remarked upon. Small Annie Thackeray, walking one afternoon with her celebrated novelist father, recalled a bright-eyed, old man with light rapid steps all 'eagerness and vividness', who kept picturesquely sweeping his cloak back over his shoulders. 'We wondered at his romantic foreign looks, and his greeting and bright eager way.' His face in its openness of expression, said Nathaniel Hawthorne, was a 'child's face'. It was with reason that this 'young-old' man was christened 'Immortal Boy'.

To visit Hunt in Kensington was like a royal audience. Young Coventy Patmore, whose father Hunt had known in his own youth, remembered waiting hours for his host to appear. Hunt entered grandly, rubbed his hands, and without apology announced airily, 'This is a beautiful world, Mr Patmore'. Francis Grundy, recalling Hunt's attraction to women, said he liked to sit enthroned in an easy chair surrounded by a court of attentive young ladies 'gently smoothing his long locks', while he sparkled with the wit for which he was celebrated. As Marianne was in seclusion, either Julia or Jacintha presided at his tea table; 'a nimble-fingered little nymph', one visitor described Jacintha 'in a stuff frock imperfectly hooked and eyed' and a crooked collar, her clothes matching the dirt and disorder. In sight of the common white jug filled with hardy yellow flowers, Hunt was fond of exclaiming how the 'commonplaces of life may be enriched by feeling and fancy'.

Not only was Hunt's demeanour kingly, but his whole mind was turning on royalism. The slayer of kings and princes had become a devoted royalist of 'the right sort', that is 'a republican with royalty for his safeguard and ornament'. He was overcome with pride when in 1852 *The Legend of Florence* was staged at Windsor Castle, and he greeted all royal occasions with suitable sonnets. A decade earlier he had dedicated his poem 'The Palfrey' to the Queen, complimenting her in a letter on her 'cheerful and liberal nature'. His friends — and he — had hoped that he might be made Poet Laureate but his subversive past was against him. Instead he called himself 'Volunteer Laureate', and Queen Victoria had his ear through her private secretary Colonel Phipps, with whom Hunt kept up a vigorous correspondence in the 1840s and 1850s. The Queen sent her thanks and admiration for his poems, granted his request to sponsor his grandson for Christ's Hospital, and privately gave him money when the Royal Bounty was denied him in 1857. Hunt's gratitude overflowed. 'I never was in receipt of a fairer fame', he wrote to an American cousin in 1851, 'or I believe a more universal good-will, than at this moment from the cottage to the throne.'

The government pension that his loyal friends had sought for him was slow in coming, and so they made their own gifts. As well as paying part of his rent, Mary Shelley, on her father-in-law's death in mid 1844, gladly honoured Shelley's promise that when his inheritance fell due he would support Hunt. Sir Timothy's protracted life had left less than they had expected, but Mary was still able to provide an annuity of £120 for the duration of Hunt's life. It was less than Hunt had hoped for and he was momentarily disappointed, but he was 'now certain of having something to retreat upon in case of illness', and he accepted it with gratitude. 'Oh my God! what blessings!' he exclaimed. Meanwhile Forster and his close friend, the rising novelist Charles Dickens, had other schemes for relieving the usual tide of pressing debts. Dickens, himself the son of a feckless father, had begun to glimpse the endless ramifications of Hunt's finances, and concluded that 'Hunt should have received long ago, but has not yet, some enduring return from his country for all he had undergone and all the good he has done'. In the summer of 1847, Dickens himself set out to organise amateur theatricals with the aim of benefitting Hunt. Two years before, he and friends had presented the play *Every Man in His Humour* to raise funds for a London nursing home, and fashionable London had vied for seats; and now he proposed to do the same for Hunt. He soon had another performance organised with friends like Lewes in the cast and Dickens himself in a leading role. Barely were rehearsals underway when Lord John Russell's government at last granted

Hunt his civil pension of £200 a year. Should the play go on? A manic Dickens was incapable of stopping: he cancelled the London performance in deference to the pension but performed in Manchester and Liverpool and collected a clear profit of 400 guineas.

Hunt continued to be an enthusiastic miscellanist and anthologist, setting aside passages from his daily reading and adding his own commentaries for a wider public. Thus in 1849 he provided an anthology entitled *Readings for Railways*, consisting of 'Anecdotes and other short stories, reflections, maxims, characteristics, passages of wit, humour and poetry . . . Together with points of information on matters of general interest'. Other books like *Men, Women and Books* were collected reprintings of his own articles, sketches, essays and critical memoirs. He also brought out Christmas miscellanies called *Stories from the Italian Poets* and *A Jar of Honey from Mt. Hybla*. 'The older Mr Hunt grows', wrote the *Examiner* critic, 'the pleasanter his books become'.

Readers eager for his earlier works could buy two valuable books in 1844. One was Moxom's edition of his *Poetical Works* with the major poems of his youth and many more of his old age. It was 'truly delightful', he told a friend, 'to think that I am going at last with the prestige of a cheap popular verse as well as prose writer, headlong into the pockets of the community'. He himself considered his latest poems his best, especially the favourite 'Abou Ben Adhem' which to succeeding generations was to symbolise the noblest sentiments of Hunt's philosophy:

> Abou Ben Adhem (may his tribe increase!)
> Awoke one night from a deep dream of peace,
> And saw, within the moonlight in his room,
> Making it rich, and like a lily in bloom,
> An angel writing in a book of gold: —
> Exceeding peace had made Ben Adhem bold,
> And to the presence in the room he said,
> 'What writest thou?' — The vision raised its head,
> And with a look made of all sweet accord,
> Answered, 'The names of those who love the Lord.'
> 'And is mine one?' said Abou. 'Nay, not so,'
> Replied the angel. Abou spoke more low,
> But cheerly still; and said, 'I pray thee then,
> Write me as one that loves his fellow-men.'

The angel wrote, and vanish'd. The next night
It came again with a great wakening light,
And show'd the names whom love of God had blessed,
And lo! Ben Adhem's name led all the rest.

Hunt's other important work of 1844 was an anthology of his favourite poetry, rounded out with his own critical comments and prefaced by an essay where he formulated the question 'What is Poetry?' In his answer he summarised his artistic philosophy of cheer and the beliefs which had guided his pen for 35 years. He called the book *Imagination and Fancy; or, Selections from the English Poets, illustrative of the first requisites of their art; with markings of the best passages, critical notices of writers*; and the title explained his method. His literary theory, like all else in his life, revolved around education through enjoyment. Through intense pleasure in poetry the reader was emotionally exalted, he believed, into a finer person. Empathy between poet and reader and a sympathetic understanding of the text were therefore vital. To promote empathy Hunt offered a detailed and engaging discussion of his favourite passages. Thus of Shelley he exclaimed: 'He had sensibility almost unique . . . For my part, I can never mention his name without a transport of love and gratitude.' Coleridge he now found 'sweetest' of the poets of his lifetime, and Shelley 'the most ethereal and most gorgeous', while Keats 'was a born poet of the most poetical kind'. Wordsworth, his former 'Prince of Bards', was forgotten.

Hunt also reworked the historical and literary guide books on London that he had begun to write nostalgically in Italy. *The Town: Its Memorable Characters and Events* appeared in 1848 and would be reprinted twice more in his lifetime. Some years later the *Old Court Suburb* was also given to an enthusiastic public. At the end of 1850 Hunt began another journalistic venture, *Leigh Hunt's Journal*, which ran for four brief months. But the best of his books of this period was his *Autobiography*, published in 1850 and revised shortly before his death. He had been jotting his own reminiscences since 1810, and had written a full account of his early life in *Lord Byron and Some of His Contemporaries*, and now, in tranquillity, he read again the revengeful episodes in that book and reinterpreted them in the light of an elderly serenity. He not only regretted the reforming violence of his youth and the bitterness of his middle age: he made amends with benevolence and blessed the suffering that had driven him from 'petulance and pride of the will and . . . fancied superiority' into 'the arms of good and beauty'. Emotionally the book took its toll. Much of what he wrote distressed him; some passages he could only recount at a safe emotional distance. In fact the *Autobiography* is remarkably charming but strangely distant. Hunt, the 'firesider' famous for his closeness to his readers, found intimacy impossible when writing of his own life. He narrated and interpreted, he forgave and begged forgiveness, but he did not reveal his innermost feelings, and he compelled the reader to sit many feet away. Three volumes of graceful, seductive, and self-effacing reminiscenses, they were adored by most of his friends, most critics, and an army of enthralled readers. Carlyle likened it to 'an exercise of *devotion*' and gave thanks 'in the name of all men', while the much-moved Novello vowed that it bound 'the flowers of the present and the fruits of the past on one stem'.

Early in 1851 the family moved from Edwardes Square to Phillimore Terrace in Kensington. In 1849 Jacintha had married a wood-engraver turned journalist, Charles Cheltnam, and only Julia and Vincent were now at home. Hunt's affection for Vincent, 'full of honour and trustworthiness and zeal', was probably the most wholehearted love he would ever give. Gentle, caring, literary and musical, Vincent had become to Hunt a Shelley reincarnated, a soul in harmony with his own. And Vincent in turn reciprocated with devotion, as he showed most movingly in these lines to his father:

> Alas! that that so loved fine face should be
> Scor'd by life's sufferings more than by its years,
> So that in calmest sleep it is not free
> From sorrow-marks that dim mine eyes with tears;
> And yet (thank God!) that patient kind face wears
> A youthful vigour still, divine to see.

Vincent coughed badly and was often ill, but Southwood Smith was hopeful and Hunt nursed him devotedly. But by the summer of 1851 Vincent was dangerously ill, with 'a sudden wasting illness'. Hunt was devoured with anxiety and 'the dread of losing him has become what I cannot describe'.

He sought a healthier region in which to spend the autumn and discovered an inn in the rural village of Ewell in Surrey, a 'sloping scene of field and cottage, nestling in trees' that at once delighted father and son. For a time Jacintha and her baby stayed with them and Vincent regained some of his strength. Closer to his dear Vincent than ever before, Hunt found this autumn in Surrey both a blessing and a source of pain. Vincent rallied sufficiently to return to London but late in November he suffered a severe relapse and Hunt too fell ill. They struggled through the cold months, but Vincent was clearly doomed. Sinking beneath 'the dreadful burden of one thought', they both clung to the philosophy of cheer as spring and summer passed. In July 1852 an agonised Hunt wrote to Dr George Bird, wondering whether the new electrical treatment for tuberculosis might work a miracle on Vincent. He knew that both Bird and Southwood Smith had 'done everything for the dear one that skill and zeal could do' and to no avail. In the autumn Vincent seemed to fade with the leaves, and late in October in the little house in Phillimore Terrace with Leigh Hunt beside him, Vincent died. It was a cold and beautiful dawn when he died and his last words were 'I drink the morning'.

Hunt was broken. No other death — except perhaps his mother's — had so touched him. He could not speak of it — he could scarcely write. 'I saw him wasting before my eyes for two years', he told his American relatives, 'and as the fatal time approached — how can I write of it?' He himself now longed to die, to 'sleep myself if I could, away'. Each night he prayed that he 'might drop as calmly into the sleep of death, and wake to an eternal morning'. But he half knew the dangers of emotional escapism and he acknowledged that 'my cheerful principles, my religion, everything forbid it'. In the following years Vincent was present in his thoughts 'on and off, throughout the day', but increasingly with 'tranquiller feelings as he would be gladder, and I endeavour to persuade myself, he *is* gladder, to see'. The thought gave him a foretaste of Heaven. Previously it was his mother and Shelley whom he imagined he would meet there — now it was Vincent who welcomed him to heavenly bliss. On many days he felt in closer communion with those three than with any living.

Even before Vincent's death Hunt had considered another printing of *Christianism*. They had discussed it together in 1850, and so precious was the book to both that Hunt confessed to thinking 'intensely of every *note* while revising'. In 1853, after Vincent's death, any word he altered had to be wrung from the depths of his grief. He organised its meditations into a set of practical spiritual exercises and ceremonies to be recited morning and evening, in sorrow, in sickness, in remorse and bereavement. Called *The*

Religion of the Heart, it became the authorised prayer book of cheer. Though condemned by magazines like the *Athenaeum*, its doctrine of love and positive living spurred a fan mail from friends and strangers. G.J. de Wilde, a faithful correspondent of many years, told Hunt it was 'a beautiful, earnest, and truly religious book, its heterodoxy nothwithstanding'. The reformer George Holyoake described how in November 1854 an audience of 3,500 crammed the City Hall at Glasgow to hear a debate during which he read out Hunt's 'Prayer of our Lord'. 'Nothing said during the debate on either side produced such an effect', wrote Holyoake.

Hunt still oscillated between elation and anxiety, and sometimes the anxiety came from unexpected quarters. While Hunt almost sank under his ordeal in 1852, Charles Dickens sat in his lavish study, writing with an ease that astonished even himself, and in a few months the first instalments of *Bleak House* were finished. As he wrote, Leigh Hunt was sometimes in his thoughts, for they had seen each other often since their first meeting in 1837 at John Forster's house. It was widely acknowledged that Hunt had influenced Dicken's early work with its emphasis on conviviality and its sharp but benevolent observations of character. 'He has derived some of his best notions from you', wrote the novelist and journalist Harrison Ainsworth to Hunt in 1844, 'and is, so to speak, reaping your harvest'. Hunt had early felt sympathy for his young disciple, and when Dickens's young sister-in-law Mary Hogarth died tragically in May 1837 Hunt sent him delicately chosen quotations and consoling words. Dickens was moved. 'That beautiful passage', he wrote, 'which you were so kind and considerate as to send me, has given me the only feeling akin to pleasure — sorrowful pleasure as it is — that I have yet had connected with the loss of my dear young friend'. He also begged Forster to tell Hunt 'how much he has affected me, and how deeply I thank him for what he has done — you cannot say it too strongly'.

After such a sensitive launching their friendship was truly afloat. In July 1838 Dickens sent Hunt a parcel of his books — *Oliver Twist*, *Pickwick*, and part of *Nicholas Nickelby* — for comment: 'If only you can find it in that green heart of yours to tell me one of these days if you met . . . anything that felt like a vibration of the old chord you have touched so often and sounded so well, you will confer the truest gratification.' Hunt found much that did vibrate his heart and, though ill, read through the three books, marking the margins with his approval. 'I admire you for your wit and humour, and love you as a *humanist*', he wrote back. 'You have made me laugh heartily in the midst of trouble, and shed painful and yet hopeful tears.' He gently chided Dickens for his fondness for melodrama but commended his 'true genius' and rejoiced that he was full of heart: 'God bless you my dear sir.'

At the start of 1839 Dickens invited Hunt, along with half a dozen other close friends and relatives, to his twenty-seventh birthday party; throughout the following years, affectionate letters flowed to and fro, and Hunt made more visits to Dickens's house. One memorable summer's evening in 1842 they walked together into the country, dining at a rustic inn, and an informal poem which Hunt composed to commemorate their walk was published that October in the *Monthly Magazine*. Dickens wrote to Hunt with delight, recalling their happy time.

> A crowd of thanks, treading on each other's heels and tripping one another up most pleasantly, — a crowd of thanks, I say, for the Rustic Walk which I have just taken again with you, and for the dinner, and for no mention of the bill, or of the squat little doll-looking tumbler which you knocked over with your elbow when you were talking so merrily, and broke . . . Good God how well I know that room! Don't you remember a queer, cool, odd kind of smell it has, suggestive of porter, and even pipes, at an enormous distance . . . Oh Hunt I'm so lazy and all along o'you! The sun is in my eyes, the hum of the fields in my ears, and the dust on my feet, — and a boy, redolent of the steam engine and sweltering in warm ink, is slumbering in the passage waiting for 'Copy'.

There can be no doubt that Hunt was one of Dickens's close friends, and yet one must put in a word of warning. As Dickens's biographers have recognised, to be his close friend did not necessarily signify closeness in the normal sense of the word. His poverty-stricken youth had somewhat hardened him to friendship as well as disappointment. Rarely did he lay himself open to the vulnerability required in a really close relationship. Instead, he displayed a dramatic and imaginative exuberance, and the affectionate avowals that crowded his letters to Hunt were probably part of his vivacious, hyper-active mask. Hunt was understandably taken in, believing himself to be 'in as sure possession of his regard, as he was owner of mine'.

Dickens, through Forster, began to know the peculiarities of Hunt's financial position, but the revelations did not seem to have lessened his affection. On the contrary, Dickens in July 1840 wrote a reference for Thornton, which dwelt enthusiastically on the great esteem and regard the son had for his father. He also enclosed an affectionate note for Hunt, requesting him to send the reference back if it were not adequate and adding as a postscript: 'I send an imaginary old shoe, which please to throw after your son for luck.' A year later, when Hunt was in particular need, Dickens sent money and, in reply to Hunt's thanks, responded: 'In Heavens name don't imagine there is any man alive from whom you could possibly, if you knew his heart, accept a favour with less reason for feeling it a burden, or a cause of uneasiness, than your faithful friend, Charles Dickens.' In 1847 it was Dickens who enthusiastically organised the benefit performances of *Every Man in His Humour* to raise money for Hunt and honour 'all the good he has done'.

The eyes of Dickens might show the strain under which he lived, but his sumptuous home, and his enormous popularity proclaimed him the ultimate in success. As the list of god-parents to his children bears testimony, there was scarcely a famous literary figure who was not his friend. Artistically he was on the threshold of his greatest writing. In 1850 he and Hunt came together professionally again when, realising a long-held dream, he began a weekly magazine of popular and educational reading known as *Household Words*. He invited old friends in the most cordial manner to contribute, and Hunt was happy to oblige.

So it was that Dickens, in the early months of 1852, sat in his study and worked on his novel as Hunt watched Vincent dying. Dickens quickly wrote those first instalments of *Bleak House*, and as usual Forster read them before they went to the printers, but unusually he begged Dickens to show certain passages to Bryan Procter, a barrister who for three decades had been a friend of Hunt. Forster had been distressed at what he read: Procter also was worried. Staring from the novel was a barely disguised portrait of Leigh Hunt: not the Hunt of 'Abou Ben Adhem' whom they revered, or the dogged survivor whom they admired, or the child-like Hunt whom they pitied, but the escapist and eccentric Leigh Hunt gliding cheerfully about in his flowered dressing-gown. The character, named Leonard Skimpole, was instantly recognisable as Hunt.

He was a little bright creature, with a rather large head; but a delicate face, and a sweet voice, and there was a perfect charm in him. All he said was so free from effort and spontaneous and was said with such a captivating gaiety, that it was fascinating to hear him talk . . . he had more the appearance, in all respects, of a damaged young man, than a well-preserved elderly one . . . he must confess to two of the oldest infirmities in the world: one was, that he had no idea of time; the other, that he had no idea of money. In consequence of which he never kept an appointment, never could transact business, and never knew the value of anything! Well!!! So he had got on in life, and here he was! He was very fond of reading the papers, very fond of making fancy-sketches with a pencil, very fond of nature, very fond of art. All he asked of society was, to let him live. *That* wasn't much. His wants were few. Give him the papers, conversation, music, mutton, coffee, landscape, fruit in the season, a few sheets of Bristol-board, and a little claret, and he asked no more.

Forster and Procter were adamant. Skimpole must be changed. Dickens himself was disturbed and read through the relevant pages, deleting adjectives, toning down judgements, and changing the name from Leonard to Harold Skimpole. He also instructed the artist who had to illustrate the novel to draw Skimpole in such a way that he did not resemble Leigh Hunt. But these repairs were insufficient. Harold Skimpole was already in the novel and was allowed to breathe and grow. A little later he was arrested for debt, and his new companions were cleverly manipulated into paying the debts. Skimpole's response was one with which Hunt's friends were familiar. He felt no gratitude and suggested that they instead should be grateful to him. Unperturbed by the incident, Skimpole sat down at the piano and joyfully began to play. 'He *is* a child', exclaimed his charmed but bewildered companions. Dickens later described a visit to Skimpole's house, and again the loud echoes of Hunt could be heard:

It was dingy enough, and not at all clean; but furnished with an odd kind of shabby luxury, with a large footstool, a sofa, and plenty of cushions, an easy-chair, and plenty of pillows, a piano, books, drawing materials, music, newspapers, and a few sketches and pictures. A broken pane of glass in one of the dirty windows was papered and wafered over; but there was a little plate of hothouse nectarines on the table, and there was another of grapes, and another of sponge-cakes, and there was a bottle of light wine. Mr Skimpole himself reclined upon the sofa, in a dressing-gown, drinking some fragrant coffee from an old China cup — it was then about mid-day — and looking at a collection of wallflowers in the balcony.

He was not in the least disconcerted by our appearance, but rose and received us in his usual airy manner.

'Here I am, you see!' he said, when we were seated: not without some little difficulty, the greater part of the chairs being broken. 'Here I am! This is my frugal breakfast. Some men want legs of beef and mutton for breakfast; I don't. Give me my peach, my cup of coffee, and my claret; I am content.'

When the serialised instalments of *Bleak House* reached the streets in a flood of 35,000 copies, Skimpole was noticed and his mask fell from his face. One reader remarked that he recognised him instantly, as did every other of his acquaintances who knew Hunt. Successive instalments appeared, and Skimpole's character grew darker. An idler and social parasite, he even acquired a hypochondriac wife, run-away sons and three improvident daughters. Dickens's alterations to the novel had been to little avail.

Hunt was unaware of the gossip. Absorbed at Vincent's bedside, or grieving at his death, his scant interest in anything as trivial as a new novel was understandable. His friends, distressed lest he should discover the truth, went to some lengths to keep it from him. Successive monthly numbers of *Bleak House* appeared and Hunt heard not a whisper from wagging tongues.

In the last months of 1853 Hunt began to go a little into society. This was the moment that his friends feared. An American paper had already revealed the scandal in detail; so had one in Aberdeen. Soon a supposedly well-meaning acquaintance thrust this paper into his hands, with the explanation that it was something Hunt should know. Hunt later described how he felt at that moment. At first he discredited it as preposterous. Why should one who had been a close friend for nearly 20 years thus attack him? But as he heard the rumours and saw the story spelled out in cold print, his world began to crumble. He wrote to his friends and begged their honest opinion. His friends rallied, and even now it is touching to read the loyal reassurances. J.W. Dalby, an old correspondent, wrote that he had heard rumours, but he and his friends had quickly discounted them. For one thing Skimpole was no gentleman, and everyone who knew Hunt knew that he was a gentleman in every true sense of the word.

In the end it was Dickens to whom Hunt turned for enlightenment. Dickens replied with what Forster described as 'an earnest eagerness' and assured Hunt that the character was not him and that Skimpole's traits were shared by thousands of people. He had not fancied that Hunt would see a resemblance; he deeply regretted causing any pain. Hunt was still hurt but he preferred to believe Dickens's reassurance than to think that he had been betrayed by one who had so long been his friend. So the sore was bandaged, Hunt began to write again for *Household Words* at — significantly — the highest rates of payment, and a meeting was arranged between Hunt and Dickens. In his last few years Hunt was worried only fitfully, if at all, by the portrayal in the novel, and he was able to describe himself once more as Dickens's 'faithful friend'.

In September 1853, just about the time when Hunt was discovering Skimpole's existence, Dickens wrote privately to Mrs Richard Watson, whose home Rockingham Castle was the original of Chesney Wold in *Bleak House*:

> I must not forget Skimpole — of whom I will proceed to speak as if I had only read him and not written him. I suppose he is the most exact portrait that was ever painted in words! I have very seldom, if ever, done such a thing. But the likeness is astonishing. I don't think it could possibly be more like himself. It is so awfully true that I make a bargain with myself 'never to do so any more'. There is not an atom of exaggeration or suppression. It is an absolute reproduction of the real man. Of course I have been careful to keep the outward figure away from fact; but in all else it is the life itself.

Clearly, Dickens in the grip of his novel had not been such a 'faithful friend' to Hunt.

Hunt could not bear Phillimore Terrace after Vincent died. Jacintha was living with her husband and two children in Cornwall Road, Hammersmith, and it was to a small, cheap house in that street that Hunt moved his family and books in 1853. Though she was alive there for four years, Marianne was never to see more than her bedroom. Rheumatism was the official diagnosis, but George Bird had described her in 1851 as 'sodden from drink'. Hunt, he noted, turned a blind eye: his loyalty to her was splendid. Horne said that he never heard Hunt say an angry word about Marianne or any of his children, no matter how provoked he was. His remedy was silence, but that too could take its toll, and one remembers a pathetic entry in Marianne's diary when she bewailed that her husband had sent her to Coventry again and treated her as if she were 'made of Stone'. As in any marriage there was a case for both sides, and drink-sodden Marianne deserves sympathy.

Hunt nursed Marianne devotedly. He feared she would set fire to the house and every night searched for unsafe lamps and candles, confessing to Thornton that each time he arrived home he expected to see the house in flames. Hunt relied increasingly on the generous Southwood Smith who for years had been happy to come 'from a distance to her at any call, and through all obstacles; deliver her from racking pains; strengthen her through long tranquil intervals to bear more . . . do all which skill and zeal could possibly do for her'. Hunt blessed him with tears in his eyes. At the end of 1856 both Hunt and Marianne were ill with bronchial infections. With Hunt these were perennial, and in 1853 he had briefly grown a beard to keep his chest warmer, but Marianne's lungs were still consumptive and she could not cope. She grew steadily weaker, without pain, without mental unease and not 'the slightest touch of fear'. Hunt, watching by her side, brought all 'the solace and help which affection and love could bring'. She died on 26 January 1857, aged 69, and Hunt wrote nobly of her: 'My wife was a woman of great generosity, of great freedom from every kind of jealousy.'

Hunt was saddened but not shattered, and comforting tears were able to flow. He considered living with Thornton, or taking lodgings in the heart of London nearer his friends, but in the end Jacintha, her husband and the children moved into his house. The children he found 'a great relief to my weariness'.

Now feeble, he seldom went out, but many visited him, including literary Americans for whom he was one of the sights of London. The novelist Nathaniel Hawthorne and the publisher J.T. Fields have left sharp accounts of their conversation with this vivacious, careworn old man. His long hair was silver white, and in his black swirling cloak his figure was more romantic than ever. Though his lustrous eyes were a little dim and his body a little bent, his serenity and cheerfulness did not falter: his spirit was triumphant. An ascetic streak in him was more visible and Thornton noted that the innocent pleasures which had habitually cheered his father's life were no longer so vital. He seemed to look forward to them, but when they arrived he denied himself in the same way that his ascetic mother had denied herself so long ago.

In the summer of 1858 Hunt was ill. To recuperate, he went with Jacintha and her children to the farm at Putney of the printer Charles Reynell, where he was 'very much pleased' by the fields and trees and animals and all those friends who came from London to visit him. A year later he was ill again, and Reynell renewed his invitation to come to Putney. On what was his last evening at home in Hammersmith, Hunt invited the writer Charles Kent to call. Kent has left a moving account of this visit. He recalled Hunt writing a letter, eating a squashy nectarine, discussing the *Examiner*'s attack on the Prince Regent, and talking obsessively but serenely of his hopes of an after-life. Outside in the rain a street organ played 'Home Sweet Home'.

At Putney Hunt complained of 'the greatest internal pain I ever suffered'. However, he insisted on writing in his pain-free intervals, and he reassured his family and even welcomed young Percy Shelley's wife, weeping to see her. By 24 August he was in great pain and unable to leave his bed. Thornton sat with him. Hunt questioned him about Mazzini in Italy, listened to music and sent messages to those he loved. At the end he believed that the spirits of 'his beloved dead' were in the room with him. On 28 August 1859 he joined them and was buried as he had wished, beside Vincent and Marianne in Kensal Green cemetery.

They called him the last survivor of a race of giants.

BIBLIOGRAPHICAL NOTES

The following abbreviations have been used:

AES: Hunt, J.H. Leigh. *Leigh Hunt's Autobiography: the Earliest Sketches,* ed.Stephen Fogle with introduction and notes (University of Florida Press, 1959)

Auto: Hunt, J.H.Leigh. *The Autobiography of Leigh Hunt,* ed. J.E. Morpurgo (London, 1948)

Brewer: Brewer, Luther A. *My Leigh Hunt Library* vol. 2. *The Holograph Letters* (Cedar Rapids, Iowa, 1932-8: privately printed)

BL: The British Library

Blunden: Blunden, Edmund. *Leigh Hunt, A Biography* (London, 1930)

Brotherton: The Brotherton Library, University of Leeds: The Novello – Cowden Clarke Collection

Corr: Hunt, J.H. Leigh. *The Correspondence of Leigh Hunt,* 2 vols., ed. Thornton Leigh Hunt (London, 1862)

Cornhill: Hunt, Thornton Leigh. 'A Man of Letters of the Last Generation', *Cornhill Magazine* I (Jan. 1860), pp. 85–95

ExE: Blunden, Edmund. *Leigh Hunt's 'Examiner' Examined* (London, 1928)

Fenner: Fenner, Theodore. *Leigh Hunt and Opera Criticism: the 'Examiner' Years, 1808–1821* (University Press of Kansas, 1972)

First Editions: Brewer, Luther A. *My Leigh Hunt Library* vol. 1. *First Editions* (Cedar Rapids, Iowa, 1932–8: privately printed)

H Diaries: *The Diary of Benjamin Robert Haydon,* 2 vols., ed. William Bissell Pope (Harvard University Press, 1960)

Holmes: Holmes, Richard. *Shelley. the Pursuit* (London, 1974)

Huntiana: Brewer, Luther A. *My Leigh ̆Hunt Library* vol. 3. *Huntiana and Association Books* (Cedar Rapids, Iowa, 1932–8: privately printed)

JH: John Hunt

Kendall: Kendall, Kenneth E. *Leigh Hunt's 'Reflector'* (University of Florida Press, 1971)

KSJ: *The Keats Shelley Journal*

KSMB: *The Keats Shelley Memorial Association Bulletin*

Landré: Landré, Louis. *Leigh Hunt. Contribution à l'histoire de Romantisme anglais*, 2 vols. (Paris, 1935–6)

LBSHC: *Lord Byron and Some of His Contemporaries* (London, 1828)

LH: Leigh Hunt

Marginalia: Brewer Luther A. *Marginalia* (Cedar Rapids, Iowa, 1926: privately printed)

Marshall: Marshall William H. *Byron, Shelley, Hunt and The Liberal* (Philadelphia, 1960)

MH: Marianne Hunt

MLBL: *Byron's Letters and Journals*, 7 vols., ed. L. A. Marchand (London, 1973, 1976)

MS Jones: *The Letters of Mary W. Shelley*, 2 vols., ed. F. L. Jones (University of Oklahoma Press, 1944)

Pforz: *The Carl H. Pforzheimer Library: Shelley and his Circle*, vols. I and 11, ed. Kenneth Neill (Harvard University Press, 1961); vols. 111 and IV, ed, Kenneth Neill (Harvard University Press, 1970); vols. V and VI, ed. Donald H. Reiman (Harvard University Press, 1973)

Rollins: *The Letters of John Keats 1814–1821*, 2 vols., ed. H. E. Rollins (Harvard University Press, 1958)

ROW: Cowden Clarke, Charles and Mary. *Recollections of Writers* (New York, n.d.)

Rylands: Sanders, Charles Richard. *The Correspondence and Friendship of Thomas Carlyle and Leigh Hunt* (The John Rylands Library, Manchester, 3 MCMLXIII)

S Jones: *The Letters of Percy Bysshe Shelley*, 2 vols., ed. F. L. Jones (Oxford University Press, 1964)

Stout: Stout, George D. 'Political History of Leigh Hunt's *Examiner*', *Washington University Studies*, New Series no, 19 (1949)

TH: Thornton Hunt

UILHC: University of Iowa Libraries: Leigh Hunt Collection

1. Bluecoat

LH's un-Englishness: *Auto* 22, 86.

Ancestors: *Auto* Ch. 1; *AES* 1–10.

Childhood: *Auto* Ch. 2; *AES* 10–32; J.T. Flexner, *America's Old Masters* (New York, 1980) 19–97 for an account of the early career and marriage of Benjamin West, also LH, 'The Sale of the

Late Mr West's Pictures', *Indicator*, 14 June 1820; *Huntiana*
317–20 for Isaac Hunt's treatment by the Philadelphian mob;
S.F. Fogle, 'Leigh Hunt's Lost Brother and the American
Legacy', *KSJ* XVIII, 1959, part II, 95; *First Editions* 326 and
Landré I, 17fn. for Isaac Hunt's poverty. For family letters see
Brewer 2, 4, 6, 7; Blunden 9 for LH's entry to Christ's Hospital.
School: *Auto* Chs. 3 and 4; *AES passim*.

2 Fit for Nothing but an Author

On leaving school: *Auto* Chs. 5 and 6, esp. 108 ff; *AES* 22–3.
Brothers' careers: M. Hunt to S. Shewell, 28 June 1799, UILHC.
Fogle, 'Leigh Hunt's Lost Brother' 98–9; *AES* 35–8.
Early literary career: JH *Juvenilia; or, a collection of poems written
between the ages of twelve and sixteen by J.H.L. Hunt* (J.
Whiting, 1801); *Pforz* I, fn. 275; LFH 13–15 for a discussion of
LH's possible mixed race, also *Auto* 20.
Harriet: *AES* 35–40.
Exploring London: *AES* 41–2
Marian: TH, 'A View of Leigh Hunt's Intimate Circle', published in
Blunden 358–67; *AES* 46–9; *Auto* 461 and *Corr* I, 46 II, 174 for
MH's age and LH, *Poetical Works*, ed. Thornton Hunt, (London
1844,) 256 for place of birth; *AES* 46–9 for early courtship;
Brewer, 39.
Earliest love letters: Brewer 9–12, 19–20; *Corr* I, 3–5.
Insecurity: *Corr* II, 165.

3 The Stormy Courtship of Miss Kent

Early journalism: *Auto* 138, 140.
LH and JH: Brewer 378; Blunden 300–1 for JH's obituary; Blunden
360–1 for TH's view.
Independence in journalism: *Auto* 154–7; LBSHC 401–3; *Auto* 136
for LH's life as a reviewer; *Auto* 178–9 and Landré I, 45–6 for
post in War Office.
Nervous breakdown: *Auto* Ch. 8; *Auto* 26–7 for mother's death, also
Brewer 37, 38, and LH, 'Memoir of Mr James Henry Leigh Hunt
written by himself', *Monthly Mirror*, April 1810, N.S. VII, 243–
8.

Courtship: Brewer 14, 26, *Corr* I, 20–1 for MH's illiteracy; Brewer 35 for LH's longing to marry; Brewer 44 for MH's attempt to joke; Brewer 39 for LH rebuking Field; Brewer 44 for LH's sense of MH's desertion; LH to MH, 7 June 1809, BL, for their marriage plans; Brewer 13 for LH at Papendiek's. A. Blainey, 'The courtship of Marianne Hunt', *Books at Iowa*, Nov. 1975, 3–10.

4 Gloom and Cheer

Robert Hunt: Blunden 361 for description by TH.

Attacked by dramatists: *Auto* 160.

Examiner: for Aims of *Examiner* see *Corr* I, 78–80; LH, 'Explanation and Retrospection: the Examiner Twenty Years Ago', *Monthly Repository*, October 1837; Francis Wrangham to JH, 19 Oct. 1808, BL; Stout for the most complete discussion of the *Examiner*: Landré II, 59–97 for excellent discussion of the political background; Kendall 35ff for LH's political aims; A. Aspinall, *Politics and the Press 1780–1850* (London, 1949) esp. 40–2 for government threats to the press; *ExE* 5ff; *Auto* Ch. 9.

Early trials: Patrick O'Leary, *Regency Editor: Life of John Scott* (Aberdeen, 1983) Ch. 3; Carl Woodring, 'The Hunt Trials: Information and Manoeuvres' *KSMB* X, 1959, 10–13; LH to Secretary of War, 26 Dec. 1808, BL; Stout 5–17.

Bluecoat coterie: Kendall 91 ff; *AES* 33; B. Field to LH, 3 Dec. 1812, BL.

Thomas Hill's coterie: LH to T. Hill, 30 Sept. 1810, UILHC; *Auto* 180–92.

At Hunters: Claire Tomalin, *The Life and Death of Mary Wollstonecraft* (London, 1974) Ch. VI on Joseph Johnson; *Auto* 195–6.

Deaths: *AES* 4–5 for Elizabeth West's death; *Auto* 18–19 for father's death.

Letters to Marianne: Brewer 49–51.

Marian to Marianne: LH's wife appears to have been born plain Mary Anne, as shown on a power of attorney, signed 20 Dec. 1809, UILHC. All her mother's letters to her in UILHC are addressed to Mary Anne. LH called her Marian through their courtship and early months of marriage. In LH to MH, 10 Oct. 1810, UILHC, he addressed her as Marianne for the first time.

Thornton's birth: B.R. Haydon, to LH, 'Monday morning', n.y., BL; E. West to LH, 20 August, n.y., UILHC; H, *Wishing Cap Papers*, (Boston, 1873) 52.

Charles Lamb: LH, *Leigh Hunt's London Journal*, 7 Jan. 1835, for obituary of Lamb.

The *Reflector: Auto* Ch. 12; Kendall *passim; Prefaces by Leigh Hunt Mainly to His Periodicals*, ed. R. Brimley Johnson (New York, 1967) 39–47.

Philosophy of Cheer: *Corr* II, 172–3 for TH's comments; LH, 'Explanation and Retrospection', *Monthly Repository*, October 1837, for LH's comments; LH, 'Fatal Mistake of Nervous Disorders for Insanity', *Indicator*, 24 Nov. 1819.

The Feast of the Poets: *Auto* 214–24.

Shelley: *Pforz* II, 769–75; Holmes 52, 63

5 The Bigot of Virtue

Marianne's health: LH to W. Knighton, 13 Jan. 1812, Pierpont Morgan Library.

Financial position: LH to JH, 14 July 1812, Pierpont Morgan Library; LH to W. Knighton, 11 Feb. 1812, UILHC.

Prince Regent attack: *Auto* 231; *ExE* 21–30; Landré I, 66.

Friend's support: B. Field to LH, 31 Aug. 1812, BL; H. Brougham to LH, Lancaster, Saturday n.y., BL; *Corr* I, 67.

LH's condition: *Corr* I, 60; Brewer 90.

Mother's grave: LH, 'Memorandum', in *Corr* I, 78.

John's birth: B. Field to LH, 31 Aug. 1812, BL.

Taunton visit: Brewer 49–56; LH to MH, August 1812, BL; *Pforz* VIII 105–7.

Haydon and LH: *H Diaries* I, 288.

In court: *ExE* 24–6; *Auto* 233–5; Corr I, 77; Landré I, 67–8, 79. Woodring, 'The Hunt Trials'; Stout 17–26; *Annual Register for a View of the History, Politics, and Literature for the Year 1812* (London, 1813) 278–9.

6 The Wit in the Dungeon

LH in prison: Brewer 58–87 for the sequence of letters between LH
and MH; *Corr* I, 69–100 for more prison letters; Brewer 91–2 for
Haydon's reaction; Brewer 152–3 for JH to LH; *Pforz* III, 133–8;
B. Field to R. Gooch, 'Friday night' n.y., BL; LH to C. Cowden
Clarke, 2 Nov. 1814, Brotherton; Henry Robertson, 'On the
Poet's Residence in Surrey Jail', 5 Oct. 1813, BL; Charles Lamb,
Essays of Elia (London, 1906) 91 for comments on TH; A.
Blainey, 'The Wit in the Dungeon', *Books at Iowa* April 1981,
9–14; P. Henderson, *Swinburne* (London, 1974) 6–7 for a
description of Sir John Swinburne; *Pforz* III, 265–8 for Shelley's
offer of money; *H Diaries* I, 350; J. Swinburne to LH, 2 June
1814, BL.

Byron: L Marchand, *Byron, A Portrait* (London, 1971) I, 388–9,
424; *Letters of Thomas Moore* (Oxford University Press, 1964) I,
309; MLBL III, 188–9, 228.

7 Days by the Fire

Mary Florimel's birth: *Pforz* VI, 907; *Auto* 245, 247; LH, *Wishing
Cap Papers* 201–2; LH, *Indicator*, 2 Feb. 1820 for meaning of
Florimel.

Hunt's poetic theory: LH, *Feast of the Poets* (London, 1814,
1815), see 'Notes' to the poems.

Wordsworth: W. Wordsworth to LH, 12 Feb. 1815, Harvard University Library; *Auto* 253–4.

The Descent of Liberty: LH, *Descent of Liberty* (London, 1815);
Ex E 55–6 for attitude to Napoleon; LH to R. Gooch, 3 April,
1815, BL, for reception and also Ollier, Robertson, Havel to
LH, 22 Jan. 1815, BL.

The Story of Rimini: LH, *The Story of Rimini* (London, 1816) and
for later ending LH, *Poetical Works. Auto* 257–9; *H Diaries* II,
63; LH, *Foliage or Poems Original and Translated* (London,
1818), see preface for remarks on *Rimini* and poetic theory;
Clarice Short, 'The Composition of Hunt's "The Story of
Rimini" ', KSJ XXI, 1972, 207–18.

Rimini and Bess Kent: *Blackwood's III*, July 1818, 453–6; *Corr* I,
112, 223–34; Blunden 359; *H Diaries* II, 81, 83.

Byron and *Rimini*: LH, 'The Story of Rimini', ms, BL; J. Medwin,

The Journals and the Conversations of Lord Byron (London, 1824) 187; MLBL IV, 294, 319, 330, V, 32, 35, and VI, 44–7.

Maida Vale: *Auto* 250–6; LBSHC 304, *Pforz* V, 640–52, MLBL VII, 86.

Hampstead: H.C. Bentwich, *The Vale of Health on Hampstead Heath* (London, 1977) *passim*; LH, *Poetical Works*, 232–5; LH, *Wishing Cap Papers* 235.

LH in society: LH, *Wishing Cap Papers* 27 on Lamb; R.M. Wardle, *Hazlitt* (Nebraska, 1971) 183 and *passim* on Hazlitt, Haydon to LH, 4 Sept. 1816, BL; *H Diaries* II, 47, 62–3, 81, 134–5; Colbert Kearney, 'Benjamin Robert Haydon and the *Examiner*', *KSJ* XXVII, 1978, 108–21; LH, *Poetical Works*, 262, 265; *The Essays of William Hazlitt*, ed. F. Carr (London, n.d.)106–7, 224–5 for Hazlitt on LH; *The Letters of William Hazlitt*, ed. H.M. Sikes, W.H. Bonner, G. Lahey (London, 1978) 204–6; P.P. Howe, *Life of William Hazlitt* (London, 1949) 323, 293–4.

LH and music: Fenner *passim*; LH, *Musical Evenings*, ed. D. Cheney (Missouri, 1964) esp. introduction; *Cornhill* 85 for LH's musical capacity; *Auto* 190 for description of Novello; *ROW* 16–27; Lamb, *Essays of Elia* 54–64; LH, *Wishing Cap Papers* 41–2; LH, *Essays*, ed. A. Symons (London, 1803) 359–68.

LH and debts and publishers: Samuel Smiles, *A Publisher and His Friends* (London, 1911) 124–7; J. Murray to LH, 1 Jan. 1816, and 'Thursday' 1816, 'Saturday' 1816, 'Friday' 1816, all BL; A. Constable to LH, 27 Aug. 1816, LH to Constable, 19 Aug, 1816 both in National Library of Scotland; *Pforz* VI, 530–9; Brewer 106–7, 117; *H Diaries* I, 35

Marianne's illness: Brewer 98; LH to Mary Novello, 11 July. n.y., Brotherton.

8 Realms of Gold

Rimini Reception: *Quarterly Review* XIV, Jan. 1816, 473–81; B.R. Haydon to LH, 21 Feb. 1816, BL; *Edinburgh Review*XXXVI, June 1816, 476–91; *Auto* 259–60; W. Howitt, *Homes and Haunts of English Poets* (London, 1847) 595–6.

Examiner: *ExE* 57–66.

Young poets: Holmes Ch. 13; R. Gittings, *John Keats* (Boston. 1968) Chs. 5–7.

ROW 120–40; *ExE* 125–8; *LBSHC* 247–51.

LH and Shelley: Holmes Ch. 14; S. Jones I, 516–19, 259; MS Jones I, 22–3. *Mary's Shelley's Journal*, ed. F.L. Jones (Oklahoma, 1947) 70 ff; *Pforz V*, 399–409.

LH's sexual theories: *H Diaries* II, 81, 83; Brewer 165; B.R. Haydon to E. Barrett, n.d., in Keats–Shelley Memorial House Rome for account of Bess Kent's suicide attempt; Doris Langley Moore, *Lord Byron: Accounts Rendered* (London, 1974) 301–2, quotes Haydon.

Keats's disenchantment: *ROW* 135–6; Gittings, *John Keats* Ch. 9 passim.

At Marlow: Holmes Ch. 15; *Pforz V*, 225–31; *ROW* 196–9; TH 'Shelley by One Who Knew Him' *Atlantic Monthly* XI, 1863, 190; *Pforz* VI, 522.

Shelley and LH's finances: *Pforz* V, 226–8, 262–8, *Auto* 269; H. Smith to LH, 3 Jan. 1818, UILHC.

'Nymphs': C. De Witt Thorpe, 'The Nymphs', *KSMB* X, 1959, 33–47; *Pforz* VI, 1081.

Foliage: LH, *Foliage, or Poems Original and Translated* (London, 1818), reviewed *Quarterly Review* XVIII, Jan. 1818, 324–35, *Blackwood's* , VI, 1819, 70–6; MLBL, VI, 44–7.

Shelley leaves: *Pforz* VI, 523–30, Holmes 408–13.

9 Friend of Shelley

LH at Lisson Grove: *Pforz* VI, 553–63, 696–703; Rollins I, 259 for Keats on Bess Kent.

Cockney School: *Quarterly Review* XVIII, Jan.-1818, 324–34, XIX, Aug. 1818, 204–8; *Blackwood's* II, Jan 1819, 414–17, III, May 1819, 196–201, III, July 1819, 453–6, Aug. 1819, 519–24, V, Sept. 1819, 627–720, VI, Oct. 1819, 70–5; *Auto* 275; *Corr* I, 166 for Shelley's refusal to defend himself; LH, *Examiner*, 10 Oct., 1810, for LH's reaction; O'Leary, *Regency Editor* Chs. 8–9 for duel; *Pforz* VI, 739–45; *Auto* 215–19, for LH's view of Gifford, and *Literary Examiner*, 13 Dec. 1823, for review of *Ultra Crepidarius;* R. Baldwin to LH, 3 Nov. 1817, and JH to R. Baldwin, 11 Nov., 1817, National Library of Scotland.

Reactions to Cockney attacks: Rollins I, 217, 224, 251–2, 294, 378, II, 8 for Keats's reactions. *The Letters of William Hazlitt*, 204–7 for Hazlitt's reactions; MLBL VI, 44–7.

Novello's circle: LH, *Wishing Cap Papers* 252–3; Blunden 362; *The*

Athenians: Correspondence between T.J. Hogg and Friends, ed. W.S. Scott (London, 1943) 70–2.
Shelley 1819: *Pforz* VI, 837–74, 877, 886–92, 879–92, 904–16; MS Jones I, 74–84;
Literary Pocket Book: Pforz VI, 739–44, reviewed *Blackwood's* VI, 1819, 233.
JH's retirement: Howe, *Life of William Hazlitt*, 283.
Mask of Anarchy: Holmes 531–41, 561, 569; *Pforz* VI, 1080–94, 1106–11.
LH's finances: *Pforz*, VI, 937–9; S. Jones II, 187.
Poems 1819: LH, *Hero and Leander* and *Bacchus and Ariadne* (London, 1819) reviewed in *London Magazine* II, July 1820, 45–55.
Indicator: *Indicator* 13 Oct., 20 Oct. 1819 for its aims: *LBSHC* 432–3; *Pforz* VI, 912–16; Blunden 147–9.
Keats 1820: Gittings, *John Keats* Ch. 27 *passim*; LH, *Wishing Cap Papers* 239, Rollins II, 297, 302–11, 316–17; *Corr* I, 107; *Auto* 276.
LH's health: LH, 'Fatal Mistake of Nervous Disorders for Insanity.' *Indicator*, 24 Nov. 1819, for LH's views on cause and treatment; Corr I, 163–9.
JH: sole proprietor of Examiner: *Corr* I, 161–3, 167–9; Howe, *Life of William Hazlitt*, 347.
Decision to go to Italy: *Corr* 1, 167–73.

10 The Wren and the Eagle

Cockney reaction: *Blackwood's* XI, Feb. 1822, 236–9, XI March 1822, 369–71, XII, Dec. 1822, 693–709, 775–81.
Departure and voyage: *Auto* 280–313; *Corr* I, 173–83; *ROW* 206–14; LBSHC 433–89; Notebook containing 'Ultra Crepidarius' ms and notes on voyage at Yale University Library; S Jones II, 379, 382, 392–4, 404–5, 434–6, 442.
Arrival in Italy: S Jones II, 437, 443–4; TH, 'Shelley by One Who Knew Him' 190; *The Works of Lord Byron, Letters and Journals*, ed. R.E. Prothero (London, 1904) VI, 11–12, 22; *The Liberal: Verse and Prose From the South* (London, 1822–3, I, 269; *Auto* 313–26; Holmes 725–30.
Shelley's burning: *Auto* 327–8; *LBSHC* 195–202; LH to Mary Shelley, 17 Aug. 1822, BL; Sylva Norman, *Flight of the Skylark*

(London, 1954) 15–16.

With Byron at Pisa: *Corr* I, 189–95; Marshall *passim* – the entire book is relevant to this chapter; *Unpublished Diary of Mrs Leigh Hunt, Pisa 18 September 1822 – Genoa 24 October 1822* (London n.d.), and also a single ms page in Bodleian Library, Oxford; *LBSHC* 18–45; *Works of Lord Byron*, ed. Prothero 119–20.

Albaro: *Auto* Ch. 20; *Corr* I, 195–211.

Bess Kent: Brewer 125–45; LH to E Kent, 1 Feb, 12 Feb, 1825, BL; Blunden 195. M. Tatchell, 'Elizabeth Kent and *Flora Domestica*', KSMB, XXVII, 1976, 15.

LH and Mary Shelley: MS Jones, I, 209–11, 219–21, 222–4, 232–61 for Bess Kent taking opium.

11 Poetical Tinkerdom

At Brompton: *ROW* 238; *Auto* 421; LH to F. Place, 3 Nov. 1833, BL, for account of the *Tatler*; Brewer 248 and J. Forster to MH, 'Thursday' n.y., BL, for friendship with Forster.

LH's poetical works: *Corr* I, 264–6; *Letters of Thomas Moore* 742–3 for Moore offering a 'subscription'; B.R. Haydon to LH, 12 March 1832, BL; Landré I, 197–9 for quotes from *Atlas* and *Athenaeum*; LH to C. Cowden Clarke, 13 Dec. n.y., Brotherton; T.J. Hogg to LH, 16 Nov. 1832, BL; Mary Campbell to LH, 27 March 1832, BL; Rylands 4, 14.

At St John's Wood and Marylebone: *Corr* I, 268–9 and 274 for John Hunt junior; LH 'The Bond of Health and Honour', UILHC, and *Corr* II, 172 for principles of cheer.

Chelsea: *Froude's Life of Carlyle* ed., J. Chubbe (London, 1979) 308 for Carlyle's description of Chelsea; *Auto* 420–8.

LH and Carlyle: Rylands 5–6 for Carlyle on LH; Rylands 15–22 for TH's Scottish trip; Rylands 60–1 for LH on Carlyle; Rylands 15 for LH on marriage; *Cornhill* 89 for LH's sexual attraction and Rylands 53–4 for Susan Hunter incident. Rylands 35–7 for Carlyle and John Hunt junior.

Bess Kent's suicide threat: Brewer 100–2.

Indestructible cheer: Rylands 8.

12 In Heart and Hope

LH's magazines 1832–4: *Auto* 420–1, 428–9; Rylands 4–5 for demise of *Plain Dealer*; *Leigh Hunt's London Journal*, 2 April, 3 Sept. 1834 for the paper's aims; Brewer 108 and Blunden 262–3 for LH's reviving reputation.

Captain Sword and Captain Pen: *Auto* 431–5; the poem is dedicated to Henry Brougham, 'always a denouncer of war'; reviewed in *Spectator*, 11 April, 1835, 353; James R Thompson, *Leigh Hunt* (Boston, 1977) 45–7.

Craven Hill group and W.J. Fox: A. Blainey, *The Farthing Poet* (London, 1968,) Ch. 6; *Leigh Hunt's London Journal*, 3 Sept. 1834 for Egerton Webbe's poem to LH; LH to F. Place, 8 June 1836, BL, for LH on Blanchard.

In debt: David R. Cheney, 'Leigh Hunt Sued for Debt by a Friend', *Books at Iowa*, Nov. 1977, 30–56.

LH's pension claim: *Auto* 442; Brewer 197; Rylands 64 for Carlyle's 'Memoranda concerning Leigh Hunt'.

Hunt family: *Pforz* V, 260–2; MS Jones II, 141; George Craik to MH, 6 March 1840 (postmark), BL.

LH's attitude to money: *The Oxford Book of Literary Anecdotes*, ed. J. Sutherland (Oxford, 1975) 183–4; Blainey, *The Farthing Poet* 90–1.

Monthly Repository: Blainey, *The Farthing Poet* 68–9, and 73–4, 83, 86–88 for Horne's attitude to LH; *Auto* 435–6.

Legend of Florence: *ROW* 86; MS Jones 11, 140–1; Rylands 55; for LH's reading of his play. For performance *Auto* 437–40; R.H. Horne to LH, 1 Nov. 1839, BL; L. Blanchard to LH 'Friday night' n.y., BL; *Corr* 11, 332 for Haydon's comments, MS Jones 145.

LH leaves Chelsea: Rylands 62, 63 fn.

LH's family in Kensington: Molly Tatchell, *Leigh Hunt and his family in Hammersmith* (London, 1969) 58–69; Brewer 304; LH to T.N. Talfourd, 26 July n.y., Harvard University Library, for Mary Florimel's death; LH to Kate Hunt, n.d., UILHC, about grandson Walter; M. Tatchell, 'Thornton Hunt', *KSMB* XX, 1969, 13; *Corr* II, 1–2; Brewer 262–4; *Huntiana* 330, for Vincent's health; MS Jones II, 157–8, 161–2, 170, 181, 197, 200–1 and 215 for Henry Sylvan's marriage; For John Hunt junior's career see Records of the Royal Literary Fund, also J. Hunt to Mr Thomas, 20 Oct. 1840, UILHC, Brewer 234–5, and J. Hunt

to American Ambassador, 9 May 1840, Harvard University
Library.
JH's death: Brewer 402, Lord Leigh to LH, 21 Sept. 1848, BL;
Huntiana 220.

13 The Last Survivor

LH's appearance: *Thackeray's Daughter*, compiled by Hester
Fuller Thackeray and Violet Hammersley (Dublin, 1952) 55 ff;
Landré I, 240–1; *Cornhill passim* for LH in old age; *Huntiana*
221.
LH and Queen Victoria: LH to Queen Victoria, 15 July 1842, and C.
Phipps to LH, 7 Jan, 24 Jan. 1852, BL; also 7 letters in Jan. 1857
from C. Phipps to LH BL; *Auto* 449.
LH's fame: *Corr* II, 151–2.
Shelley annuity: LH to T.N. Talfourd, 7 May 1844, Huntington
Library; LH to Percy Shelley, 9 July 1844, UILHC; MS Jones II,
163, 178, 217, 210, 222, 228.
Dickens's theatricals: Edgar Johnson, *Charles Dickens: his Tragedy
and Triumph* (London, 1953) II, 616–18; *Auto* 443.
Imagination and fancy: LH, *Imagination and Fancy; or, Selections
from the English Poets* (London, 1845) 293–4, 297 for comments
on Shelley; Thompson, *Leigh Hunt* 103–28.
Autobiography: V. Novello to LH, 6 Jan, 1849, BL.
Vincent's death: LH to Henry Cole, 11 Sept. n.y., UILHC; *Corr* II,
140–4, 152–5; *Corr* II, 144–7 to Dr Bird about electric treatment;
Auto 456–8.
The Religion of the Heart: *Auto* 451–5, 458–9; *Corr* II, 129; De
Wilde to LH, 18 Nov. 1853, UILHC; Brewer 355.
Skimpole: H. Ainsworth to LH, 9 May 1844, BL, for Dickens's
deriving from LH's popularity; *The Letters of Charles Dickens*,
ed. M. House and G. Storey (London, 1965) I, 340, 414, 685–6,
II, 66–7; Charles Dickens, *Bleak House* (London, 1896) esp.
introduction on Skimpole; LH to Charles Dickens, 8 Nov. n.y.,
UILHC; Dalby to LH, 14 Oct. n.y., UILHC; LH to Duke of
Devonshire, n.d., BL; Sylvere Monod, 'When the Battle's Lost
and Won: Dickens v. the Compositors of "Bleak House", *The
Dickensian*, no. 369, Jan. 1973, 3; *Huntiana* 162; C.Dickens, 'A
Remonstrance', *All the Year Round* 2 1859–60, 206; *Leigh Hunt
and Charles Dickens: the Skimpole Caricature*, ed. Luther

Brewer (Cedar Rapids, 1930) *passim*; Blunden 313–21.

Marianne's death: Blunden 328–9 for quotes on MH's drunkenness, also *Corr* II, 277; R.H. Horne, 'Leigh Hunt: In Memoriam', *Southern Cross*, 10 Dec. 1859, Sydney; S. Smith to LH, 24 Feb. 1855, BL; to LH to S. Smith, 28 Jan. 1857, BL; Landré I, 269 for date of death.

LH's death: *Cornhill*; Charles Kent, 'Leigh Hunt's Last Evening at Home', *Dublin University Magazine* CCCXLVII, Nov. 1861; *Corr* II, 308.

INDEX

Note: Leigh Hunt is abbreviated to LH. Books, plays and poems are indexed under their titles.

DATE DUE			

Blainey   197268